THE KLANSMAN'S SON

THE
KLANSMAN'S SON

MY JOURNEY FROM
WHITE NATIONALISM
TO ANTIRACISM

A MEMOIR

R. DEREK BLACK

ABRAMS PRESS, NEW YORK

Published in 2024 by Abrams Press, an imprint of ABRAMS.

Library of Congress Control Number: 2023950102

ISBN: 978-1-4197-6478-3
eISBN: 978-1-64700-836-9

Printed and bound in the United States
10 9 8 7 6 5 4 3 2 1

Abrams books are available at special discounts when purchased in quantity
for premiums and promotions as well as fundraising or educational use.
Special editions can also be created to specification. For details, contact
specialsales@abramsbooks.com or the address below.

Abrams Press® is a registered trademark of Harry N. Abrams, Inc.

ABRAMS The Art of Books
195 Broadway, New York, NY 10007
abramsbooks.com

Allisoni, quae post est numquam,
Parentibus, qui me uicturum uoluerant,
Rosae, quae me ad saltandum inuitauit,
Marco, qui mecum cibum cepit,
Elishae, qui patri gaudium fecit,
Matthaeo, cui antea hoc dicere debui,
Eli, cuius historia etiam narranda est,
Omnibus qui me fouentes mutauerunt,
dono dedi

CONTENTS

Time said: *You must transform to survive.*
We said: *Not over our dead body.*
What can we call a country that destroys
Itself just because it can?
A nation that would char
Rather than change?
Our only word for this is
Home.

AMANDA GORMAN

THE JENNY JONES SHOW

MY DECADE OF POLITICAL ACTIVISM on behalf of White nationalism began in October 1999, when I was ten. I gave my first public interview to the salacious daytime talk show *The Jenny Jones Show*. It was a trip of firsts: one of the first times I left my home state of Florida; my first trip to Chicago; and my first time in the North at all. It was the first time I rode in a limo, when they picked us up and dropped us off at our hotel. At that hotel, on the morning before we headed to the studio for filming, I got to order my first pay-per-view movie (the remake of *The Mummy* with Brendan Fraser and Rachel Weisz). At the studio, it was my first experience in a greenroom. It was my first time in the public eye, my first time out front, and my first time claiming publicly my intention to lead White nationalism into its next generation.

The experience was genuinely fun. It was also terrifying, and it taught me terrible lessons.

The Jenny Jones Show was a nationally syndicated daytime talk show filmed in the same studios in the NBC Tower in Chicago as its rival *The Jerry Springer Show*. *Jenny* and *Jerry*—and *Geraldo* and *Maury* and others like them—often brought on unsophisticated guests to face a shouting and brawling live audience, to great commercial success; *The Jerry Springer Show*, by far the leader of the genre, ended that season with ratings just behind *Oprah*.

The episode they invited me and my dad for was titled "Hateful Websites on the Internet" and ran on October 4, 1999. Several years before, David Duke, my dad's oldest friend, had negotiated to appear on *The Jerry Springer Show* in a one-on-one interview, away from the jeering audience. Thanks to that negotiation, David was able to speak to Springer's huge viewership without having to face the demeaning taunts of the studio audience. For my first interview, my dad negotiated something similar, allowing me to give a one-on-one interview offstage. In addition, the producers also offered to pay for a trip to DisneyQuest, the virtual reality amusement park that had recently opened downtown.

My dad asked me over and over, even up to the day of filming, if I was sure I wanted to give the interview. I felt listened to and respected, and I felt like I was fully consenting to my participation. I believed in the cause, as much as a curious child can believe in any ideology, and I was excited to begin advancing it myself. A month earlier, I had created a kids' page on Stormfront, the website my dad had founded. I had already seen reporters coming to the house to interview my dad, and I'd become familiar with the hostile way they wrote about us as "hateful."

When we arrived at the set, my dad went out with the other guests, including other White power leaders and two daughters of Fred Phelps, the founder of the Westboro Baptist Church, a group known for picketing the funerals of soldiers and queer people. The studio was built in the middle of a large open room, so the crew, the guests who hadn't gone on yet, the kids of the Westboro family, and I could stay in the greenroom or walk all around the set. I watched the lighting crew and cinematographers, while I heard the echoes of the angry crowd through the thin prop walls. The crew were friendly and asked me if I needed anything while I hung out with them behind the scenes. I refused the makeup artist's offers several times, because I didn't think makeup was for boys. I remember her explaining that it wouldn't be visible, and was only meant to keep the glare of the stage lights from shining off my face. I held firm, committed to upholding my sense of gender norms, and she relented.

When the time for my interview came, the crew turned on fog machines that produced a dramatic cloud around the stool the producers led me to. I was near the corner of the stage, behind two panels they slid open to reveal me there. Jenny Jones implied my separate interview was a last-minute decision: "He didn't want to come on the show, and we'll see, uh, he's backstage, he is ten years old, his name is Derek. You've been listening to us back there, Derek? Okay, you—you want to go out there in the audience? Sit next to your dad? You're welcome to."

Watching the interview now is an almost unbearably mortifying experience. It feels like I am watching it simultaneously through my eyes both then and now, from two different vantages and two different worlds. I tried to present my family's cause with as much care and responsibility as I could muster. I had told the pre-show B-roll interviewers the night before, "I designed the website for White children. Most people think that my father has taught me to hate other races. He's just taught me to be proud of my heritage and to be proud of my race. Since I designed my website, I've had virtually no problems except for—except for hateful and vile emails." Jenny asked me how I decided to create the kids' page of my dad's website, and I recounted, "There was a newspaper article with another racist kids' page on— that I saw in the newspaper, and I wanted— wanted to make another one to have other— to have kids have another way of being able to see ideas and other opinions."

I knew immediately I had messed up by using the word "racist." My family was strict about messaging, and nothing was more fundamental than their position that "racist" was a word only our enemies used to describe us. Jenny asked me what ideas and opinions I was hoping to send, and I told her, "I'm sending a message to be proud of your her—"—momentarily forgetting the word "heritage"—"history and your ancestry, just to be proud of all the things that your ancestors have done, because the news media and schools never say any of it."

Finally, Jenny asked me again if I wanted to go out in front of the live audience, and I shook my head with a look of fear. "No," I responded, "I've been hearing all the audience. They boo— they boo when you come on, they boo when you're talking." She responded, "You understand why, though?" and I responded, "Yes." I knew immediately I'd made another messaging mistake. She got up. "I'm going to go back and talk to your dad," she said, and I tried to add quickly, before she was gone and I lost my chance, "They don't understand us."

Looking back now, it's overwhelming to watch the moment I first plunged into public activism for White nationalism, on behalf of my family and the community that raised me. I remember feeling mature and capable. I had answered affirmatively every time my dad checked in along the way, making sure I wanted to join him on this show. All the years that have cascaded down since then were on display in that moment. Even all this time later, I can't help being shocked to hear myself slip up and use the forbidden word "racist" in my first-ever interview. When my family gathered back home in Florida to watch the broadcast, they were disappointed to hear it and gave me feedback to remember to be careful not to use the enemy's wording, but instead to use the word "racialist" to describe our "pro-White" movement. The next decade trained me in how to stay on message. There's a part of me that still leaps to the fore unbidden when I watch it, wanting to coach that kid through their first interview. Or to tell them not to do it at all.

Once I overcome the twinge from watching my younger self spout talking points of a movement I've now spent nearly as much time opposing as I had supporting it, my next feeling is empathy. It's hard to listen to my younger self call out, "They don't understand us," to the back of Jenny Jones as she walked away. I loved my family. I wanted to stand up for them, and that day I felt like I had.

After filming wrapped, my dad came backstage, and we met again in the greenroom. We barely had time to talk about our two interviews because we needed to be ushered out of the studio by security. In the limo, he said repeatedly that he never wanted to do a daytime talk show like this again, and that he couldn't believe they had put him on the same show as the Westboro Baptist Church. They had risen to national prominence for their homophobic protests of the funeral of Matthew Shepard, a gay college student in Wyoming who had been brutally tortured and murdered the year before.

I remember feeling relieved that we could draw a line between our community and other communities people collectively called "hate." I appreciated how he felt so totally unconnected to them. In part that was because of their religious conviction, which he didn't share, and their vitriol toward queer people, which he just didn't think was a pressing social issue. That's not to say he privately respected or empathized with gay people any more than he did Black people or Jews. Instead, he was committed to seeing himself as maintaining the higher ground, not seeing himself as cruel, gratuitous, ignorant, or—as the show was trying to paint us by including us in the larger group—hateful. He didn't agree with homophobic slurs, in the same way that he opposed his own people using racial slurs. In an interview nearly fifteen years earlier, he had once complained about "drunk people" making it into KKK rallies where he was speaking and shouting the n-word. He wouldn't go out of his way to attack or condemn or verbally harass anyone, and he'd say that was wrong, but he'd also say it wasn't his responsibility to defend or protect anyone but his "own" people.

The question of how expansive the circle of my "own" people could be stuck with me, but I rarely voiced it. I didn't like excluding people from my life before I knew them. Thinking about that limo ride, talking with him about our interviews and what we were accomplishing, it's ironic to think that I've now given antiracist talks on polarization right alongside kids from Westboro who were backstage with me that day. It turned out the distinction between us wasn't absolved by our rhetoric.

IT TOOK YEARS BEFORE I felt comfortable revisiting that experience and that first trip to Chicago. After I condemned White nationalism in 2013 at the end of my college years, I moved to the city in my mid-twenties to attend graduate school for a history PhD at the University of Chicago. For the first few years there, I didn't look up where my dad and I had gone on that first trip. It was a part of my life that I was still trying to leave behind.

When I finally did look up where we'd been, I had lived in Chicago for several years already. I had built memories with friends throughout the city, and it was odd to learn that the NBC Tower on the riverfront in downtown had loomed over me every time we'd gone downtown to walk the Magnificent Mile, Chicago's fancy shopping strip. It was a block from the theater where we'd seen movies that the small cinema in Hyde Park wasn't playing. The virtual reality theme park Disney-Quest had been short-lived—Disney closed it less than two years after we visited—but it was in a building near a couple coffee shops where I wrote several of my grad school papers.

When I look at these early moments, it makes me want to break through the glass and tell my dad to stop this immediately. No matter how many times he asked if I was confident that I wanted to do the show, and no matter how many times I told him that I did, and meant it, I can't imagine how he couldn't realize just how little I knew what it meant to give up my privacy and to make a name for myself in our cause. My path wasn't set in stone then, or for many of the years that came after, but it felt like it was from the moment Jenny Jones walked up to my interview chair.

Appearing on that show was the beginning of a life that increasingly boxed me in over the next decade. As I became more entrenched in the White nationalist movement, I gained more power to cause more harm to people and society in ways I came to deeply regret. Each additional interview, each choice to go deeper and become a more involved leader of the movement that my parents had helped create, constricted the possibilities I saw for myself. A decade later, when I arrived at college, I had become an internationally recognized leader of the White nationalist movement. I had won local public office and had given interviews to newspapers and television shows around the world. I had created and run a White nationalist radio broadcast for years. I had become so confident in my beliefs in our family's ideology and movement that I knew my future was to help lead it. I couldn't yet imagine any other path.

Researching this book, I set out to find the dates and milestones of my life and of the generations of White nationalists that came before me to figure out how we got here, and what takeaways there might be to help the fight for antiracism. I expected to find, and indeed found, the glossy public face of a movement I had grown up in, but I also found a personal record in the archives that was more revealing than I expected. In college, I learned from history professors to read ancient and medieval letters with caution because the writers, the recipients, and broader society understood that letters would be saved and read by the public—unlike modern correspondence, which carries some assumption of privacy and intimacy. Given my life experience, that assumption of privacy seemed absurd. One of the earliest and most consistent pieces of advice that my dad ever gave me was, "Never say anything that you wouldn't be willing to see published in the *New York Times* the next day."

I always knew my interviews would be public, of course, but part of having a public life also meant remembering that even "private" correspondence might one day be published widely. Letters, texts, emails, and private conversations were still no place to let down our guard. We all became our message.

Several years ago, I worked at the Facebook headquarters in Menlo Park, California, focusing on helping people build relationships and community across identity divides. One day, while sitting around a table, a coworker who became a friend said she thought it was funny that I mentioned guarding my privacy so often while I also participated in so much publicity both before and after leaving White nationalism. I understood the irony, but I responded that it was pockets of privacy—no matter how fleeting or how briefly that I believed they'd last—that allowed me to lower my mental guard to hear things that challenged my core beliefs.

My now wife, Allison, factored high in those moments. She was the person on the other side in many of those pockets of privacy and, therefore, trust. When I told her I thought writing a book would be a good way to get my thoughts in order, she reminded me that privately journaling was always an available option for me. It reminded me of my friend at Facebook, perplexed about how I parsed my privacy with my public speaking and appearances. I hope this book bridges the gap between the veil of a "public profile" that makes me the medium of my message, with the intimacy that's possible in a personal relationship. By going back through my experiences of community, legacy, and family, I hope to show the ways that these things have not only shaped me, but also drive change from the largest social movements to the smallest individual relationships. I'm not telling their stories to justify them or seek redemption. While I believe it is essential to understand the White nationalist movement to counter its continued influence on our society, I am motivated to tell this story by more personal reasons as well. I am telling it because it is my story, as much as I have tried to run away from it, and I can't share what I've learned without sharing the context in which I learned it and how it felt.

When I started writing this book, I thought that my dad's maxim would mean that I wouldn't have records of my private thoughts. As I read through the archives, I realized what he had actually shown me was how to speak our thoughts and feelings where no one would recognize how personal they were, to translate them into forms that could and did appear on the cover of the *New York Times*. Our diaries were easy to find in databases of old newspapers, or in my scared face on *The Jenny Jones Show*. Some personal records could fade or be lost, but ours were reprinted, archived meticulously, and immortalized. My dad's records go back to the 1960s, when he joined a movement that was still nascent. His history and choices shaped mine, setting a course for my life that I'm still working to correct. This book is a part of that.

CHAPTER 1

A PERSONAL HISTORY OF WHITE NATIONALISM

THREE DAYS AFTER I WAS born in 1989, David Duke won his race for the Louisiana state legislature. David was thirty-eight years old, and he won despite having led the Ku Klux Klan (KKK) just a decade prior, despite continuing to espouse White power positions, and despite powerful figures in the Republican Party condemning him. Former president Ronald Reagan recorded a robocall that ran against David, which was highly unusual in a state representative election. Reflecting the international furor and fascination that surrounded that election, President George H. W. Bush spoke out against him as well, and Republican Party chairman Lee Atwater did the same.

The next year, David ran for the US Senate seat in Louisiana unsuccessfully. The year after that, he ran for governor and again lost. In those campaigns, however, he won 55 percent and 60 percent respectively of the total White vote statewide.

My dad worked on David's 1989 campaign, making the 800-mile drive from South Florida to New Orleans to pitch in. But he missed the victory party because he had driven back to Florida to be with my mom (who was also David's ex-wife), as she went into labor with me.

By that point my dad and David had been friends for twenty years. They met in the fall of 1969, when David was nineteen and my dad was sixteen. They had each written to the National Socialist White People's Party (NSWPP), a White power organization originally established by George Lincoln Rockwell as the American Nazi Party, struggling in the fallout following the 1967 assassination of its founder. In response to their letters, the NSWPP invited them to their conference in Arlington, Virginia, in the suburbs of Washington, DC, and helped facilitate their travel by coordinating a ride share.

In the era before computers or cell phones, this was all done through letters and postcards. The NSWPP wrote to my teenaged dad, telling him to get himself to a central meeting spot in Birmingham, the largest city in Alabama in the late 1960s, ninety-five miles south from his hometown of Athens, near the Tennessee border. David would be driving up from Baton Rouge, Louisiana, where he was in his second year of college at Louisiana State University (LSU). He would pass through and pick him up on his way to DC.

Birmingham had been at the epicenter of the civil rights movement. In May 1963, when my dad was ten years old, Birmingham's commissioner of public safety, Eugene "Bull" Connor, unleashed dogs and directed fire hoses on nonviolent civil rights marchers led by Fred Shuttlesworth and Martin Luther King, Jr. National coverage of those assaults and mass arrests galvanized national attention on Alabama's violent enforcement of White racial supremacy, and helped buoy passage of the national Civil Rights Act of 1964. Birmingham's Sixteenth Street Baptist Church was bombed in retaliation for the community's role in organizing the desegregation protests. The bombing killed four girls and wounded over twenty other church members. Though three men would later be convicted, an investigation into the church bombing had been completed with no prosecutions in 1968, the year before my dad arrived with his parents to make his way to his first White nationalist conference.

My grandmother told me how my dad first got involved in what she always called "politics," and that she and my grandfather Sport had been against my dad going to the Nazi conference at all. My dad told them that he'd be going with or without their consent. The compromise he offered was they could drive him south to Birmingham for the pickup, where they could assess the safety of the situation, and meet the other teen boys he'd be riding north with.

Sixteen years later, when my dad was thirty-two years old, living in Birmingham, and the leader of the Knights of the Ku Klux Klan—the particular KKK group that David had founded and, by that point, already stepped down and passed to him—he recounted his youth in an interview for a doctoral dissertation that he didn't expect to have wide public readership. He described growing up in a family that was "typically Southern conservative," and "very middle class." He described his parents as products of their environment: "Their attitudes reflected that of the community." They opposed the civil rights movement that was happening all around them, "as almost everyone did—all Whites in that community."

My dad described how, as an adolescent, he had "rejected a lot of what my parents held to be dear." Initially, that meant rejecting their religious views and declaring himself an atheist, as well as adopting, perhaps unexpectedly, more liberal, or less conservative, views than his family or community. As a young teenager, he would walk down the street to the small library on the corner, where the librarian knew him well and would order away for books that he requested, including lots of sci-fi and fantasy, but also political books. Most of them "took the other side of the race issue . . . and, for a while, I concluded that was probably correct . . . [T]he way to eliminate the discord, and the violence, was for all the races to mix together, and ultimately to achieve the time when there wouldn't be any individual races, so there wouldn't be any racial problems."

I've never heard my dad describe the response of his parents or his community to his contrarian adolescent years, but as he grew, he aligned with the foundational racist attitudes of his community. He said his newfound radicalism came from "what I saw around me, plus whatever else I could find to read," and that he felt Black inferiority was an objective reality: "[D]espite guaranteed equal treatment, and ultimately, as we've seen, preferential treatment, [Black people] were never going to be the same as White people. There was a profound innate difference, and the solution was not forced race mixing or forced integration."

My dad added there was "no specific incident that I could recall that would cause me suddenly to want to join" White power organizations, but rather, "I didn't understand the reasons for some of the things going on. I felt very strongly for my people and for my country, and I was concerned that something was badly wrong, and from there I read fairly extensively." My dad said he was not "in touch with any organization at the time. In fact, I felt pretty lonely."

I recognize in this trajectory both his fierce independence and simultaneously a very familiar need to belong. My dad's ideas about White superiority were obviously based in the beliefs and assumptions of his family, his community, and the White power structure of Alabama society. Yet my dad found their worldview incomplete and lacking, and he found their vision for society that came out of those beliefs uncommitted, unimaginative, not radical enough. So he reached out to the nascent White nationalist movement. "It was quite enlightening in that it was the first time I had actually seen any literature or books which expressed the ideas that I had suspected for a couple of years." He saw the world around him in discord, and he wanted better answers and people who cared enough to offer solutions and a vision. Perhaps, at one time in his life, that could have been civil rights activists, but the influences and avenues he found didn't lead him there. Instead, they led him and his parents to a meetup spot in Birmingham, where another teen who would be joining the drive was already waiting.

My grandmother would recount this story decades later, when my dad and I visited her on our frequent road trips around the country. She'd mention the detail that the boy they met in Birmingham that day had been wearing a wrinkled shirt and seemed poor. My dad would always intervene and remind her that that boy's wrinkled shirt should have been the least of her concerns. That boy, James Clayton Vaughn, Jr.—he later changed his name to Joseph Paul Franklin—was a high school dropout who had already ridden 250 miles north from Mobile, Alabama. He cursed and used racial obscenities, but he'd later explain in an interview that his family likewise "weren't members of any White supremacist organization or anything. Just about everybody in Mobile at that time during the '50s and '60s when I was growing up, used the N-word."

Franklin's grandparents had immigrated from Germany after World War II, and they had been unrepentant supporters of Adolf Hitler and the Nazi Party. He and his sister reported years later that both his parents beat, hit, and slapped them throughout their childhoods, and he carried many scars from his parents. In 1968, when he was eighteen, federal legislation against discrimination in housing had passed and had integrated the subsidized housing project where he lived. Amid the White backlash to integration, an older friend gave him White power literature that connected him to the NSWPP in Washington, DC. Looking back on those years, he recounted how "I just started hanging out with other people with similar beliefs, and when you hang out with people . . . who believe what you do, you are constantly reinforced. Once you consciously go over the stuff over and over again, it just goes down in your conscience and you begin to think that Blacks and Jews aren't even people at all."

Eight years later, in 1976, he legally changed his name to Joseph Paul Franklin, naming himself after two of his heroes, Hitler's propaganda minister Paul Joseph Goebbels and the American founding father Benjamin Franklin. After having left the Nazis to join the National States' Rights Party in Georgia, followed by a period with the violent United Klans of America, Franklin quit all White power organizations. He said, "I found out that most of the organizations are often infiltrated, so I had to take a different course of action."

Instead, he set out on a solo murder spree across the country that lasted for nearly four years, using a sniper rifle to kill Black people, Jews, and interracial couples, robbing banks, and bombing synagogues. The seeming randomness of his murders and his distance from his victims made connecting the murders difficult. He said from prison, "It was my mission. I just felt like I was engaged in war with the world. My mission was to get rid of as many evildoers as I could. If I did not, then I would be punished. I felt that God instructed me to kill people." Two years after Franklin was executed by the State of Missouri in 2013, my dad told an interviewer, "We weren't friends. He was a real creepy guy when I met him in '69. He didn't become a serial killer, a sniper of interracial couples, until the '70s."

DAVID DUKE, IN THE DRIVER'S seat, was named after his father, an engineer for the Dutch-owned Shell Oil Company. They had lived in the Netherlands for a few years when David was little and, when he was five, the family moved to a White suburb of New Orleans. Like my dad, David shared the experience of having considered himself liberal, committed to social justice and antiracism before he came to his views of White superiority as an adolescent. Also like my dad, he was raised in a family and community that upheld the "traditionally conservative position of the South."

Looking back, David credited his youthful liberalism to "practically everything written about the subject [of race] in books, newspaper and magazine articles, as well as everything on television led me to believe that the civil rights movement was based on lofty principles of justice and human rights." Consequently, "Because I was idealistic and aspired to be fair and generous and chivalrous—and because I was under the influence of the media—I came to believe that racial integration would elevate the Black people to their true ability and thereby guarantee justice for them and progress for all." In a trajectory remarkably like my dad's, however, in his early teenage years David accepted the opinions of racial superiority of Whites and inferiority of Black people that his community believed.

David's path to connecting with the White nationalist movement itself likewise was through seeking out literature that could explain and provide him supposedly "authoritative" evidence for White racial superiority and a worldview to justify it. He'd often describe how he'd been almost forced to seek out White nationalists, because literature from mainstream sources only took the pro-integration side.

In an experience similar to my own—at least at first—David arrived at Louisiana State University with his White nationalist views and having read White nationalist literature for years, but he spent his freshman year private and unassuming: "It was one thing having a discussion with a few guys in a dorm room, quite another to contemplate giving a speech." He was nineteen, like Joseph Paul Franklin, when he arrived in Birmingham, making my dad by far the youngest in the car at age sixteen. In DC, they found a White nationalist community that was already making headlines and formulating the ideology they'd foster for the rest of their lives.

When David returned to campus, he found his nerve to protest publicly and make himself known as a White nationalist spectacle. I grew up hearing about the legendary Free Speech Alley at LSU, where anyone could stand up and give a speech. One Wednesday at the start of his second year, David stood up and started giving a speech on White racial superiority and his arguments for the threat of a global Jewish conspiracy. Week after week, he kept coming back until he started to dominate the Alley. The LSU student newspaper, the *Daily Reveille*, reported that students had begun to complain that

Free Speech Alley had "become a soapbox for David Duke's own brand of racism." David went on to protest a campus speaker while wearing a swastika armband, shocking his parents when news and photos reached them. With a friend on campus, he founded a student organization they called the White Youth Alliance, along with a newsletter called the *Racialist*. They tabled on campus, looking for kindred students and offering books and pamphlets as reading material for passing students to take.

My mother—a year older than David—approached one of their tables that year and introduced herself. She borrowed a book, and David suavely put his number inside. They met a few days later. She was already a member of the conservative student group Young Americans for Freedom. He remembered her telling him that night that "she readily understood that if the White race was not preserved, that neither could conservative principles be saved." He wrote in his autobiography, "By midnight, I was telling her my dreams for the future and about the things that I so fervently believed. I could see that my words expressed her own feelings, and that they burned just as bright in her own heart."

I remember my mom mocking David's version of their wedding night, taking her small sunfish sailboat to a mangrove island in the Florida Keys. They camped on a dock of a barrier island that turned out to be infested with rats that came out once the sun went down, and overnight they got caught in a rainstorm. Sailing back to their car the next morning, David remembered, "Chloe began to cry, but we hung on until the storm had passed." My mom would remind us that she knew how to sail, not him, and she had not cried. My mom was twenty-three and David was twenty-two; she had graduated, and he still needed to complete a final year of college. So my mom opened a day care center and supported David through his final semesters of college. Together they set up a Klan office, buying books and office supplies, as well as a printing press to produce flyers. David began traveling to give paid college campus talks and, when my mom became pregnant with my eldest sister, he remembered years later (without a hint of self-consciousness at his absence), "It was difficult for Chloe, who had to contend with the day care center and the Klan office work while she was pregnant, but she never complained. She was ecstatic over the thought of our first child."

That same year, 1975, David ran unsuccessfully for Louisiana state senate in Baton Rouge, organized a media spectacle "Klan Border Watch" that drove along the US–Mexico border like a volunteer Border Patrol, and filed a free-speech lawsuit supported by the American Civil Liberties Union (ACLU) after the East Baton Rouge Parish School Board canceled one of his Klan events. The school board had canceled his rally after the civil rights branch of the US Department of Health, Education, and Welfare had threatened to cut federal funding if they didn't. In 1980, the case made it all the way to the Supreme Court, which ruled in David's favor and demanded the school district compensate David and the Klan. By that point, however, my mom had left David and New Orleans, taking my two sisters with her back to Florida. It would be a few years before my dad, who had regularly visited the Dukes during the years she was running the administrative side of the Klan, would reconnect with her. They would marry in the late '80s. David was the best man at their wedding.

First as adherents to Hitler, readers of *Mein Kampf,* and as new acolytes of the American Nazi Party, my father and the two boys riding in that car from Alabama diverged as they built what the modern movement became. David and my parents became founders of a new generation of the Ku Klux Klan, then suit-and-tie-wearing political organizers. Franklin became a mass murderer, condemned by my parents and David, but nevertheless represented the most abject violence that this movement logically produced. They were the founding generation of the next fifty years of the White nationalist movement in all its forms. Over the ensuing decades, they stood at the center of all the convulsions and expansions of a movement they each tried to define called "White nationalism." It carried their revolutionary fingerprints at every turn.

WHAT THEN, IN DETAIL, IS White supremacy and White nationalism? White supremacy is society's undercurrent. White supremacy is everywhere, and has to some extent touched every household with its insidious implication that White people have somehow earned their spot at the top of the social pecking order. It is the social system that leads to the manifold ways that our society denies rights and resources to people who aren't White. Everyone is affected by White supremacy, because it is woven into the fabric of our society, and its history has a strong legacy. It is what props up the "garden-variety" racism you can find in any majority-White suburb, workplace, or institution, and it is what props up White nationalism.

White nationalism is built on White supremacy. It is a specific social movement with a particular ideology, and its members label themselves as White nationalists. The White nationalist movement was created by people inheriting centuries of White supremacy instilled and preserved by a racist legal hierarchy. Laws began to formalize race and racist hierarchy in colonial America and White supremacy and racial slavery were perpetuated in the Constitution after the American Revolution. The civil war, despite five years of war and 600,000 people dead, didn't end the legal imposition of authoritarian White supremacy. Instead, state and federal governments produced completely new and horrifying forms of that oppression. Jim Crow segregation lasted for a century, and the withdrawal of explicit laws that codified race hatred came only reluctantly. It was in the context of the 1950s and '60s that White nationalists created a revolutionary movement that turned on the government it felt had betrayed them with even the mildest overtures to racial equality.

White nationalism can be amorphous and hard to recognize, but the particular mash-up of racial and antisemitic hatred plucked from different eras of history that drives it is one of the most reliable ways to define the movement. White nationalists believe:

1: Race is a biological category, the primary division of humanity that predicts people's behaviors and capabilities;

2: Jews are not White; that they are a separate racial group, not a religion;

3: Jews control global media and finance, and Jewish people collectively have used this power to orchestrate racial integration and antiracist movements and convince the American public to accept it;

4: Racial inequalities are not structural, meaning racial discrimination has ended, and any wealth or outcome inequalities in society should be explained only by individual and group ability and merit;

5: The color of your skin and other "racial" phenotypes are more important to preserve than culture, because they are the most significant quality of personhood; that a mixed-race child is "diluting" Whiteness, even if this child grows up in "White" culture;

6: Whiteness is under attack and that White people are being discriminated against;

7: Most White people would agree with White nationalist principles if their message were broadcast louder and without a negative spin;

8: Immigration by people they don't see as White to countries with a majority they see as White, and legal toleration of intermarriage, constitutes a "genocide" of White people; and

9: If everyone were separated by racial category, then White people and White majority countries would be at the top of the pecking order globally through sheer merit, and not because of historical legacies of colonialism.

The White nationalist movement arose in response to the civil rights era. In many ways, White nationalism was established on the view that the racial supremacist hierarchy set up after the Civil War wasn't extreme enough. Their ideology was based on the model, or at least on their understanding of the rhetoric, of Black liberation ideology, of "Black nationalism." Among the extensive library in my dad's office was a collection of the speeches and papers of Marcus Garvey, the pan-Africanist, Black nationalist founder of the Universal Negro Improvement Association. I had seen the book on the shelf for years, but I only realized who he was, after reading it as a teenager, when I discovered it was Garvey who had written the words that appeared in Bob Marley's "Redemption Song": "Emancipate yourselves from mental slavery. None but ourselves can free our minds."

Before World War I, Garvey had advocated for a mass exodus of Black people to Africa on his Black Star Line, inspiring a "Back to Africa" movement. He was controversial among other Black leaders of his time for his willingness to collaborate with White supremacist groups, including the Klan, arguing that they had shared interests in separation, but those separatist roots went even further back.

In the nineteenth century, the American Colonization Society established the West African nation of Liberia and proposed to facilitate the travel of free Black people to Africa. The society had been supported by American founders including James Monroe, James Madison, and Thomas Jefferson. In some ways, the White nationalist movement picked up where the Colonization Society left off, but while the Society upheld slavery by removing free Black people and thus maintaining the rigidity of the racial barrier, the White nationalist movement wants to uphold that racial barrier by removing all people whose bodies they see as challenging it. Its members want separation and a revolution to get it. The "nation" of White nationalism is not the American or any other state, but the nation of White identity, with only White bodies represented within it.

Rockwell's American Nazi Party wasn't the only group to capitalize on resistance to integration, nor the only influence on David, my mother, and my father. Citizens' Councils, often referred to as the White Citizens' Councils (though Council members are especially prickly that the word "White" was never part of the name), were formed by southern elites in the 1950s to oppose integration of schools and businesses. The Councils created private schools for White families, often called "segregation academies," in response to the Supreme Court's *Brown v. Board of Education* decision in 1954. Southern elites who didn't want to be a part of—or at least speak publicly as representatives of—the KKK or engage in direct illegal or violent actions could more proudly claim membership in the Councils.

In 1956, a year after the start of the Montgomery bus boycotts that elevated the profile of activists Rosa Parks and Martin Luther King, Jr. as they put pressure on the city to end segregation of public transit, W. A. Gayle, the mayor of Montgomery, joined the Citizens'

Council and publicly announced, "I think every right-thinking White person in Montgomery, Alabama and the South should do the same. We must make certain that Negroes are not allowed to force their demands on us."

King described the Councils as a "new modern form of the Ku Klux Klan." In response to the bus boycott, the Councils attacked the organizers using the multifaceted power of their economic control, including suing civil rights organizers, canceling insurance policies for their vehicles, evicting them from apartments, denying them lines of credit, and directly firing them when White business owners discovered employees attending marches or leading groups. King demanded the Councils be "held responsible for all of the terror, the mob rule, and brutal murders that have encompassed the South over the last several years." He asked President Eisenhower to investigate the bombing of his membership's homes and the hanging in effigies of Black and White integration activists in downtown Montgomery, but the US attorney general exonerated the Councils, declaring, "the activities of the White Citizens Council . . . [do] not appear to indicate violations of federal criminal statutes."

THE POWER OF THE COUNCILS eventually receded, as the fight to preserve legalized segregation increasingly lost steam. King had felt their power receding. He saw the dramatic victory of Lyndon B. Johnson with 61 percent of the popular vote over the far-right conservative Barry Goldwater in 1964 as a rejection of "representatives of . . . the White Citizens Council. It is my honest opinion that this same majority still finds repulsive persons who strive to impose 19th Century standards upon our society."

The true believers in racist ideologies didn't go away, however, and they found each other in the 1960s. They came from many disparate backgrounds, but what they had in common was a vision that the concessions to the civil rights movement, such as the opening of European-dominated immigration laws, the desegregation of schools, and the abolition of laws that banned interracial marriage constituted an existential threat to the White race. After Rockwell was assassinated by a disgruntled fellow member of the American Nazi Party, his followers picked up the pieces. A former nuclear physicist at Los Alamos named William Pierce, who had given up a tenured faculty position to follow Rockwell, hosted the conference my dad, Joseph Paul Franklin, and David Duke attended in 1969.

MY DAD'S FIRST PUBLIC ACTIVISM after returning from his teenage pilgrimage to meet movement leaders was to volunteer on the campaigns of openly segregationist politicians in the South. While the 1970s and '80s saw a decline in explicitly White supremacist politicians, my dad and other White nationalists recognized the more covert signaling that the GOP adopted after passage of the civil rights acts. White nationalists never felt fully supported by these new sorts of Republican politicians, and some drifted off.

My dad got to know Asa Carter, the speechwriter for Alabama governor George Wallace, who wrote Wallace's famous "Segregation Now!" inaugural speech in 1963. After Wallace toned down his racist politics, Carter protested his 1970 reelection, calling him a traitor to White people.

In 1974, my dad and David formed a Klan group that showed up to political events wearing suits and ties. The KKK had seen its political apex in the 1920s when it could count millions of members around the country, but in the 1960s, new Klan groups rose again nationwide. Not only did they grow across the South in response to desegregation, but some of the largest chapters came together outside of the South, such as in the Rocky Mountain West. These new Klansmen became a part of this new mix of radical White power ideologies. My dad and David's group were a major part of this movement, along with its attempts to mainstream White nationalist ideology.

And as David began his drive to break into politics, my dad ran for mayor of Birmingham, Alabama, in 1979. He only got 2.5 percent of the vote in an election that elevated the first Black candidate to become mayor of the city, which had been a stronghold of segregation. The headline about that election in the *Tuscaloosa News*, ironically, nevertheless was "Black Wins B'Ham Race."

One year when my dad and I visited my grandmother in Athens, Alabama, on one of our road trips, I asked her about all the news clippings I'd found in the closet, and she said she just wanted to make sure he saw all the publicity he was getting even back home. She then asked him pointedly, "Why did you run for mayor that year? You didn't think you could win, did you?" and he explained, with a slight eye roll that only his mom elicited, that it hadn't been about winning, but about raising consciousness and awareness of his group and their activities.

In the 1980s, the White supremacist network of the Citizens' Councils were re-formed and hosted Republican governors, senators, US representatives, and state legislators. My first introduction to mainstream politicians was at their meetings, where my dad took me every year from the time I was nine years old.

As teenagers, my father and David watched this movement coalesce, and over the coming decades they came to define its future, ultimately trying to build something new that united all these disparate factions—Klansmen and Nazis and skinheads, heirs of the old White supremacist political systems—to create a more radical ideology and social movement, which they called "White nationalism."

My dad adopted "White nationalism" as the description of the online community Stormfront that he founded in 1995. He rejected both Rockwell's founding term "White power" as well as the segregationist-era term "White supremacy," which he held, and which the Stormfront FAQ reported for decades, was a term for "a White who wishes to subjugate other races by force." He argued that his movement only wanted self-determination and geographic separation "as a means of defending themselves." The FAQ further clarified that the "formation of a White nation removes any possibility of White dominance of other races," ignoring the obvious implications for international hierarchy.

White nationalists were the one group that reliably could be expected to argue for open White separatism long after the last vocal segregationist politician recanted or was driven from office. Often White nationalists continue to be covered in the nightly news in contrast to the movement for antiracism.

As White Americans watched the slow turn away from explicit political White supremacy, members of the White nationalist movement rose consistently from outside mainstream politics to speak the unspeakable forms of racism that polite elites claimed were a relic of the past.

At the same time, the lessons of the David Duke campaigns were adopted and sanitized by Pat Buchanan in the 1992 Republican presidential primary, in which they both ran. Buchanan pitched himself to GOP donors as the safer alternative to David, and in his speech at the Republican convention that year, Buchanan sounded the White nationalist alarm: "Block by block, my friends, we must take back our cities, and take back our culture, and take back our country."

Buchanan and David both spent the rest of the '90s unsuccessfully running for office and promoting a White nationalist agenda. During the Clinton years, that agenda did not enter the mainstream of the Republican Party. When Buchanan ran for president again in 2000, Donald Trump told *Meet the Press*, "He's a Hitler lover. I guess he's an antisemite. He doesn't like the Blacks. He doesn't like the gays. It's just incredible that anybody could embrace this guy. And maybe he'll get 4 or 5 percent of the vote and it'll be a really staunch right wacko vote." Sixteen years later that agenda had clearly become a winning strategy.

I KNOW THAT THE HISTORY of the White nationalist movement is my history and exists somewhere inside of me. It's the part of me I feel the most shame and responsibility for. It wasn't just my inheritance, but also part of the legacy I had passed on. It was the unspoken recognition that no matter how much I wanted to disconnect and disappear into an academic life studying medieval history, I was still part of the thread that connected everyone inside and outside of the movement into a lineage that apparently existed below the awareness of most of the people I met.

I am haunted by the legacy of the White nationalist movement I inherited, and whose future I helped advance. Its violence is a source of infinite guilt and irreparable harm. I fear for our future, because I know that its ideology is not isolated or fringe—it rises up every time a politician talks about "woke ideology," a columnist writes about "the immigration invasion," or a radio host rants about "crime in our inner cities." No matter what choices I make, I cannot escape its impact on our society, and none of us can. I used to say on my teenage Internet radio show that, even if I didn't believe the rightness of White nationalism, I would believe in its power to impact society. I left it, and I have done what I know to condemn it and push back against it. But I continue to recognize the ways that it impacts our society.

Before I began to study history, I tried to understand my place in it. That wasn't difficult in a family like mine. The drive to know our place in White nationalist history was constant. I was born into a legacy that my parents had been building for decades before they had me. And they had inherited the legacy of at least a couple generations of White nationalist activists before them. Their whole worldview was based on a sense that America was founded as a White supremacist nation, and that they carried that legacy with them and wanted to fulfill it.

The White nationalist movement that I grew up in is constituted by relationships, both between current activists as well as their equally strong feeling of inheritance and responsibility to those who came before them. It's impossible for me to truly separate an objective sense of this destructive ideology from the fact that I understand their self-identity, love so many of them, and can never really separate myself from their story.

No matter how thoroughly I disassociate from White nationalists— I rarely even talk to my own family now—or how long I work with antiracist groups, who often embody the benevolent work I strive to see in myself, I still feel self-conscious about my history. I follow my values to fight for inclusion wherever I can in the spaces I influence, but I feel conflicted at every turn knowing that I have deep compassion for many of the individuals of the White nationalist movement. I try to act on my knowledge that nothing changes except when we strive actively to change it, and that we cannot change our past but can change our future. These people's lives only remain caught in that mire because they don't believe they could ever change.

Yet I have never lost the sense that the history of this movement has caught me up in a web whose threads connect me to everyone else. Maybe my consolation is the realization that no one else is free of those connections either. No White nationalist, no antiracist, no moderate progressive or conservative, and no one who thinks they are neutral to all of this is outside of the influence of the collective history.

WHY SHOULD WE TRY TO understand White nationalist ideology? Like many social movements, White nationalists have always relied on public attention for their oxygen. During the Donald Trump administration, journalists wrestled with whether covering the community only fueled the latent prospects of an ideology many viewed as politically impotent. On November 25, 2017, a few months after the Charlottesville Unite the Right march drew international attention and linked Trump and his movement more closely to White nationalism than ever before, the *New York Times* ran a story with the title, "A Voice of Hate in America's Heartland." It profiled a White nationalist Ohio couple preparing for their wedding. The journalist described the items on their gift registry, focused on the fact that the bride-to-be was taking the threat of Antifa activists breaking up their wedding more seriously than her fiancé was, and quoted her explaining that many of her best friends would still be attending, because "a lot of girls are not really into politics."

The publication of the *Times* story drew harsh criticism and backlash claiming that it was "normalizing and even glorifying hate." I stood—and continue to stand—behind that criticism. White nationalists are, for the most part, "normal" enough people. They watch the same popular movies, go to the same stores and schools, wear the same clothing brands, live in the same suburban neighborhoods as many other White people. The fact that this couple believed in White racial supremacy and also ate dinner at chain restaurants was a pointless and misleading connection to emphasize. It actually served one of the main media strategies of White nationalist activists: to present a public face of their movement that looks welcoming to prospective members who hold racist beliefs but are hesitant to join a fringe movement. It is not my goal to replicate those mistakes in this book or to underemphasize the harm caused by this ideology.

White nationalists have committed murder and perpetrated terrorist attacks around the world over a period stretching back over sixty years, resulting in hundreds of deaths. At the same time, running for electoral office and advocating brutally racist, harmful legislation has been the parallel goal of the White nationalist movement. These twin impacts on society continue to have lasting, deep, intergenerational effects today.

The people who joined that movement, who continue to join it, come from our collective society, and were taught the racist beliefs that led them there the same as everyone else. The way White nationalists are apparently normal is exactly why this movement can be appealing to other White people. It is made up of people just like them. No household is immune to the messaging of White supremacy; the ideas behind racism are entrenched because inequality is entrenched.

The assumption that extremists will be easy to spot or will stand out from a crowd because of their caustic behavior, unusual clothes, tattoos, or haircuts helps the White nationalist movement in two powerful ways. First, it tells people to expect racism to be distinguishable from "normal" behavior, when in fact structuring things to treat people differently based on their bodies is one of the most fundamental ways our society has been formed. Second, when the mainstream press says it's notable or surprising for an extreme racist to be reasonably smart, articulate, put together, or in some other way relatable, it implies that that person is somehow more reasonable or worth taking seriously than someone else with less education or money.

The assumption baked into that bafflement is less a critique of racism itself than a feeling that otherwise sensible people shouldn't openly declare themselves to be racist. Being smart, however, has little deciding power in whether someone is prejudiced or not. That is a question of experience and empathy. Smart people often construct the most elaborate justifications for the racism they learned from their community and family. Both of these problems are well understood by White nationalist organizers. The subjects of that 2017 *New York Times* piece themselves most likely knew exactly what they were accomplishing.

CONSIDERING THAT WHITE NATIONALIST ORGANIZERS are often media savvy, and have long used the ways they can appear relatable and familiar to many White people as the basis of their recruitment, there's an obvious question: Could we suffocate White nationalism by ignoring it, by depriving it of that oxygen it gets from public attention? That's a question I've contended with not only in writing this book, but over the past decade of my life since I publicly condemned the movement I was raised in.

My dad taunted me when I first began speaking out against White nationalism. When I published a *New York Times* opinion piece in the days after Donald Trump's election about the insidious nature of White nationalism, he mocked me, saying that by publicly describing his movement and its beliefs, I was actually recruiting new members from readers who find that description appealing. Both of us knew that dynamic played out in a lot of the coverage he and I received over the years supporting the movement. As a kid, I watched mass media attention jump-start Stormfront, the online community that he created in 1995. Although it has declined in relevance in recent years, replaced by new, younger online spaces, his website went on to be the largest and most influential space to grow and develop the White nationalist movement for twenty years during the formative years of the Internet.

I'm confidently writing the stories in this book as part of my anti-racist activism because of the two foundational things I've learned over the past decade since I condemned the movement I now write against.

The first is that it's not simply attention itself that boosts their movement, but rather attention that acts like we all don't already live in a society with widespread racist beliefs—that is, attention that ignores context. Journalists themselves often write on White racism as if it is a personal character flaw that they themselves are exempt from. The banality of White nationalism is the point, not an oddity to remark on. The choices of White nationalists are ethical failings, but they're also beliefs and decisions that are easily explained by recognizing that these people grew up in a society where the average White family has six times the wealth of the average Black family. Ours is a world in which Black people are imprisoned at five times the rate of White people, in a country that consequently has the largest prison population in the world.

None of the arguments that White nationalists employ to justify this world were invented by them. The historian Khalil Gibran Muhammad describes how, beginning in the 1890s, elites in American academia created statistics and social surveys to transform "racial knowledge that had been dominated by anecdotal, hereditarian, and pseudo-biological theories of race" into something that seemed more legitimate. Attending a White nationalist conference today, you'd hear that same late nineteenth and early twentieth-century pseudoscience. In this book, I work to provide that societal context.

The second insight that drives me is that it's never too late for someone to change their fundamental values and worldview. Although I recognize "changing your mind" on something fundamental to your community or personal identity is a difficult and painful thing to do, I also know it's possible. I want to tell this story because I myself want to be known, and to know me, you have to know where I came from.

After I condemned the White nationalist ideology and apologized for my advocacy for it in 2013 at age twenty-four, I tried to vanish into graduate history programs. At first, I thought that the fact that most White people didn't seem to be aware of the movement, beyond a few Nazis on daytime TV in the '90s or skinheads in movies like *American History X*, meant that I had seriously overestimated its significance.

Then, it began to feel like the mainstream culture that I had tried to disappear into began to reflect my extremist past that I had tried to ignore. I started to worry I was suffering from the Baader-Meinhof phenomenon, where something you've focused on seems to start coming up everywhere. After years of believing that this movement had an enduring hold over our culture, I had almost convinced myself of the mainstream mantra I'd heard my whole life. Racism and White supremacy were supposedly fading with time, replaced by a more open society that didn't need to cling to them. My goals as a leader within White nationalism had largely been about seeding conversations so that the ideas would pop up everywhere. I had failed to recognize we were not seeding the ground so much as reaping what generations before us had planted and which had grown so high around us we couldn't see anything beyond it.

CHAPTER 2

OPERATION RED DOG

THE INDIVIDUALS AND TYPES OF communities within the White nationalist movement vary widely. Organizations are as different as rural compounds, suburban political organizations, academic think tanks, radical Christian communities, militias, or skinhead youth finding each other at heavy metal concerts.

It is a decentralized movement, and few groups or organizations have formal memberships that would make it easy for an outsider to identify who is a part of the movement. Adjacent fringe or conspiratorial ideologies often share many of the social features of the White nationalist movement, which leads to a lot of the confusion about just how structured and organized it can be. The historian Kathleen Belew described White nationalism as "a broad-based social movement united through narratives, symbols, and repertoires of war," and that rings true with my experience. White nationalists are united by their agreement that they are the only people who see the world as it really is. Ultimately, the definition of whether one is a part of the White nationalist movement comes down to a question of relationships and identity, to whether someone shares the personal connections and stories that have accumulated and carried the movement through many tumultuous decades. Over the last sixty years, it is hard to name any particular event more important than the basic fact that so many historically different groups and communities coalesced at all.

White nationalism can offer a sense of purpose and identity that stands up against all reason and causes people to live miserable lives for decades, because they believe their sacrifices are so deeply meaningful. As a movement, it has an endless supply of potential new members willing to ruin their lives because of how many White people in America hold garden-variety racist beliefs affirmed by its ideology. White nationalist organizers know this explicitly. My dad always told me that we were looking for people who started sentences with the phrase, "I'm not racist, but . . ." Whatever they said after that was the foundation of the most extreme versions of the ideology.

DR. BELEW'S OTHER CLASSIFICATION OF the movement now gives me chills: "a broad and organized social movement supported by decades of networking, deep belief, and a shared sense of the coming end of the world." People tend to hear the word "apocalyptic" and think only of the violent, destructive, chaotic ending that such prophecies seem to always declare. Its original Greek meaning is simply "uncovering," in the sense of future events being perceived. That sense appears in the English translation of the last book of the Bible, the Apocalypse, the Book of Revelation. The community of White nationalists, and specifically my family who raised me, brought me up with the conviction that they knew the inevitable course of the future.

My family prided themselves on being well read, well researched, and intellectual. They draw on historical examples to build their arguments—in retrospect, often cherry-picked, presented out of context, or blatantly inaccurate. They tried to present a worldview that they thought was validated by facts beyond their own gut instincts. Despite being smart people, they could not ever engage seriously with the plentiful evidence that their beliefs about race aren't real.

In interviews and speeches, David Duke and my dad constantly referenced the racist views of the founding fathers to present a world in which White nationalist thinking was the historical norm. That drumbeat of historical references certainly got under my skin and influenced the academic direction of my life. Yet, for all their work to construct a world of the past, their real motivation was an inalterable confidence that their racist ideology foretold the outlines of the future. The job of movement activists like my family was to provide a nudge.

Everyone in the movement agreed that racial integration was death for White people. My family claimed to abhor violence, which helped them build a public groundswell of political victories. But their ideology was identical to those who declared war on the government, bombed civilians, and terrorized the nation. They are all the same movement, recognizing each other and trying not to get in the way of each strategy, because they recognize that it is only their degree of pessimism in the current system that divides them. It is a symbiotic system, and it is dangerous and ignorant to accept the common movement argument that you can draw firm lines between illegal revolution and political elections.

Every White nationalist, by definition, sees the wider world as an edifice that is disintegrating. White nationalists have watched the dissolution of European colonial societies in their own lifetimes, and perceive an ongoing end to White supremacy in America and around the world. They see their movement as encompassing all the resentful Rhodesians who lost their colonial farms and left Zimbabwe after its independence in 1980, and all South Africans who felt the end of Apartheid in 1994 as a threat to their way of life. White nationalists sensationalized news articles about brutal murders of any Whites there for years after they occurred, dwelling on the most lurid details of torture and violence. For White nationalists, there isn't any line between inclusion of non-White people and literal violence and death.

Seeing the world around them as so much loss, they are convinced that civil violence and social collapse are inevitable. That belief, the bedrock of White nationalist ideology, could erroneously justify nearly anything as an act of self-defense.

Both threads within White nationalism, the political organizers and the violent revolutionaries, are invested in a vision of a future White utopia, which they may or may not believe ever existed before. They all believe that a coming cataclysmic social destabilization will provide the opportunity to build it. They see the commitment of the United States to an idea of multiracialism, of equality, of financial systems that tie everyone together and theoretically try to level old divisions of race and ethnicity, as hypocritical at best and malevolent at worst. They point to the history of White flight from majority-Black cities, White people literally sacrificing their homes in order to isolate themselves in suburban enclaves, as proof in itself that the majority of Whites agree with them.

I once heard a well-read attorney, who had used his legal practice to defend my dad and David Duke over the decades, give a speech in which he claimed he wished for nothing more than that multiracialism and immigration would create a stronger society. He concluded his speech, however, by saying that, as Thomas Jefferson declared in his autobiography, "nature, habit, and opinion have drawn indelible lines of distinction between the [races]." Eventually, he told us, the ideas of egalitarianism would collapse under the reality of racial differences, as everyone fell back into the security of racial group loyalty. "Let the bad times roll," he declared, because then it might come soon enough for a unified White voting bloc in America to legally inaugurate a renewed White power government.

The policies that White nationalists want draw as much from American history as from Nazi laws. Their vision of a White nationalist government would focus on nothing else before trying to repeal the Fourteenth Amendment to the Constitution, not just because it guaranteed equal treatment, but to repeal the principle that anyone born in America is a citizen. Secondly, White nationalists are focused intensely on an immigration moratorium, followed by implementation of policies that only allow immigration from European countries with people they consider White. The brutality of their deportation policies would rival Nazi Germany, but the foundation of all their earliest policies would be based on reinforcing race as a primary social and legal category.

My family believed that a last-ditch effort could change the future politically, so they were considered more "optimistic." Their violent compatriots thought they were naïve. Like Bolsheviks on the eve of the Russian Revolution, they didn't see much worth saving in the world as it is. They welcomed its overthrow, and no one around me seemed to have an argument against them other than a wish that things might go slightly differently if they organized things now. In his speech hoping that the "bad times would roll" as soon as possible, the attorney had condemned conservatism as a lost cause, because, he said, there was no longer something left to conserve.

THIS SENSE OF THINGS DYING, of the end of a people and of a history, was always present in my household. I absorbed it on a personal level as a background anxiety. When I was nine years old, soon turning ten, the idea suddenly overwhelmed me that I would likely not live to see the number of digits in my age change again. Time was running out. That realization led me to a moment of existential dread.

I remember asking my mother when she and my dad would die, whether she was afraid of it, and how long it would be before I died. Few of my other memories of conversations with her are as candidly emotional and protective as that one. I remember her crouching down in the kitchen, telling me that I was right, that life was limited, and that both of them were much further along in what life they had left to live. Even so, she said, it would be a long time before they died, and even longer until I did. She told me that a lot of life would happen between those two points, and that I would understand it more after having experienced everything in between.

Death was also personal because of how it seemed to stalk my dad's stories. Many of the people he had met when he was young in the movement had already died. The violence that made up the backdrop of most everything he had experienced unnerved me. My dad had a long pink scar across his stomach where a surgeon had extracted a bullet when he was sixteen. As a young staffer on a segregationist political campaign in Georgia, he had been tasked with stealing the mailing list for an opposing White power organization. He was caught on his way out by their security guard, Jerry Ray, whose brother, James Earl Ray, had assassinated Martin Luther King, Jr. eleven years earlier.

My dad described the shot from the hollow-point bullet as feeling initially like nothing, making him more angry than scared or hurt. Then he felt the warm blood on his hands. He stumbled to a nearby laundromat and collapsed. He told the story of waking up in the hospital, seeing his parents, who had flown on their first airplane to come get him, and doctors telling him he had almost died on the operating table. He'd interject dark humor about how ludicrous that statement sounded to him at the time. He couldn't imagine dying. He was in a hurry to get out of the hospital and back to working for the cause, albeit preferably with people who valued his health and safety.

Once he recovered, he came home, and for his senior year his parents transferred him to Madison Academy, a private high school in Huntsville, Alabama, about thirty-five miles away. He drove fast on the country roads back and forth every day. Huntsville was and is well known for its space research facilities, and it was in that environment that he became enamored of the development of the rockets that had landed Americans on the moon the year before. They were designed in Huntsville by Wernher von Braun, a German scientist seized by the US Army in the last weeks of World War II.

Von Braun had previously designed the first liquid-fueled rockets in the world for the Nazis, creating the V-2, which bombarded the UK in the last months of the war. My dad often quoted the line that von Braun supposedly said as he watched his rockets shell England: "The rockets worked perfectly except for landing on the wrong planet." It always struck me as somewhat incongruous with the apocalyptic predictions of race wars my dad always made, but it did fit with his claim that he wanted to avoid that kind of war. Space travel for my dad always seemed like his most lofty exit plan out of the world he thought was doomed. He idealized von Braun as a figure who, he presumed, agreed with his beliefs about race—von Braun had joined the Nazi Party and the SS—and who also saw interplanetary travel as a way out of the conflicts, pain, and hardship he had experienced on earth. Yet, like von Braun, his idealism masked the painful detachment and lack of empathy he showed for the harm his ideology caused.

OVER A DECADE AFTER HE was shot, when he was twenty-eight years old, my dad joined nine other Klansmen trying to overthrow the government of the newly elected prime minister of the Caribbean island of Dominica, Eugenia Charles. Growing up, this story contrasted with the quiet man I knew.

Prime Minister Charles was the first woman in the Americas to be directly elected as head of government. The White power mercenaries my dad joined planned to reimpose former prime minister Patrick John, who had led the small island to independence from the British Commonwealth in 1978. John had been replaced by Charles in an election the previous year in 1980. In exchange for bringing weapons and support of this small band of White power mercenaries, John had apparently agreed to fund White nationalist groups in America afterward.

My dad and his co-conspirators were stopped in the New Orleans harbor in a boat filled with "Nazi and Confederate flags, dynamite, and thirty high-powered rifles." The press dubbed it the "Bayou of Pigs." Seven of the men pleaded guilty, but Mike Norris, Danny Hawkins, and my dad refused a plea bargain and went to trial, charged with violating the 1794 Neutrality Act, a felony.

During his trial, my dad turned the case into an international news story by claiming he and the others had been working in the direct service, covertly, of the State Department. He and Danny tried to "muddy the waters," as they'd both describe it to me years later, on our frequent stops at Danny's house in the woods in Mississippi. They tried to implicate mainstream officials as supposedly knowing about and approving their plot, from the newly elected President Ronald Reagan to the libertarian Texas congressman Ron Paul. I always loved staying with Danny more than anyone else, because I could run through the woods that we didn't have at home, playing with his pack of dogs, catching fireflies, and leading the adults on nightly tours of the firefly "shows."

My dad and Danny had defended themselves based on the federal government's inconsistent enforcement of the Neutrality Act, which they were being charged under, throughout the twentieth century. Signed into law by George Washington, the Neutrality Act forbade "any military or naval expedition or enterprise to be carried on from thence against the territory or dominion of any foreign prince or state, or of any colony, district, or people with whom the United States is at peace." The law was famously used by Thomas Jefferson in 1807 to indict Aaron Burr for attempting to make war on the Empire of Spain along the borders of the Ohio River, three years after Burr had killed Alexander Hamilton in a duel and stepped down from the vice presidency.

At the time of my dad's trial, the federal government had a very public recent history of using mercenaries and training insurgents for covert wars. The post–World War II Cold War order saw a string of wars not formally declared by the United States. Many of these operations armed and trained guerrilla combatants to wage war on regimes that were friendly to the Soviet Union. The failed Bay of Pigs invasion of Cuba had been led by 1,400 exiles, covertly trained and funded by the US government, and had seemed to violate American neutrality. In response to such accusations, Attorney General Robert Kennedy stated at the time that the Neutrality Act was "not designed for the kind of situation that exists in the world today." By the time of the Reagan administration, in the political climate in which my dad and Danny were defending themselves, there were calls for the government to enforce the law in order to constrain CIA actions.

The year my dad went to trial, the *Washington Post* broke the news that President Reagan had authorized the CIA to train Nicaraguan exiles in Florida and California and send them to attack the Soviet-friendly Sandinista government. The news lent support to the Dominican conspirators' claims that they were acting on behalf of the US government, or had at least credibly believed they were. At the trial, my dad and Danny spoke to the jury about how their mission had been patriotic and in the anti-Communist interests of the United States. Still, they were convicted of violating the Neutrality Act, but found not guilty by the jury on five firearms charges.

The next year, President Reagan invaded the nearby island nation of Grenada with the support of Prime Minister Charles of Dominica. From prison, my dad balked at seeing Charles standing with Reagan as he announced the invasion: "Prior to our arrest, she had made overtures to Cuba and her statements were published in the press in this country. . . . Apparently, since then she has been mollified by offers of U.S. aid."

Thankfully for my dad, and therefore later for me, the colonial origin of the Neutrality Act meant that it capped sentences at "not more than $3,000 or imprisonment not more than three years, or both." This was a far cry from the decades to life in prison that modern "war on drugs" laws impose, which have contributed to cruel and racist punishments in the modern era. My dad served a two-year prison sentence at the minimum-security federal prison in Big Spring, Texas.

THE DOMINICA CONVICTION WAS MY dad's greatest embarrassment, but it was also an event he revisited frequently, almost like he was trying to vindicate himself. It was clearly a major part of his self-image, his regrets, and a mark against the person he could have been. Although he usually added that he thought being twenty-eight years old was past the cutoff for youthful indiscretions.

When my dad and Danny were both older and more docile, they each gave me accounts of how they'd gotten to know each other in the plot. Danny was older, already gray-haired, and seemed to become a little more paranoid every year. He worried that federal agents were watching him from the woods, and he was convinced they occasionally killed his dogs to send him a message.

I knew Danny had a long Klan history in Mississippi, but it seemed hard to believe this gray-haired man with a Santa Claus beard would still warrant that kind of attention. In private, my dad reassured me there were no federal agents out there. Instead, my fears when I slept on his couch at night were of the strange sounds from the unfamiliar animals in the woods. I would stay awake as late as I could, while both of them talked and told stories of old times, until I fell asleep from exhaustion while they were still awake and had the lights on. I'd wake up in the daylight ready to go exploring again.

I didn't realize until I was a teen that his nickname for me when I was small, Red Dog (after my red hair), had also been their code name for the coup attempt: Operation Red Dog. When I started going through classic movies on Netflix, I made a list and rented all my dad's favorites. A film about mercenaries from 1980, *The Dogs of War*, was one I remember him talking about most. The plot follows American mercenaries hired to overthrow a country in Africa, and it felt especially poignant.

The relationships my dad made then lasted a lifetime and were the earliest mentors I had in the movement. The first time I saw fireflies was while running with Danny's chow chow dogs in the woods. My mother once broke her ankle by slipping down the steps from Danny's trailer porch while carrying too much luggage and infant me. She laid me safely in the grass, but she carried a large scar and metal pins in her ankle ever afterward.

I HEARD PIECES OF THE story of Operation Red Dog throughout my life, and I absorbed it all. Like many of my dad's stories, the tale of his conviction eight years before I was born gave me knowledge of a whole series of radical talking points about American incarceration and undeclared wars that served me well when I went to college and found myself in conversations with activists on the left who were concerned with many of the same issues, albeit from a totally different social justice orientation. His conviction for such a bizarre mission always felt especially challenging to integrate into the version of the man I knew. He described it as a mistake, so I filed it away as an aberration. I didn't wrestle with his history as deeply as I needed to, with the broader violent implications and intentions of the movement he was a part of.

In some ways, Operation Red Dog's failure felt like a relief to me, considering the even darker history of the White nationalist movement. In the early 1980s, a group called The Order engaged in a violent crime spree. They robbed armored cars and a bank, and assassinated Jewish radio host Alan Berg. White nationalists revered members of The Order such as David Lane, who created the famous "fourteen words" that served as a White nationalist mantra: "We must secure the existence of our people and a future for White children."

I picked up on the conflicted ways that my family talked about Lane and the other Order members, but that didn't stop them from allowing me to quote Lane on my White nationalist kids' page. In his more contemplative and private moments, my dad sometimes later described his two years in prison as the luckiest thing that could have happened to him, because he wasn't available to be approached when Order members started recruiting and organizing their plots.

I used to often say that White nationalists never want to talk about the end. They never want to describe the moments of breaking down people's doors, the trains, the rounding up of families in large numbers that would be necessary to impose a racial state on a land that has no homogenous ethnic regions, and never has in its colonial history. But I'm not sure that's fully true. We had Pierce, and we had the problematic posters who showed up on Stormfront regularly and were only banned if they explicitly advocated for direct violence now, against living people today. When they said that the future would be like the Nazi era of mass deportation, many of them got very explicit.

Beyond the violence, or the illegality of invading another nation, what I never really understood was how the overthrow of the Dominican government fit within the goals, as I understood them, of White nationalism. Some of the leaders talked about setting up casinos in Dominica, or about other sources of funding for the Klan that would follow a successful reinstallation of the old prime minister. That wasn't something my dad ever talked about. The idea of a younger version of him sailing across the sea and risking his life to impose a Black dictator on an island nation few Americans had ever heard of so he could raise millions of dollars as a kickback just seemed weird.

No matter how in line with the anti-Communist mission of the Reagan administration my dad's plan may have been, its ultimate goal was the same as every part of his political career: the eventual recognition of a new racial nation within the United States. Whether that be the American government adopting an entirely new direction, a new one to subsume it, or some process of carving out a new White racial state from within it, White nationalism was fundamentally not a patriotic movement. As the government of the United States made efforts to move away from its racial supremacist roots, members of the White nationalist movement saw it as illegitimate for doing so.

After my dad was released, he initially returned to running the Klan—he had never formally given up his leadership, even while in prison. For the two years that he was gone, he had left it to "lieutenants," as they were called in the movement, who ultimately would seize control in their own administrative coup and push him out. In 1985, while he was still running the Klan, my dad described David Duke's reasoning for resigning from the Klan several years earlier in an interview. He reported that "David felt that the Klan was—was not as effective as it previously had been and had a lot of—many things that would have to be overcome. . . . And there are a lot of people that would—that do join an organization such as NAAWP [National Association for the Advancement of White People, David's successive group], that would be reluctant to join the Klan." He didn't mention the scandal that had surrounded the way David left the Klan, trying to sell the organization's mailing list to a rival Klan. The privacy of member information is always highly important for an organization that carries social and professional consequences for being outed. My dad had planned to join him in that exit, but stayed after David's gambit backfired—his buyer turned out to be an FBI informant.

Ultimately, David's reasoning would become my dad's as well. By 1987, he had resigned the Klan, and in 1988, he moved to Florida and married my mother. The next year, he helped out with David's campaign using an important new skill he'd learned while taking computer classes while in prison. He had learned to code.

CHAPTER 3

STORMFRONT

IN 1989, MY DAD ESTABLISHED a dial-up bulletin board system, called a BBS, for David Duke's campaign for Louisiana state representative. It was designed to serve as the digital communications hub for the campaign volunteers, and users literally dialed in by connecting their phone receivers to modems anywhere in the world, before the phase of AOL and dial-up Internet. They then posted text messages that were routed through a server running on a computer my dad operated. Users could log in to see what news, messages, and information others had recently posted.

The Internet had existed in various forms for decades, developing slowly as more powerful computers joined the network. It was not immediately obvious to computer enthusiasts, including my dad, how fundamentally the graphic interface and hyperlinked "webpage" format of the World Wide Web would radically alter our culture and escalate wider personal computer and Internet adoption. In 1994, he set up a server on his desk at home in Florida, similar to the one he'd run for the campaign, and opened the Stormfront network again as a dial-up BBS for the use of tech-savvy White nationalist activists across the world. Having left Alabama and his Klan leadership at the end of the 1980s, his next project became building and expanding a community for himself and for everyone who came to it.

While our plumbing rarely worked perfectly, leaving us without hot water for months at a time, the windows were broken and couldn't open despite not having air conditioning, and our roof often leaked, we always had the latest technology, most up-to-date desktop computers, and fastest available Internet access at our house. When ADSL connections became available over telephone lines, my dad had the phone company set up a new distribution box down the street and run new lines specifically to our house, so we could become the first people in the neighborhood to have broadband and leave dial-up speeds and limitations behind. When I was a small child, he'd warn me not to accidentally unplug the computer on his desk, because it would cut off hundreds of activists from around the world.

To make our home such a central nexus of the movement made us a publicly identifiable target, not only as the organizers of the largest network of White nationalist communication, but as one of the most prominent families of the movement. In addition to having two family dogs, a German shepherd my parents got me when I was three and a Belgian shepherd mix we'd adopted a few years later, my parents were explicit that someone always had to be at home and on guard. If we all left at once, even with our dogs at home, we were leaving ourselves open to invasion. Most directly, this meant that my mother usually stayed home while my dad and I went on multi-week road trips a few times a year.

I was familiar with the paranoia that I saw in Danny on our trips to Mississippi, but many of the threats on our house were undeniably real. Letters and packages to my dad's post office box sometimes came with loaded mouse traps, loose razor blades, or bags of feces or urine waiting to burst when we opened them. My parents taught me careful techniques for inspecting and opening anything that arrived so that I wouldn't get hurt.

Since age ten, when I'd set up Stormfront for Kids, I had received a constant stream of terrifying threats of violence or death in my email inbox. We'd had threats to the house. An obsessive stalker had called our phone hundreds of times a day for years, leaving endless voicemails that vacillated between professing her love for me and threatening me with vicious obscenities, detailing the ways she would rape and murder me. I had spoken to her while I was answering the phones for David's 1997 congressional campaign and someone on the campaign had explained to her who I was. Her obsession began; I was eight.

At the beginning of the 1990s, the rhetoric of far-right violence in the 1980s continued and escalated. In 1991, the White nationalist Idaho survivalist Weaver family had undergone eleven days of siege by federal agents on their land in Ruby Ridge, Idaho. The father, Randy

Weaver, had been charged with selling illegal guns to an undercover ATF agent posing as a member of the Aryan Nations White supremacist group. Weaver didn't show up to his court date, and then refused to surrender to federal marshals when they showed up at his property. During the siege, Weaver's wife and son were killed by federal agents. I knew their story as a child, both from legends inside the movement as well as the CBS miniseries about them. Four years after the standoff, in 1995, Timothy McVeigh cited the deaths of the Weavers at Ruby Ridge as a reason for his terrorist bombing of the civilian Alfred P. Murrah Federal Building in Oklahoma City, the deadliest terrorist attack in US history until September 11, 2001.

A month before the Oklahoma City bombing on April 19, 1995, the *New York Times* ran a story on how the White nationalist movement was using "electronic tools" to spread its message. The main thrust of the story had been following the founding of Resistance Records the year before, a label that produced and marketed skinhead music and video content, which had rapidly grown in sales, influence, and revenue. The *Times* described the new company as an operation that "[runs] its own record label, produces video documentaries, promotes its bands and publications on its own Internet site and publishes *Resistance* magazine, the slickest periodical in the White supremacy movement." The anti-hate organization the Simon Wiesenthal Center called it "a new model for purveying hate."

My dad told Stormfront members the origin story of their community. The record label had set up their own dial-up BBS, which the *Times* reporter called an "Internet site," following the one my dad had established the year before, but their main business was selling CDs. The reporter, my dad remembered, "called me as an afterthought to get a quote about this newfangled Internet."

The article became the first one to report the tech backstory that was becoming his primary interest, calling my dad "a former Ku Klux Klan leader from Tuscumbia, Ala., who learned computer technology while serving a two-year prison sentence in the early 1980s on a Federal sedition charge. Mr. Black now operates Stormfront, a White supremacy computer bulletin board in West Palm Beach, Fla."

My dad's words struck precisely the articulate fear of new technology and its malevolent purposes that the article had intended: "All this has had a pretty profound effect on a movement whose resources are limited," he said. He then reported to the *New York Times*, apparently as the sole authority, that "a third of households have computers, and with the phenomenal growth of the Internet, tens of millions of people have access to our message if they wish. The access is anonymous and there is unlimited ability to communicate with others of a like mind."

He always enjoyed telling the story of what happened next, how he leveraged the power of the traditional mass media against itself to bootstrap his creation of the first and largest White nationalist website and community. It was a near-symbiotic tale. Stormfront existed then only as a public-dialup BBS, sitting on his desk, tempting my six-year-old curiosity to knock down or unplug. He had made it public in 1994, only a year prior. It was this article, and the interest in his tiny "White supremacy computer bulletin board," that jarred him to set up the first White nationalist website, and one of the earliest websites in general. He remembered, "I hadn't quite managed to get a website at that point. I'd registered the domain name months earlier, but my local internet service provider hadn't gotten his webserver working."

Following the *Times* story, he got calls from the *Miami Herald* and the Fort Lauderdale *Sun-Sentinel* to run "competing front page Sunday features . . . about my dialup BBS . . . with my background spicing things up. The wires picked that up. Then ABC News called."

He knew a website on the World Wide Web would spice up the story of his cutting-edge technology: "I called an internet service provider in New Orleans, whose owner had been a David Duke campaign supporter, and they had the account ready that day." Even more important than the website itself was a large and showy graphic. He remembered, "I spent all night manually coding the website, which I'd never done before, and had it ready in time for Mike Von Fremd, and his ABC camera crew the next day."

In order to have something to show them, he created a website and filled the front page with a stark Celtic cross designed by a local

Cuban White nationalist graphic designer, meant to fill the screen, surrounded by the words "White Pride World Wide." The striking logo was beneath the domain name written in a red German Fraktur font, created by the same designer.

MY DAD ALWAYS TOLD ME that story as a lesson to think through what media crews need from you in order to get what you want. What they often need, to this day, is visually striking imagery. The design of Stormfront's new homepage made it more likely that the editors would show it on-screen, which guaranteed that viewers would get the URL address, and be more likely to find their way to join the community.

This was the same savvy that made him drape a Confederate flag in the corner behind his desk for interviews, creating a more visually striking scene to encourage them to leave in more of his interview. The press got the story they wanted, and he got exposure for his movement and his website's library of White nationalist content. Quickly, Stormfront rocketed to become the largest online White nationalist community.

Landing on the site, new visitors saw a declaration: "Stormfront is a resource for those courageous men and women fighting to preserve their White Western culture, ideals and freedom of speech and association—a forum for planning strategies and forming political and social groups to ensure victory." It was a message that had called to him as a teenager, and that he believed would draw in an entire new generation. It made me curious to understand the subtleties of his choices, of the meaning behind using an archaic German Fraktur script. I read about the history of the Celtic cross, trying to understand how it had come to be so tightly associated with this movement, but also appeared in Irish pubs and on some churches. As I moved between the White nationalist community and the wider world, sometimes it was critical to understand when a symbol I knew from Stormfront was considered scandalous, like a swastika; when it was only slightly questionable, like a Confederate flag; and when it was a code few beside White nationalists knew, like the numbers 14 (standing in for the quote "We must secure the existence of our people and a future for White children"), 88 (for

the eighth letter of the alphabet, H, standing in for "Heil Hitler"),
or the acronym WPWW (standing for "White Pride World Wide").

THE OKLAHOMA CITY BOMBING HAPPENED only a few weeks after my
dad established Stormfront on the back of media coverage. The attack
sent national media on a quest to cover the movement that had motivated McVeigh to act out one of the nightmare scenes from William
Pierce's novel *The Turner Diaries*.

For at least the first decade of Stormfront's existence, those media
appearances could double or triple traffic and exposure for days. The
initial enormous spikes would dissipate, but, like an outgoing tide, they
deposited new people who became fixtures of our community. In the
early years, I could have a fun conversation with most senior members
of Stormfront by asking them what major interview they saw my dad
on that lit their way to us.

For one woman who became a senior moderator and a close family friend, that was my dad's interview on *Nightline* in 1998 with Ted
Koppel. After a pre-edited opening montage—they recorded it in our
home, it took all day, and blew out a fuse when they tried to run the
lights—they invited my dad on air to speak in the live interview portion that concluded the show. I was nine and watched the broadcast at
home with my mom, while my dad spoke live across town at a studio.
The show had sent a limo to our house to pick him up in the front
and drop him off back home once it was over. Afterward, I ordered a
VHS recording of it and the network mailed it to us a few weeks later.

The segment was about whether or not to censor hate off the
nascent Internet. I remember being so proud to see my dad debating
a constitutional lawyer who despised what Stormfront stood for but
who defended its First Amendment right to remain available instantly
in the growing number of homes buying computers.

After years of clawing for attention, my dad's observation from the
year before, "tens of millions of people have access to our message if
they wish," was becoming a reality. Even so young, I remember how
it felt like the sun was breaking through the clouds. All the adults were
shocked at how quickly their fortunes and dreams were changing. It's
a strange experience, at nine years old, to know with certainty that

these moments you're sharing with each adult in your life are just as new and shocking and confusing to them as they are to you.

In that interview, it struck me even then how my dad talked about "we" in response, every time Koppel or his other guest referred to him as "you" or "Mr. Black." That "we" felt like it expanded out to encompass not just our family, but in some way all the Stormfront members I had begun to chat with in the evenings on the Internet Relay Chat server that he routed through another computer on his desk. I had learned to touch-type when I was seven, so I prided myself on my speed, although the adults told me my spelling was terrible. When I leapt into my own first interview on *The Jenny Jones Show* the next year, it was *Nightline* that I remembered.

WHEN I WAS EIGHT, I had built my own desktop with my dad's help, using parts we bought together at a monthly computer fair and from the specialty computer parts shop. When I came home after school, I'd play pinball on my Windows 95 computer. I'd practiced touch-typing with the Mavis Beacon software, which sparked my whole family to joke that a Black woman was teaching me typing. I knew the Stormfront members, some of whom were even young themselves, the children or relatives of adult members. I connected with people across the world, and although I was only six, then seven, then eight, then nine, I was already a veteran of the community before most of them arrived.

When I logged on that night, during and after his triumphant interview, I didn't have to imagine my family's larger community. I knew they were watching in their own homes, because I could see their live commentary.

Beyond the circles of elated White nationalists, Koppel and the other guest must have known that, among the millions of viewers of the show there were certainly potential new adherents who agreed with "Mr. Black" but didn't know where to go until they saw that interview and the URL along with it. My dad delivered the full version of his favorite quote from Thomas Jefferson live on TV, only the first part of which is engraved in the Jefferson Memorial in Washington, DC: "There is nothing more certainly written in the book of fate than that these [the Negro] people are to be free."

The redacted but genuine second half, he noted indignantly, continued, "Nor is it less certain, equally free, they cannot live under the same government." He added, "In fact their views . . . weren't that much different from my own." Koppel's interruption, "If you'll forgive me, most of us won't have trouble distinguishing between you and Thomas Jefferson," ended the show on a slightly dejected anticlimax. My dad had the last word to opine on free speech: "The truth will win the debate. There's no controlled point of view on the Net."

At home, it seemed clear that the White nationalist community—which was coming to feel more like the Stormfront community—felt like they had won the night. Their numbers were growing by the minute as the live broadcast continued. At the time, hearing that quote and others like it from America's founding fathers gave me comfort and security that our ideas and community weren't as wrong as the world wanted us to feel. Now I hear them as a founding curse that allowed a family and community like mine to see rallying around inhumanity as moral and noble. Denying charity and kindness to others should never have come so easily. A social heuristic like that should have died as soon as it was created in colonial laws centuries before. Racism should have been intuitively wrong.

Afterward, the webmaster for the New York Anti-Defamation League criticized the way the show handled everything: "[Don Black] was like an honest computer consultant with a different point of view. I believe in contextualizing this stuff. Most Americans will reject this garbage when they understand what it is. But people do elect demagogues—and any soapbox only serves to fan the flames."

The producers may have felt like their program offered a reliable format to marginalize what seemed like a ridiculous group of extremists. The steady hand of the interviewer and the network could telegraph just how repulsive they found my dad and his followers. Yet, in advertising Stormfront to such a large audience, this new technology, a website, which a growing majority of that live audience could immediately visit, *Nightline* offered White nationalism a gift. Like the *New York Times* the year before, that broadcast was in large part responsible for the rapid growth that Stormfront and the White nationalist community experienced over the following decades.

Few people in the audience likely would have ever shown up at a physical Klan event, or have written to a Nazi group's address, or overcome the social taboos and hesitations of going headfirst in any way. The number of people who made the anonymous move to visit a website at the dawn of the Web was instantly multiples bigger and faster than the laborious searching and waiting that had been necessary before.

MY DAD WAS A RELATIVELY assured and calm figurehead of a community that he hosted nightly, in his home, through the computer tower that he ran on his desk. Back then, the homepage of Stormfront featured an FAQ including questions like "What is White Nationalism?" and "Who Rules America?" that tried to reassure readers that the community wasn't committed to "hating" other groups. The introductory material introduced readers to the antisemitic conspiracy theories that underlie White nationalism's racism. After reading those primers, or maybe sooner, depending on their attention spans, they could click on the "Discussion" tab, and find themselves immediately in a forum among thousands of other posters. The list began with discussion of the news, but the subjects branched out into areas for music, recipes, hobbies, youth discussions, or new categories that were regularly added once enough requests for them were made. The forum was meant to provide a space not just for racist and antisemitic beliefs, but a communal space that could foster those beliefs no matter what aspect of life someone needed a community to share.

Suddenly they'd found a place where people would never shame them if they complained about immigrants, never ask them to rethink their double standards, never give them a moment to wonder what might improve in their own lives if the lives of the people around them weren't so tilted away from fairness. It was a space that reinforced their fears, told them they were right to seek out a sense of security in being White. If their kid didn't get into their preferred college, they had a community where they could demean strangers and feel better about themselves. Almost any subject that *Nightline* considered beyond the pale was open for anyone coming to Stormfront to bond and connect over.

The time from seeing a story on the news to standing at the edge
of a (virtual) room, wondering whether you should introduce yourself,
had gone down to seconds in an instant. It was not a kind environment
most of the time, however. There were very many extreme, caustic
personalities, toxic rage, and aggression. As a younger child, I initially
avoided the public forum for exactly that reason, preferring chat rooms.
But if someone was motivated, they could find friends.

As the years went by, and the Web itself became larger and more
connected, the impact of traditional media waned. My dad regularly
showed me the latest graphs that demonstrated how the impact of his
interviews on new traffic had decreased every year, and month over
month. The total amount of daily traffic to Stormfront had grown
to a point that almost no television or print interview meaningfully
budged our average daily numbers. As I once told a group of Google
researchers who were interviewing me to investigate anti-hate inter-
ventions, nothing in history could compare to the torrent of new users
who had found a home in White nationalism by using the basic search
engine they had created.

IN 1995, THE SAME YEAR Stormfront took off, National Public Radio's
Morning Edition visited the "small and plain home of White separatist
Don Black" that sat "on a pristine middle-class street." The journalist
had come to us seemingly confused about the early Internet, and asked
my dad's opinions about censorship and the future of networked communities. "Congress is considering a bill that would ban pornography
from computer networks," she said. "Hearings on the proposal likely
will address hate speech as well, but White separatists and Internet
advocates say the network should remain completely unrestricted."

Another article that year, in the *Wall Street Journal*, described how
the presidential election was changing "amid the usual tide of election-
year chatter on television, in newspapers and on talk radio" and also
on "the Internet's World Wide Web." Among those "cyberpundits"
was my dad, who offered his standard take: "The Web, I think, offers
an alternative medium, which is relatively inexpensive, and which
organizations and movements such as ours can use to promote our
point of view without censorship."

He saw himself from the beginning as building a new, larger community than he'd ever found before by using the low friction of the Internet. Unlike the organizations he'd headed, Stormfront assumed the shape of the movement itself, bending or expanding to make room for every facet of the White nationalist cause. If they could adhere to the ground rules that banned discussion of explicit violence or illegal activity, it seemed at first like any subset of the movement could find a niche. Increasingly, the large waves of new visitors who had no previous experience in White nationalist spaces began to outnumber the old guard who had found new organizing spaces online.

As the head of this new virtual space, my dad felt conflicted almost from the beginning about his leadership role. He appointed senior moderators to handle daily issues, and dedicated himself to technical support and to mitigating online attacks by hackers who tried to take down the server on a nearly daily basis. Eventually, the technical hurdles receded, security and bandwidth increased to make the scale of attacks significantly more difficult for the attackers.

In our living room closets were brown, moth-eaten cardboard boxes that contained souvenirs of all his leadership roles over the decades. There were Klan robes, sewn by my mother and other women in the '70s, that felt like relics of an era that belonged closer to textbook history than what I should be able to hold in my hands. It was hard for me to imagine the version of him that I saw in the old photo albums I also found in those storage boxes. In some, he was dressed in those same robes, with cadres of the press flanking the edges, hustling for placement at press conferences in the middle of a field, to hear from a national leader of the Ku Klux Klan, all of them standing in front of a flaming cross. Microphones were pointed toward him from different directions to capture his words exactly. In some slightly later photos, he wears a regular business suit, while his so-called lieutenants are dressed in the formal white hoods around him.

The version of him I knew gave plenty of interviews, but they were never on behalf of his "organization," and rarely to promote anything other than his invitation to cross the divide and join his growing community. More often, he spoke as a commentator, embodying an educated bleeding-edge tech evangelist. For journalists and television anchors, he became someone to offer context or explanation to the news. I could imagine a tweaked reality where he became a TV talking head. He would have enjoyed being asked to pontificate, but being agreeable was never his priority or strength.

In 1999, the Simon Wiesenthal Center issued what became a regular update to their growing attempt to catalog all hate sites on the Internet, and said somewhat defeatedly, "This is the bottom line: they're not overthrowing America tomorrow. They're still a limited fringe. But they have established a significant, unprecedented beachhead in the mainstream of our culture."

During the presidential election the next year, my dad told the *Washington Post* that his, and most Stormfront members', political goals were to "restore White majority rule to the U.S. while we are still a majority, during the next three or four decades." In the alternative and openly leftist newspaper *New Times*, in 1998, he had forecast, "We see the breakup [of the United States] coming in about twenty years—it's a natural progression of events," and called the Web "a means of planting seeds for the future. There are a lot of middle-class people who feel disaffected—and, in Stormfront, they can find what they can't in the mass media. It's about building a community and attracting hard-core supporters."

That online sense of community grew stronger as the website and forum grew, first from countable regulars who signed on in the evenings and recognized each other's usernames, then to hundreds of people online simultaneously every night until, by the 2000s, tens of thousands of users connected and posted in a growing list of topic and language sections, from home repair to literature to movie reviews in French, Spanish, Norwegian, Polish, Swedish, Czech, and nearly every other European language. It became impossible to know everyone. As the community grew, most people no longer knew who I was. I'd regularly run into problems when someone was shocked to realize they were debating a twelve-, thirteen-, or fourteen-year-old kid. Inevitably a moderator would join the discussion and reprimand them for being rude to "the boss's son."

As Stormfront grew less easily managed, my dad stepped back more and more from the direct work of moderating posts. As the founder of the largest and oldest White nationalist community, whose roots stretched back into the decades of movement history, he was a topic of gossip and criticism, and he took it personally. Always an insomniac, he stayed connected constantly, reading both the discussion on his own site and on the smaller communities that had sprung up over the years, essentially refuges for the people banned from Stormfront.

The old politics of the movement in the '70s and '80s sometimes played out on Stormfront, but, for the most part, new members didn't personally know that history or those old grudges. It felt to me like the expansion of the Web into something impersonal drove my dad to begin traveling more to in-person events again, where he could reminisce with old comrades. He felt driven to found Stormfront as an online community shortly after he moved away from his stomping grounds in Alabama. I only hazily remember the parties my parents hosted when I was very young, where longtime activists would come from out of town and stay over late. The parties happened before Christmas, but they formally called them winter solstice or pagan Yule gatherings, because they were all outspokenly atheist, and enjoyed being contrarian. My dad brewed beer and mead, and my parents' friends would loudly come together to drink, eat, and share their time together. One winter, the weather turned uncharacteristically cold, and the ice chest outside froze solid. They told that story for years, even as the decades went on and their house parties had long stopped.

That his community was online meant that we were both at the center of things, and yet everything felt far away. Increasingly, the visiting journalists, making the pilgrimage to ask his opinions about the future of the Internet and of White power and the ballooning numbers of new members joining Stormfront, occupied his time and his energy. And then, gradually, they grew to occupy mine.

CHAPTER 4

THE HEIR APPARENT

IN 2001, A *USA TODAY* article began, "Twelve-year-old Derek Black won first place this year in a local science fair, and he carries around an encyclopedic knowledge of frogs, snakes, fish and the Web. With red hair past his shoulders and slightly crooked front teeth, he looks like the typical tech-savvy preteen he is. Yet the thing that makes his father proudest is that Derek runs a Web site for kids—promoting White supremacy and racial hate." "I get a lot of people who think I'm just a pawn in this horrible game of lies," I'm quoted as saying to the reporter, perhaps somewhat dramatically. Anticipating that she believed my upbringing was cultish and isolated, I described a whole scenario drawn from examples in my email inbox: "One person said, 'Don't listen to what your father says. Go turn on the Discovery Channel. Find out what the real world is like.' Why would I turn on the TV to find out what the real world is like?'"

My youngest childhood memories include flashes of being cared for by my stay-at-home dad, of carrying a large glass bottle of apple juice we'd bought at Costco with a cup across the concrete terrazzo floors of our living room, heading for his office, so he could pour it for me. I still carry a scar on my thumb from tripping and breaking the bottle, although I don't remember the damage or the time healing. I remember once swinging outside on the jungle gym my parents had built for me, when the chain broke. I hit the ground and it knocked the wind out of me. Terrified and gasping for breath, I clambered inside and to my dad's office to find him. He hugged me and drew a warm bath to calm me down.

I remember touring preschools with both my parents, them asking me to choose which I preferred. I remember refusing to drink the polio vaccine in a pediatrician's office, and my dad arguing with the doctor on my behalf. If I didn't want to take it, he told the doctor, then no one would make me. When I was very little, up until around age eight or nine, I'd invite the kids who lived down the street to my house to play in our yard, and we'd walk back and forth between our houses nearly every day after school. As we got older, we lost touch.

I attended a local public school through third grade. When I look back on my final year there, my memories include taking an art class outside on a cold Florida day, working at a picnic table with my best friend Manuel, whose family came from Mexico, and a Black girl named Gretchen who was, for reasons I can't remember, my constant frenemy. Their signatures and kind send-offs are written in the back of my class yearbook. Their notes are also filled with descriptions of me conducting what felt like preadolescent social campaigns. They remembered, "Derek always wants to be last in line," which I started doing when I realized that the scramble for the first spot was too hard to win.

My parents withdrew me from Palm Beach Public Elementary School at the end of the third grade, when I was nine. As with preschool, I remember them asking me what I wanted to do: a private school or homeschooling. They didn't like that the public school class was multiracial, or that many of my teachers weren't White. My mom heard my teacher say the word "ain't" at a parent-teacher event, and she told that story forever afterward to explain why I couldn't have stayed there. I chose homeschooling.

My parents began following the philosophy of "unschooling," a subset of homeschoolers who believe that kids should be allowed to follow their curiosity and never be forced to study. It felt incredibly freeing and respectful to me, making all my own choices about what to read and how to spend my time from the age of nine to nineteen. My dad argued with my mom about it for the first couple years after they took me out of school. She was convinced I needed a traditional curriculum, and that he needed to teach it to me while she was at work. He insisted that I was unique and was using my time in the best ways for me. I also think he was reluctant to become a manager of what I read and how I learned.

Homeschooling for me really did look like what kids imagine quitting school would be like. I could learn whatever I wanted and, more importantly to me, I didn't have to study anything I didn't want to. Looking back, it's genuinely incredible that it was only in math that I had to take any remedial courses when my mother dropped me off at our community college a decade later.

For the first few years of my homeschooling experience, my parents took me to an annual exam mandated by the county. The organization didn't report our scores directly to the state of Florida, but, rather, they passed on a recommendation for us to proceed to the next grade level or not. I got very high scores in reading and writing, high scores in science knowledge and social studies, reasonable scores in math application, and terrible scores at math calculation. That test was the only time of the year I needed to worry, once I had ground my mom down enough that she stopped trying to spend her evenings after work walking me through the homeschool math curriculum she bought and that my dad refused to make me follow. For better or worse, the homeschool organization indicated they weren't going to report me when so many of my scores were above average. My mom relented on teaching me math, but insisted she wouldn't let me get by without learning domestic skills, so I "wouldn't burden my future wife." She taught me how to make a full Thanksgiving dinner on my own, and gave me a final exam by having me make every dish one year, and bragging about me to all our relatives as they ate. She showed me how to do dishes, laundry, iron, sew a button, and house maintenance.

During weekdays, my dad took me to various homeschooler social functions, taking advantage of cheap rates for the water park, skating rink, and laser tag. And I volunteered at the local science museum years before I could officially fill out a sign-up form by just showing up several times a week and informally giving tours. I began at age nine or ten, announcing to perplexed visitors I was going to guide them through the exhibits and proceeding to do so.

When I was eight or nine, I started refusing haircuts when my mom gathered the family to give us all trims. I wanted it long enough to put behind my ears, I told my parents when they sat me down to ask why I wouldn't let them cut it. True to their style, they let me wear it however I wanted, even though strangers started consistently mistaking me for a girl. I liked the gender confusion, except in public bathrooms, where adult men always took it upon themselves to compliment my looks before telling me I was in the wrong room. After puberty started, I kept my hair long, but I was able to use the bathrooms in peace, and was relieved to stop getting the inappropriate comments.

I attended summer snorkel camp, seeing the same kids year after year, but I never tried to maintain those relationships during the year. As a homeschooled kid, I was objectively isolated, but I rarely felt lonely.

MY LEAVING SCHOOL ALSO ALLOWED my dad to take me into the complicated social world of White nationalism. He had initially left me behind when he'd go on his road trips, until I wrote an adamant letter demanding he take me with him, printed it on our inkjet, and shared it with my parents.

The most confusing aspect of navigating that world as a child were the contradictions. The nonviolence that my family, and many others in the supposedly political and intellectual activist groups, espoused didn't square with the common hero worship of genocidal dictators like Hitler or domestic terrorist organizations like The Order. As I grew into a kid who hoped to direct some of this network of personal relationships and loyalties, it became clear that the names of our heroes didn't operate in the same way that arguments and talking points did. They were a powerful means to show your membership in the group.

I conducted that first interview for the cause on *The Jenny Jones Show* around this time. Later, my dad described the experience to his online community as "going to the circus" and swore, "I know . . . I promise I won't do it again." That description felt absolutely appropriate. Like being a performer in the circus, I was rewarded, and I got to see the world, including the virtual reality Aladdin Magic Carpet ride at DisneyQuest, in exchange for a moment of my time and the sacrifice of my privacy.

A month afterward, traveling with my dad to Jackson, Mississippi, I attended a meeting of the Council of Conservative Citizens, the organization that had inherited the side of segregationist politics that tried to present itself as cultured and sophisticated. I posed next to the podium with the governor of Mississippi at the time, Kirk Fordice. In the picture, I'm looking at the camera sternly. My dad always said

I arranged the photo so I could put it up on the new Stormfront for Kids political site I had set up. I don't remember if that's true. A month after that, a reporter for an alternative newspaper from Tampa came to our house, and I greeted her at the door for my second-ever interview. "I've come expecting to find a stunted, twisted, hateful child," she wrote. "Instead of an emotional cripple, I find an easygoing, genuine young man, who makes me think 'nice kid.'" In that interview, she remarked, the family does not "call themselves racists, they call themselves racialists. They don't call themselves White supremacists. They call themselves White separatists." When she asked me, as Jenny Jones had, "why having this page was important to him, Derek says, 'White pride, keeping the race alive.'" Still a few months from my eleventh birthday, she recorded that I was convinced there was "a subtle genocide of the White race afoot," and that I wanted "to save the remnants."

I had been close friends at school with kids who were Black, Jewish, and Hispanic, but I hadn't maintained any of those relationships when I started homeschooling. Still, I got to know other teen volunteers at the science museum, including Black and Jewish kids with whom I didn't share the White nationalist part of my life. As the years went on, my family became more reclusive, and I accepted distance in my relationships as the price of living an increasingly movement-driven life. I can't discern any moments when I wasn't conscious of the expectations of my family and their movement.

AFTER MY APPEARANCE ON *The Jenny Jones Show*, I began giving more interviews, becoming a public advocate for our cause in *USA Today*, *60 Minutes*, the *New York Times*, and even *Nick News* on Nickelodeon, which was especially memorable, because I actually watched that show regularly. I appeared on a continuing stream of media for a decade.

Writing about my past now, it feels impossible to separate my own narrative from the stories written about me. They are an archive of every point, and they are a record of my conversations with my dad. Together, we gave the press a salacious story. I joked with him that they thought I was "the devil child," like a White supremacist Damien from *The Omen* movies, an Antichrist unearthing our deepest wounds.

I joked with White nationalists at conference after-parties about how funny it was that all it took to get our message out was to embrace their horror. I had to learn to be okay with welcoming my being the devil child in those interviews.

When I was eleven years old, I swore off doing interviews for months after the HBO documentary *Hate.com* interspersed clips of me with shots of lynchings and an interview with the serial murderer Joseph Paul Franklin from prison. I decided to start doing interviews again later that year after a Japanese film crew visited and gave everyone in our house gifts for welcoming them and thanked me even if I wasn't willing to talk to them. I carried the pocket watch they gave me for years. Their story felt kind and understanding; I hadn't participated, but wished I had.

Before each journalist or crew came to the house in those early days, my dad would ask if I wanted to participate. That responsibility did not feel like something forced upon me, although as I approach the age my dad was when I was born, I can't imagine acting the way he did. As a child, being asked to make those decisions felt empowering, but they were also impossible to refuse. In the face of his convictions, turning away, and not using my own outspokenness, would have felt like cowardice.

When I started giving my own interviews at our house, my dad made a point to leave the room, so I wouldn't be looking for his reactions or approval. A local elderly friend of the family would often come over when media crews were there to sit around and visit. My dad called him a crank, a category of movement person that usually translated as the older men who hung around gossiping and shooting the shit about the news. During one of the interviews, I was seated in the makeshift interview chair they'd set up in the middle of our home office. My dad had left the room, but Paul was there. When the interviewer asked me what I thought about Hitler, I started a long equivocating answer about how I didn't admire him, but that the media overplayed how evil he was. Paul interjected from the couch, saying, "Careful, Derek," and I realized my mistake and redirected my answer toward something else about our current beliefs. I was probably eleven or twelve for that interview, and Paul's caution stuck with me for years afterward. I didn't know how to square the abundant fascination and admiration for Hitler and his regime I saw all around me with the public distancing my dad and David always did.

I came by my worry about this contradiction naturally. In an interview in 1985, four years before I was born, my dad explained why he was leading the Knights of the Ku Klux Klan even though his friend David Duke had stepped away to avoid the bad reputation the Klan carried: "That's the advantage to the Klan. It's very difficult to label us neo-Nazi, because we are a completely American organization. It's very difficult for the media to taint us. . . . Well, certainly there are similarities in philosophy [between the Klan and the Nazi Party]—no question about that—but, . . . people will just not make the association."

I INITIALLY HESITATED IN STARTING my own kids' page on Stormfront because I didn't want to start receiving the hate mail that filled my dad's inbox. I'd enjoyed running an innocuous personal webpage I'd set up when I was nine. There, I posted articles I wrote about my favorite country singer, Alan Jackson, Spider-Man, my niece ("aka the cutest baby in the world!!!!!!!!!"), tornado chasing, the Chernobyl explosion, and anything else I got interested in. That site only drew other fans of those things to contact me.

As predicted, when I started Stormfront for Kids, my mailbox began to fill with messages I learned not to read. While many were from concerned adults—and I'm sure if I looked through them now, I would have a very different perspective—the only ones that stood out for me then were the brutal threats of violence. Before I even reached puberty, I had already learned how to distinguish between death threats that were just talk, ones meant to unnerve me, and ones that I should alert my parents to. Details mattered. On the rare occasion they'd mention specifics about our house, about what I looked like, or describe places they knew where I went, I'd forward them to my dad, and he'd archive them in case we ever needed the evidence. The parts of my life that terrified me were never as far away as I wanted them to be.

As the years went by, and our movement and the community my dad had built grew, our personal lives at home felt increasingly isolated. Media attention felt like a siege sometimes, and going out to play in the yard carried an intangible threat that I learned to monitor. Our house was not a place I would bring friends.

My dad's felony conviction meant that under Florida law he couldn't vote or possess firearms. This meant that I didn't grow up with guns, which always felt like a relief. The threat of violence was never far enough away to feel comfortable being close to guns. My dad's lack of personal protection was a concern he'd bring up often, and my mom would always brush him off and tell him he was being ridiculous. He speculated about getting an "antique weapon" that was in a gray area of Florida law, but he worried about law enforcement taking him to task for possessing even that.

When I hit my early teens, I discovered medieval reenactment. My dad saw a solution to our self-defense problem and asked me to look for people selling functional crossbows, maces, morning stars, and other medieval implements. When another, older volunteer at the local science museum overheard me talking to my friend about my new hobby knitting medieval-style steel chainmail inspired by *The Lord of the Rings*, he told me about the local medieval reenactment group. The reenactment group met in the park in front of the science museum. I became enmeshed in the culture and remained enmeshed for years. My mom sewed costumes and regalia for me, my dad, and herself to attend the meetings and formal events and dinners.

ONE NIGHT WHEN I WAS a teenager, while my parents were enjoying a rare date night out to see The Who, a band they'd both loved as college students, I heard someone walking outside. I was sitting at my computer, when our dog Heidi began barking in the distinctive way she did at delivery people. Heidi was both the alarm and the deterrent, and that night I heard something in the narrow passage in the back of our house.

It was obvious when people were away, because our car would be gone from our driveway. I stayed up late usually, but I often didn't keep lights on. That night I waited, growing more worried, as our dog kept focusing on one of the back windows. When the sounds outside continued, I decided I needed to do something before I found myself alone in the house with an intruder. Years of hate mail and death threats played through my mind as I drew a combat sword from my closet. We had two. One was blunt edged and rounded on the tip, meant for play combat with heavy padding and steel armor. I grabbed the other, the one that had been sharpened.

I snuck out the side of the house, quietly moved into the narrow passage behind the house, overgrown with vegetation. I held the heavy sword ahead of me, pointed forward in the darkness, and moved quietly. I edged forward until I was close to the sound, then I spoke out. No one responded, but the sound stopped.

I stomped my foot and held the sword tightly in my knuckles. Something ran the other direction down the narrow passage. It was an animal.

IN MY MOTHER'S INHERITED ANTIQUE glass-fronted cabinet, under the tall, vaulted wood ceilings of our living room was a complete bound set of the eleventh edition of the *Encyclopedia Britannica*, published in 1910 and 1911. One of my great-aunts had ordered them by mail, one at a time. Collecting the complete works felt like an impressive accomplishment. I had come home to them when I was born, and they were in the background of the photos of every Christmas present opening, birthday party, and Thanksgiving of my early childhood.

In the early '90s, when I had a question about how the world worked, my parents would lead me to the right volume of the collection. When I asked why the sky was blue, we cracked open the entry for "sky." There I learned that a whole chain of people had wondered this before me, and I learned how they tested theories through experiments and discussions.

Maybe just as important for my family, this edition of the *Encyclopedia* from the early twentieth century was open in its racism. Within the pages was seemingly the collected knowledge of a civilization. My parents told me I should use it explicitly because it was a record of knowledge before there had been a fall of knowledge of the world and our place in it. They said it was an archive of the last generation of Western thinkers before truth had been conquered.

My parents weren't unique among homeschooling families in leaning specifically on the eleventh edition to educate themselves and their kids. There were local expositions where homeschool families could buy supplies, at-home curricula in every subject, and where we could sign up for group social activities. A common product sold was a digitized version of the *Encyclopedia*.

MY DAD HAD SPENT HIS entire childhood and adolescence buried in books, and he tried constantly to find the right stories to spark my interest. He bought me collections of classics like *Treasure Island, The Invisible Man, Robinson Crusoe,* and *The Time Machine.* I remember him bragging to friends that he'd won a victory by getting me all the *Goosebumps* books by R. L. Stine, scary stories for kids that were made into a TV show I loved on *Nickelodeon.* I'd lay on the floor, engrossed in reading them, excited that I could go beyond the ones that had been adapted for TV.

My favorite in the series was *The Haunted Mask,* which I read over and over. It is about a girl who buys a hyper-realistic monster mask and uses it to terrorize her bullies on Halloween. It slowly changes her personality, making her into a more callous and cruel person, and she refuses to take it off when her friends beg her to. At the end of Halloween night, alienated from everyone, she desperately tries to remove the mask only to discover that it's become her real face. I didn't recognize at the time why the story resonated so strongly for me. The idea of a horrifying mask that gave me a sense of power, terrified even adults, but which slowly became my own face that I couldn't take off clearly mirrored the experience of my own public reputation growing over time. I wanted to preserve who I felt like I was with myself. The more I performed the role I thought I needed to to feel confident, the more I worried I'd lose the soft and curious version of me I saw myself to be.

Despite occasional passions like *Goosebumps, The Lord of the Rings* (I read my dad's copy in advance of the movies), I didn't become the voracious reader he'd hoped I'd be. I was extremely literate, in the sense that I often wrote essays online for fun. I loved words, and I wrote well enough that a lot of the hate email I got claimed I couldn't possibly have written them so young. That always made my preadolescent ego proud. By my mid-teens, however, I became concerned that I didn't actually know what I would have learned if I had been in school. I embarked on reading the multivolume *Norton Anthology of English Literature* that we had on the shelf, and I went through medieval and Renaissance poets, Victorian short stories, novels by Charles Dickens, all the collected "classic" stories like *Treasure Island* that my dad had added to my room over the years. I started to read Shakespeare's plays and was quickly perplexed why anyone should read something that was only written to be acted. I researched the "best" unabridged film versions of all of Shakespeare's plays and went through them one at a time.

Being unschooled felt like swimming in too-deep water, never knowing what stories or styles, references, or basic knowledge would be something that other people knew, or that I would wish I knew. I grew up in the culture of White nationalism, yes, but I also grew up in the context of unschooling, where I missed the fads, the music, and the adolescent peer pressure to distance oneself from one's parents; the impact of both linger today.

MY MOM WAS VERSATILE AND could learn any technique to remodel our aging house well enough to avoid paying a professional contractor. From the time I was in kindergarten until I left for college, she and I renovated the house, which her parents had built in the 1950s, fixing things one by one from the foundation to the roof ridge. When I was a teenager, she asked me to replace all our old glass and aluminum awning windows. After I discovered the hot water was leaking under the concrete floors, she and I replumbed the house room by room. Always trying to stay ahead of hurricanes and leaks, she and I reroofed most of the house section by section.

She worked long hours at her job, which meant that weekends were the only time she could commit to our projects. Consequently, she and I tried to fence in the yard one section at a time, repanel the bathroom walls and tiles area by area, build a new kitchen counter and cabinets one section at a time, install new lighting fixtures corner by corner and room by room, and replane the terrazzo floors, renting a machine to do it in one area at a time. We were never able to get our projects all done at once, and the work we hadn't finished would often degrade and need to be replaced before we had even moved on. Most projects never did get fully finished. Even after I started community college, and then when I went away to finish my bachelor's degree, every visit home was an invitation to jump back into ongoing projects with her.

Looking back on my childhood, it sometimes felt like I was an only child, but I have two sisters. Erika and Kristine are each more than a decade older than me, and their dad is David Duke, the White nationalist leader, my father's best friend and my mother's ex-husband. They lived with my mom when she married my dad and when I was born, but Erika moved back in with David in New Orleans before I was old enough to remember. Kristine left home to go on the road as a rebellious teenager when she was sixteen and I was five.

When she came home, I remember that Kristine was generous enough sometimes to let me join her with her teenage and then early twentysomething friends. I remember sitting next to her on the bench at the end of our porch at night while she smoked cigarettes, talking about our family and what she'd seen traveling the country. We talked about life and what it meant to have a purpose, and about our family and what an inspiration they were to us both. She seemed so adult, but also young enough that our mom treated us both like kids. My dad avoided interfering in their relationship, which was often antagonistic and heated. I remember hiding when that antagonism flared. In an effort to staunch their conflicts, I printed out signs to hang on the fridge commanding, "No Yelling" and "No Arguing," but my attempts had limited success.

She moved back home when she was twenty and I was eight, telling my mom she was pregnant. By then, she had already traveled the country for several years. Kristine had seen mountains and snow and met people in different White nationalist communities across the country. I couldn't always tell from her stories what that had looked like, or if those people had all been good people. I could tell that some of her experiences had been scary, and I thought of her like a hero for having gone out into the world and seen so much more than I had dreamed about.

MY NIECE WAS BORN WHEN I was nine. I spent days in the hospital with Kristine, sleeping on the guest chair in her maternity room. One of the first pages I created on my own website was about my niece, and over time, I documented each of her firsts, from her first step to her first word and writing about her personality.

My relationship with my niece was something between a younger sister and a particularly close cousin. She and I grew up together, but my trajectory led me ever deeper into a public life where my reputation grew every year, and every year White nationalism took up more of my time and mind.

I remember walking to pick her up from school one day, like I usually did in my later teens. Although I had long been active on Stormfront and in media, being recognized in day-to-day life was relatively unfamiliar. But it was increasingly evident to me that the parents and babysitters also showing up to that elementary school knew exactly who I was. No one confronted me, though. While waiting for the kids, a father approached me to explain that he and his family were from the Dominican Republic, but that I should understand that they considered themselves White, and that many other Hispanic people from the Caribbean were also White. I was already familiar with some White Hispanic perspectives, but it was striking to have a stranger approach me to tell me how many people like him supported my positions, so long as I was not racist against him or his family. My niece's teacher came up to say she had seen me on our local television, and she thought I had been very articulate.

My niece, however, had become a target of gossip in her fourth-grade class and in the school, first because some of the kids learned from their parents that her grandfather was David Duke, who was infamous, but later also because I was her uncle, notorious on TV and in the papers, and the one who picked her up from school each day. Despite that discomfort, she never asked me to stop being so public, and I don't ever remember her asking me why I did it.

Our immediate family, including my sister, were adamant about our White nationalist beliefs. It was obvious that, as the two youngest members of the tight-knit inner core that made up our immediate family, my niece and I were expected to uphold White nationalist beliefs. That included not being friends with kids of color or with Jewish kids and, especially, as we got older, to date anyone who wasn't White. For me, in my isolated homeschooled existence, that admonition had been easy enough to adhere to. I didn't invite anyone over, and I only dated girls associated with the movement until just before college. Kristine tried for a while to follow my parents' example and homeschool my niece too, but following the same free-form lack of curriculum didn't work as well for her. When the pressure grew to salvage her education, and her intense desire to socialize became clear, Kristine enrolled her in private school.

As my niece grew into adolescence, it was clear we were very different people. She wanted to be friends with anyone, and she did it whether our family approved or not. When friends at her school asked her about her family, she would explain it was their beliefs, and that they would be the first to tell you they didn't hate anyone, but that she didn't believe the same things as them.

Kristine was outraged to see her daughter indifferent to our ideology, but I told her we couldn't demand anything, and we shouldn't expect conformity. Privately, I admired how open my niece was to be friends with whoever she wanted and to like whatever music she wanted. In return, she was treated like a disobedient delinquent in our family, while I was honored as a leader and visionary. I tried to help by surreptitiously downloading the hip-hop and other forbidden music she asked me to get for her iPod.

WHEN I WAS A CHILD, my parents took me to see Stone Mountain, the enormous curving oval mass of granite and other quartz minerals that rises unexpectedly from the ground in the suburbs outside Atlanta, Georgia. I was eight or nine years old and on a road trip with both my parents, three people of the four million who visit the park every year. The mountain itself feels otherworldly, rising abruptly out of the ground like one hemisphere of a globe of stone that bubbled up from the earth's mantle. Visitors to Stone Mountain come now to hike and to see the enormous carving of three Confederate leaders—President Jefferson Davis and the generals Robert E. Lee and Stonewall Jackson. It is the largest Confederate memorial in the world, as well as the largest relief carving of any kind.

Beyond just being a large stone canvas on which to work, Stone Mountain has special significance for White nationalists. It was the place where the Klan reemerged in modern America at the turn of the twentieth century. On November 28, 1915, the *Atlanta Journal Constitution* reported on a small gathering on top of the mountain: "The new secret organization is founded with a view to taking an active part in the betterment of mankind, according to the statement of its members who are known as Klansmen. . . . The rites incident to the founding of the order were most interesting and the occasion will be remembered long by the participants."

Many of the attendees had also been present at the antisemitic lynching of Leo Frank that had taken place in nearby Marietta, Georgia, two months earlier. In 1913, Frank, a Jewish factory owner in Atlanta, had been accused of murdering a thirteen-year-old White girl and had been found guilty by a biased jury. Amidst international news coverage criticizing the ruling—the case precipitated the formation of the Anti-Defamation League to confront prejudice against Jews—and appeals that reached the Supreme Court, the governor commuted Frank's death sentence to life in prison. Then, while the guards looked on, a mob broke into the jail, took Frank, and murdered him, all while reportedly chanting "Kill the Jew." It was a moment that fostered the re-formation of the Ku Klux Klan.

Like hundreds of other Confederate monuments across the South, the creation of the relief carving at Stone Mountain was a public attack and show of White power against the growing victories and public outpouring of post–World War II civil rights activism. The carving was begun in 1964 amid civil rights marches across the country and was dedicated in 1970. Klan rallies had been hosted at this mountain, and now it stood as a Confederate monument of White power.

As my family and I walked through the museum and gift shop in the early 2000s, we lingered on the small area among the museum displays that featured black-and-white pictures of Klan rallies on the mountain in the 1920s, with captions that lamented its early Klan history. As we looked at the paltry section describing the early twentieth-century Klan resurgence on the mountain, my parents joked that they should donate pictures from their photo albums of cross lightings and annual rallies on the mountain well into the 1980s. An annual "reunion of Klan groups and individuals" met there, and all the national connections they'd made helped smooth over the factionalism that plagued Klan groups.

IN FEBRUARY 2000, AT THE age of eleven, I traveled with my father to the biennial conference of the largest gathering of academically oriented White nationalists of the 1990s and 2000s. The conference was held at a business hotel in the Northern Virginia suburbs near Dulles International Airport. It attracted more than three hundred attendees and mandated a suit-and-tie dress code, which meant that my mother got me a suit and a clip-on tie before we left. The speakers were professors and politicians from around the world, there to give talks about why they believed race was biologically determinative, and how to foster an international political movement to enforce that belief.

The leadership of the British National Party, which over the following years would win the strongest electoral victories for a far-right party in the UK since World War II, were in attendance. We heard about the organizing work of the French political party the National Front, from Bruno Gollnisch, the party's then second-in-command and close friend to leader Jean-Marie Le Pen. Gollnisch was actively serving in the European Parliament when he spoke to us, and two years later Le Pen would reach the second round of the presidential election runoff against Jacques Chirac. Le Pen's daughter Marine Le Pen defeated Gollnisch for the party leadership in 2011, then ran prominently for the French presidency against Emmanuel Macron in 2017, and again in 2022, when she received over 41 percent of the vote in the second-round runoff.

We listened to lectures from tenured professors of behavioral genetics and evolutionary psychology that could have come out of nineteenth-century phrenology classes. They complained about how embattled they felt at their universities because of their White supremacist advocacy. Attendees ranged from college students and business owners to scientists. It was the genteel face of the White power political and academic movement.

The hope for a political revolution in America and Europe that suffused such self-possessed events was only one side of this movement's coin; the other was represented by calls for violent revolution, and the lines between the two were never as firm as some adherents claimed. At the end of the conference, a caravan of some of the British politicians and my dad and I made the drive into the West Virginia mountains to pay our respects to William Pierce at his National Alliance compound, home to the largest and most successful White nationalist organization of the twentieth century. Making a visit to the headquarters of an American who was internationally notorious and blamed for inspiring terrorism was too much for these White nationalist true believers to pass up, despite their mainstream success in British and European politics.

Pierce, trained as a physicist, had worked in the 1950s at the Los Alamos National Laboratory before receiving his doctorate and becoming a professor of nuclear physics. He had given up his tenure in 1965 and moved to Washington, DC, to work with George Lincoln Rockwell. Pierce edited the American Nazi Party newsletter until Rockwell was assassinated in 1967, and afterward he helped pick up the pieces to form the NSWPP.

My sixteen-year-old father had met Pierce on his first trip to a White nationalist event as a teenager, and Pierce became a mentor. Under the pseudonym Andrew Macdonald, Pierce would go on to write the genocidal novel *The Turner Diaries*, which modeled how a leaderless and disconnected band of White revolutionaries could violently destabilize society. The book inspired decades of violence, including Paul Joseph Franklin's serial murders; the bank robberies and assassinations by The Order (who named themselves after an organization in the novel); the Oklahoma City bombing (modeled on a similar bombing in the novel); and quite likely the Capitol insurrection in 2021, which is similar to a scene in the book of an attack on the Capitol intended to disrupt proceedings and show that even the Capitol itself is vulnerable to White power resistance. As a kid, I had tried to read Pierce's book, but had stopped early on, disturbed by the paranoia, the violence, and the cruelty of its narrator. The dreams Pierce envisioned felt like the nightmare I saw my family trying to avoid.

As we entered the town, some of the most prominent politicians decided at the last moment to stay behind at a diner rather than make the trip up the mountain, afraid that the British press would make a scandal of their visit. My dad and the rest of our group made our way up past the compound gates, manned by armed skinhead guards, into the headquarters of the National Alliance. It was one of the most intimidating places I had ever been, what with all the young skinhead strangers trying to look tough. I felt more comfortable when people recognized my dad and started approaching him like a visiting dignitary.

He wanted to convince Pierce that he should add pro-White country music to the already broad catalog of skinhead records produced by Resistance Records, the label that Pierce had recently bought. As Pierce sat in his office, with one of his cats on his desk, he laughed off the suggestion and exclaimed "Johnny Rebel!" referring to the album of 1960s segregationist songs filled with racial epithets that was still widely circulated among White nationalists on burned CDs.

My dad responded that he didn't mean that level of epithets or explicitly racial language. He recounted that the country music concerts we attended in racially diverse South Florida attracted huge, nearly all-White crowds, who had waved hundreds of Confederate battle flags until the amphitheater banned all flags to avoid the bad optics. He argued they were a ripe audience who intuitively felt dispossessed and disheartened, and for whom White identity was already a powerful driving force—they just needed a more gentle, subtle, and positive message to activate it. Skinhead hate music wasn't what they wanted, nor was epithet-laced archaic hillbilly music from the civil rights era. White nationalism had grown and changed over the decades, he explained, and Pierce was unnecessarily limiting himself by targeting only alienated and disaffected youth. He could appeal, my dad said, to millions of regular middle-class White families, if only he packaged it correctly.

I absorbed that message from a young age. I saw it play out in the campaigns of my dad's close friend, David Duke. Although David didn't win his later races for senator, governor, or US representative,

I saw crowds of thousands of cheering White people fill the streets and venues of Louisiana, and he received a majority of the statewide White vote.

My dad never gave up on his goal of a White nationalist political revolution sweeping the United States, and argued its inevitability in any media outlet that would listen. Although the timeline changed, always got pushed further out as the decades wore on, and he was never as sure about the certainty of victory as he seemed in interviews, he remained convinced, because he saw how many people agreed with him if given the right opportunity. He only needed to hold out and continue building out his infrastructure and support.

His great-grandfather had fought in the Civil War on the side of the South, under General Nathan Bedford Forrest, who founded the Klan after the war ended, and whose portrait hung on the wall of my father's office. He often told a story of Forrest during the war, cornered and outnumbered, who had his troops march in a circle at the top of a hill, so that Union generals would see the same men repeatedly from a distance and mistakenly think their numbers were higher. That principle drove my father's activism. Despite feeling outnumbered, he always sought to target his resources and true followers where they would have the most impact. Among his tactics were marches within larger events—rather than explicitly racist events—in order to garner national media attention, and helping with strategic political campaigns of right-wing candidates who wanted to avoid being branded as White nationalists. He believed that nothing changed in society except through the concerted work of activists.

THE 2000 PRESIDENTIAL ELECTION TURNED my neighborhood into "ground zero" a year before that term came to be used exclusively to refer to the terrorist attacks on 9/11. Weeks of hand recounts of the flawed presidential ballots in Palm Beach County provided an opportunity for my dad to organize marches and protests, give interviews, and use the moment to promote the movement. I was eleven, beginning my second year of homeschooling, which meant I could join him in the crowds.

White nationalist supporters joined us and sometimes carried Confederate and Celtic cross flags. Other times, my dad asked them to carry inconspicuous signs and to try to blend in. It was often the White nationalists around me, in the core of the rallies, who seemed to tip the clamor in the direction of pro-Bush chants.

Over those weeks, I saw street protests and brawling, but nothing was so memorable as November 13, standing in the middle of a block-aded road at my dad's side in downtown West Palm Beach, in front of the county government building. The group of White nationalists and Bush supporters around me were trying to force the civil rights marcher Jesse Jackson from the stage.

Watching videos of that day now is surreal. Every time the cameras pan through the crowd, angles of my dad in his suit and tie, tall enough to stand a head above most people around, include me sticking close to his side.

I remember standing in the crowd, remember the warm and slightly overcast weather, the bullhorns and jeers, the shoving crowds, and the claustrophobic tension that occasionally broke into chaos. I was wearing my favorite baseball cap, a small confederate flag embroidered on the crown. I stood shorter than the shoulders of the adults around me, so I couldn't see the stage well.

The signs that the White nationalists and Bush Republicans around me used to block the view and end the event were hard to decipher. Besides the dozens of Bush-Cheney campaign signs and "Jesse Go Home" signs, one held a huge sign that cryptically read, "Those who cast the votes decree nothing. Those who count the votes decree everything," implying the election was being stolen and the majority-White Bush protestors needed to save it. They used those signs to reduce visibility for the police, the organizers, or their supporters.

After only a few minutes, the police pulled Jackson from the stage, and an announcer asked the Gore supporters to return to the amphi-theater they'd marched from, leaving the Bush supporters to celebrate.

That night, the right-wing commentator Tucker Carlson said on C-SPAN, "You have Jesse Jackson, and people like Jesse Jackson, who I have to say I consider parasites in all this, running around, claiming that there's a racial issue here." It was exactly the message my dad was giving his own supporters. He said, following the Jackson rally, that chanting or displaying explicitly White nationalist messages was neither necessary nor desirable. "That's the kind of thing that I'm sure the Bush campaign doesn't want us to get into. That's not the focus of it right now. It's an implicit racial issue here, which most people understand, but it's probably not to our advantage to turn it into an explicit one."

ALL THE WHITE NATIONALIST EVENTS that I remember from the 1990s and 2000s were planned under levels of secrecy imposed by fears of Antifa, which was a movement that affected my life long before it was a staple of mainstream conservative politics. We White nationalists described ourselves as persecuted, not by the state police—who often stood by, whether to show their support for us or simply to stay uninvolved—but by private citizens who responded to the threat of organized White supremacy with direct action, and they didn't preclude violence.

When I was in my mid- to late teens, my best friend (and eventual first romantic partner) was the daughter of a conservative White nationalist leader. We had met at one of her dad's conferences late one night and we talked on couches in a corner away from the main hotel lobby until the early hours of the morning, when her mom came down looking for her. I learned how to text on my phone for her. We'd see each other a couple times a year at conferences.

One summer, her family had organized a barbecue at a public park for White nationalist members in the area, where they got together over picnic foods under a pavilion and served themselves on paper plates. She sent photos of the get-together that Saturday afternoon. Things seemed sedate until she messaged that they had been attacked. A group of masked anarchists had shown up with a banner that read "Fuck Y'all: Social Liberation, not Anti-Immigration" and chanted "Fuck you!", "Nazis!", "Class traitors!", and "Delete yourself!" Several members of her dad's group had been hurt in the fighting, and my friend had fought with them, too. Afterward, the anarchists' write-up said that "in the end, at least two Nazis were severely beaten and bloodied, another given a killer tittie-twister (purple-nurple), and one stripped of his cane he was wielding as a weapon." White nationalists, like always, acted aggrieved at the violence, and it was legitimately scary to worry about the safety of my closest friends. Yet these same people regularly admitted the cops were on their side, and they also knew the countless times that police had stood by while White nationalists attacked antiracists. The balance of power between these two groups wasn't equal.

By my mid-teens, I was a fixture with my dad on the White nationalist conference circuit. In contrast to most other White nationalist conferences that happened on a regular schedule, David's events were sporadic, and the most chaotic. They also tended to be the largest, and they were also the spaces where my family and I felt most at home. Other conferences were more self-consciously cultured, and represented the only social venue in the broad White nationalist movement that rejected antisemitism on any level, even if that level of rejection was tenuous at best. At revived conferences descended from the original Citizens' Councils of the 1950s, I learned to distinguish the deep accents of the large Mississippi delegations from the distinctive contingents from Alabama, Georgia, Tennessee, and South Carolina.

Many of the people I met in that period as a kid had reputations that preceded them and left me feeling connected to American history in ways that were different and felt older than my family's version of White nationalism. Many of the people I grew up looking up to were men that Dr. King himself had confronted. I met the founder of the original Citizens' Councils, Robert B. Patterson, a WWII veteran and former Mississippi State College football star who had created the first chapter of the Councils shortly after the *Brown* decision came down. I regularly saw Leonard Wilson, an elderly Alabaman who grew up in Selma, who everyone called "Flagpole" because in 1956, when he was twenty and a sophomore at the University of Alabama, he'd dramatically climbed up the base of a large memorial flag mast to lead the chants of a White anti-integration mob. That crowd of over a thousand people marched through campus, lighting crosses, setting off firecrackers, and surrounding the university president's home the night after Autherine Lucy, the first Black student admitted to the school, had attended her first day of classes.

Under the pretense of protecting Lucy from that violence, the board of trustees voted unanimously to expel her. A month later, under scrutiny for caving to the will of a mob, they tried to balance the scales by also expelling Wilson. Expelled from school at twenty years old, Wilson failed in his political attempts over the rest of his life, consigned to obscure White nationalist organizing, where I met him decades later. Lucy married and had a career as a schoolteacher, and in 1988 the faculty finally petitioned the university to overturn its expulsion order. She returned to get a master's degree the next year, the same time her own daughter matriculated there.

At another meeting in Montgomery, Alabama, I joined a dinner with the leadership and a guest of honor: one of the White officers who arrested the civil rights activist Rosa Parks. He told us his story of processing her arrest on December 1, 1955, after she had refused to move to the "colored" section that the bus driver demanded she occupy according to city code. He told me how amazing it had been to see what felt like a routine arrest to him erupt across headlines around the country the next day. He was still baffled decades later that his action, which he had taken many times before, sparked a thirteen-month standoff in the city that ended in a US Supreme Court decision overturning the segregation laws he had been enforcing. All those years later, he was sitting at a chain restaurant, still baffled, regaling a crowd of White nationalists with his stories about a woman who had "used him" to fuel the civil rights movement. When Parks passed away later that year at the age of ninety-two, she became the first woman to lie in state at the US Capitol.

I regularly circulated in the hallways at these events when people got coffee and snacks, chatting with professors and movement leaders, editors, and politicians. I floated between groups of people to connect and share updates, but I also kept myself somewhat aloof. Documenting White nationalist gatherings felt like my role most of the time. One of my hobbies was photography, and my parents had dutifully gotten me a nice DSLR camera in 2005 that I carried around my neck. I enjoyed the hotel pools, but I often turned down invites to spend a day swimming so that I could attend the speeches instead.

The trips with my dad, and the people he introduced me to along the way, taught me so much more about my dad, and I don't think he had expected me to be so drawn to his world. He was a deeply loving father, but I don't remember, as a kid, him saying "I love you." Instead, he showed it through becoming my main caretaker as a baby during the day after my mother went back to work. He seemed endlessly interested in my opinions and perspectives. When I turned my interest to the world he'd committed his life to, it gave us a bond that felt like it could only become deeper and more enmeshed as the years went on. He could help launch me and my projects, and I could help him find ways to move his life's work forward.

CHAPTER 5

PALM BEACH COUNTY REPUBLICAN
EXECUTIVE COMMITTEE MEMBER

I WAS NEVER CONFIDENT THAT I wanted to attend college. Everyone in my immediate family had at least a bachelor's degree and two of my great-grandmothers had PhDs. When I turned eighteen, my mom asked me when I planned to go to college, and I told her I would rather use my home repair and blacksmithing skills to make gates and windows for the wealthy people in Palm Beach. I could see a life building beautiful things for rich people, and I thought that a job behind the scenes, building and designing as a contractor, working independently, could spare me from losing much work due to my White nationalist infamy.

As part of an effort to derail this plan after I turned nineteen, and after she started to realize I was serious about it, my mom switched tactics and tried to capitalize on my deep interest in medieval history. In an incredible show of support, she offered to fund my traveling to Europe so I could see medieval things in person.

Thus, in the spring of 2008, I traveled to Europe for the first time. It was my first time traveling on my own. The trip was possible because David was living secretly in a small mountain town in Austria. When he visited for the holidays the previous year, he had encouraged my family to send me to visit him. He had contacts in Western European universities, and he guaranteed that he could get me a placement at one of them. He told me and my family that, as soon as I saw it, I'd fall in love with Europe like he had.

We planned the trip so that I would arrive at the Munich airport in southern Germany the same day his girlfriend was also landing there. I arrived a few hours earlier, and I spent that time out of my depth, unable to speak any German or read many of the signs. I met David's girlfriend for the first time at her gate, and she guided us to the train across the Alps to meet David and settle into their small two-bedroom apartment overlooking a lake.

In retrospect, that trip set the trajectory of a lot of the next decade of my life. Landing in Bavaria meant I was confronted by German, a language I had no ability to speak or understand, but which had held a mystique and sense of danger my whole life.

Over the next few weeks—the first time I'd ever seen deep snow— David taught me to ski. Then I traveled to Germany on my own, staying with an old campaign volunteer of David's who I'd gotten to know during David's unsuccessful 1997 race for U.S. representative. Afterward, I went to London to stay with an ornery Hungarian Storm-front moderator and his girlfriend. In the evenings, they'd explain how White nationalist talking points against immigration had found traction in the UK. I spent nearly every day in the British Museum, taking pictures of objects and artifacts, experiencing that older history authentically and directly for the first time. European history had felt vaguely like a fairy tale when I was a kid in Florida, a feeling exacer-bated by the medieval reenactment scene. Seeing museum collections helped me realize history was a discipline with tangible evidence behind it. My hosts drove me to Stonehenge, and I was amazed by the deep time of prehistoric civilization. The trip made me feel small, uneducated, and inexperienced, but hungry to grow.

When I landed again in Florida, I was enthusiastic about trying to understand the ancient and medieval worlds accurately. I had navigated the language barrier in Germany and Austria with a guide-book, and I came back excited to learn German, though I stopped telling White nationalist friends that I was learning it when everyone, including my family, assumed it was because I wanted to read Hitler in the original.

I refused to read *Mein Kampf*, even in English, back then. The reverence for Hitler and the National Socialist regime that pervaded my childhood conflicted with the political agenda of mainstreaming the movement. Anything about Hitler seemed cursed, because our community shared so much ideology with a regime that had brutalized a continent and murdered millions. Holocaust denial was universal among White nationalists, but I largely avoided talking about it or reading about it. The more I learned, the less their arguments seemed true, and quibbling about how many of the millions of dead were victims of malnutrition versus murder seemed psychotic. My family asked me what I was learning about the history of White people when I began to study the Middle Ages. I told them it was Europe, so they were White, but privately I liked studying that era because I wanted to think about things disconnected from the controversies that dominated my life. Journalists tended to stop asking questions when I told them I was studying something from more than 500 years earlier.

WHEN I LANDED AGAIN IN Florida, I felt like a different person, but I was excited to be home. My mom surprised me, however, when she refused to take me home directly. Instead, she dropped me off at the admissions office of Palm Beach Community College, where the last three generations of our family had begun their own college educations. She had scheduled a placement test for me and a meeting to enroll me near the end of the eligibility period to start that summer.

I was deeply afraid I wasn't prepared for college. A lifetime of writing and publishing essays online just because I wanted to didn't necessarily prepare me to write them for a professor. When they told me I could enroll, but I'd have to take remedial algebra that summer to prepare, I signed up, and filled the rest of my schedule with writing, language, and literature classes. The state required a math sequence that culminated with precalculus, and I white-knuckled my way through the sequence, got As, was surprised I enjoyed a lot of the puzzles, and then I never took another math class. I started taking elementary German immediately.

THOSE NEXT TWO YEARS OF school were a revelation. I began with vague fears that I didn't voice to anyone. My family were convinced I was a genius, that my lack of a formal education would actually demonstrate how advanced I was. I was extremely worried that the opposite was true. Slowly, I realized that I was actually a perfectly respectable student, and I enrolled in honors classes. I found a refuge at school I hadn't expected. It gave me a semblance of stability as my White nationalist profile grew.

Several years earlier, I had founded an Internet radio network on Stormfront. What began as an experiment in setting up a server to stream audio quickly expanded into a full-time volunteer job I threw myself into. We secured a license to play music so I could create a mainstream-sounding radio station for White nationalists in the era before smartphones became common, and before podcasts were ubiquitous. I convinced my dad and David to set up a weekly program together that I engineered on a digital radio console on my desk. I patched calls through a number I set up using Skype. At the end of every episode, I'd edit the file and upload it for people to listen to when they wanted. I recruited other movement leaders and members of Stormfront who showed interest until I was broadcasting eight to nine hours every night, and then looping the lineup as reruns the rest of the day. We started to hear from truckers who would call in to our different shows to tell us we were offering an alternative to satellite radio. My own show broadcast four nights a week for an hour, and began exclusively as a program to play old folk songs. As my profile rose, I conceded to requests by listeners and my family to include more political content. I made the first half hour a profile of an American folk artist from the first half of the twentieth century, but I started using the second half to provide a White nationalist spin on the news. This work had grown to absorb most of my time, and keep me at home running the control board most nights per week. At some point the responsibilities began to weigh on me, but I didn't feel like I could let down all the people who were proud of what I'd created, including my dad. When I debuted a Sunday news show I hosted, I opened it every week with a song that I look back on and wonder how no one, including me, picked up on the bold messaging I was broadcasting. Each morning, that show opened to the words of the Pink Floyd song, "Comfortably Numb." Taken from the 1979 album *The Wall*, about a kid who felt the expectations of their parents and who then rose to become a White power leader, that song marked the point in the album when the protagonist finally broke and embraced the identity awaiting them.

THE SUMMER I STARTED COMMUNITY college I registered to be on the ballot for my neighborhood precinct's seat on the Palm Beach

County Republican Executive Committee, the administrative body of the county GOP. I would be representing the Republicans in my voting precinct of roughly 1,000 people, which itself was dominated by Democratic voters.

I applied for a spot on the ballot almost on a whim. I needed the form notarized, so I rode my bike to the bank where my parents had accounts and had a bank officer sign my form in his office. I then dropped off my notarized paperwork at the Palm Beach County Supervisor of Elections office, where I had protested the 2000 presidential election between Gore and Bush with my dad eight years earlier. Now nineteen, I registered to vote at the same time as I registered as a candidate.

Applying to be on the ballot was in retrospect remarkably bold. I hadn't even begun community college classes yet. Once I was on the ballot, along with the incumbent who lived in a condo down the street, I requested the voting rolls from the supervisor of elections. They would only issue them to me in hard copy, which turned out to be multiple poster-sized sheets of printer paper. I folded up the list of all registered voters in my neighborhood, which included their addresses, genders, records of whether they had voted, registration dates, and other demographic information. Registered Republicans were the only people who would see my name on the ballot, and they were outnumbered on our streets, so I could instantly cross out most of the names. Over the next few weeks, my mom helped me make a database of the information and I mapped out a schedule to knock on the doors of the hundreds of eligible voters. I sometimes rallied my mom, sister, and niece to knock with me, but most of the time I went alone after my college classes let out and I finished my homework. I printed little cards on our color printer with my picture on them, wearing my brown leather hat that I hoped would make me more memorable, named the office I was running for, and made a promise to represent them.

When people answered the door, which they did most of the time, I'd apologize for bothering them, introduce myself, and hand them a card. Usually, they'd thank me and go back inside. Occasionally I'd wake up a baby and then I'd get an angry parent. Once, I mistakenly knocked on the door of an older woman who promptly told me she was a registered Democrat. I apologized and tried to leave, but she asked if I would stay to chat. She was fascinated that a young person in our neighborhood would be running as a Republican when Barack Obama was such an inspiring candidate. I told her I appreciated the offer, but I needed to keep campaigning, and she wished me well. When Republican voters gave me the time to talk about my issues, I told them I was always against immigration, which was overwhelming Florida. I was opposed to affirmative action, because it was reverse discrimination. I thought the violent crime in our city was due directly to liberal policies, which didn't recognize that it was certain neighborhoods where most of the violent crime happened. They'd usually name the northern part of the city I was alluding to, the part that was majority Black, and I'd nod in agreement.

Halfway through the summer, I came home late in the afternoon and my mom told me my dad couldn't get up from bed. I asked him what was happening, and he wasn't sure, but said he wasn't able to move. He hadn't called anyone, because he didn't want us to worry. My mom called an ambulance, and the doctors told him he'd had a stroke that hadn't affected his speech or thinking, but had paralyzed half of his body. They were annoyed he had waited hours to call the ambulance.

The rest of the summer, the house was often empty, a stark shift from our prior security policy that someone always had to remain home. I visited my dad at the hospital and then in rehab, continued my classes, and continued knocking on doors. Election night was in August 2008, late in my first summer college semester. It was a Tuesday, and my mom was at the hospital. I didn't have any plans, so I went to an open mic night at a tiki bar near my grandparents' house. My parents had let me start guitar lessons three years earlier, and I liked to write and record songs using my radio equipment, but I hadn't ever performed for anyone. I introduced myself to the group of performers, who told me they were mostly regulars, and I promised to start coming often. Late in the evening, when the performances were almost done, I refreshed the election results on my phone and discovered I had won.

I hadn't expected any congratulations or recognition except from my family and maybe the wider White nationalist movement. I was used to being treated as an obscurity, and it didn't even occur to me to contact a journalist about my victory. Nevertheless, the next morning, our local paper ran a story under the headline, "Did We Witness the Birth of a Mini-David Duke in West Palm Beach on Tuesday Night?" followed by another, "Teen Son of Klansman Wins Vote for GOP Post." With 58 percent of the vote—final tally 167 to 120—I had beaten the middle-aged incumbent and would now represent the hundreds of Republican households in my district. My duties, I was now being reminded, were to keep in touch with GOP voters and encourage them to vote in every election. The news coverage about my family history that began the morning after the election in the local paper quickly expanded to the *New York Times* and international press that fall.

Because of the ambiguous relationship between parties and the state government, the board of elections managed the vote, but it was the party that decided how to handle the winners. Reporters called the GOP chiefs that morning to ask them if they knew about my family and my personal background.

I had realized that it would be the first time I was trying to take White nationalist activism to people directly, in particular to people who hadn't come to it themselves, but doing that had always been the dream of my family. I had gone door-to-door each afternoon and, while not naming our ideology, I had won the election using all of our talking points.

OVER THE NEXT FEW MONTHS, I was frequently in contact with journalists for the local *Palm Beach Post* while I managed my college course load. I would drive to conduct an interview at a local restaurant and rush out at the end to go take my exams. Headlines about the local Republican committee refusing to seat me appeared in the *New York Times* before my final grades were posted that first semester. For the first time in my life, people regularly recognized me when I left the house. My frequent morning stop at Dunkin' Donuts to get a sandwich and tea now came with people in line murmuring to each other. Cashiers would do a double take and tell me they recognized me.

Sometimes someone in line would offer to pay for my order and tell me it was an honor to meet me. At first I felt proud to receive congratulations and praise from strangers, and it made me feel important to become a local celebrity overnight, but the novelty wore off and soon that routine just made me self-conscious and I missed anonymity.

Both my role as a local celebrity and having to take exams in formal classes were new experiences I was learning how to balance. I had, unfortunately, made it easy for the GOP chairman to deny my seat when I hadn't signed a loyalty oath to the party before submitting my paperwork to the County Supervisor of Elections. The party previously required its members sign the oath before being seated rather than before getting on the ballot, but they had made the change, wary of attempts by fans of Ron Paul's failed GOP presidential primary campaign to establish control of the Republican Party at the local level. I had actually learned about the executive committee elections in the first place from one of the private email lists of former Ron Paul volunteers in Florida. I'd gotten added to the list at a Ron Paul rally that spring, where my dad and I had our picture taken with Paul during a meet and greet. When we posted the photo online, it went viral and caused Paul to have to address how he felt about being beloved and supported by racists. That media scandal, of course, was what we expected.

My dad and I had not been especially enthusiastic for Paul's platform, which was filled with obscure and seemingly irrelevant planks like returning to the gold standard and abolishing the Federal Reserve. But his campaign had obvious overlaps with our movement—his platform also called for annulling the Civil Rights Act of 1964 for violating individual liberty, and his *Ron Paul Political Report* newsletters from the '80s and '90s were filled with racist rants against "animals" that "play Whites like a piano."

The minimum donation that compelled a campaign for federal office to report the donor in 2008 was $500, so my dad quietly donated exactly that much to Ron Paul's campaign. When the campaign filed their donors, reporters found my dad listed and broke the story. The Paul campaign distanced themselves from us, but their repudiation was nevertheless softer and more friendly than I had expected. The campaign refused outraged calls to return the donation, and they justified it to reporters only by saying, "Dr. Paul stands for freedom, peace, prosperity and inalienable rights. If someone with small ideologies happens to contribute money to Ron, thinking he can influence Ron in any way, he's wasted his money. Ron is going to take the money and try to spread the message of freedom." The AP headline "Paul Keeps Donation from White Supremacist" did the intended work of drawing attention to the movement and simultaneously demonstrating a perverse sort of respect from a popular candidate.

THAT NOVEMBER, A FEW DAYS after Obama won his first presidential election, David called me "the heir" at his 2008 conference in Memphis. He had planned to host a conference just four days after the presidential election. It became clear leading up to that week that Barack Obama would likely win. The Republican candidate that fall, John McCain, wasn't popular among White nationalists, who generally supported third-party candidates in that election, but the symbolism of his defeat to the first Black president caused despair and anger. When the election results came in on Tuesday night, it shifted the event—and the Memphis city and suburban governments where it was being held—into a feeling of high alert. In the days leading up to it, the conference rapidly went through three hotels, who canceled the contracts after each one was found and outed by antiracist activists.

I had stayed home during the early planning of that conference because I didn't want to miss a week or more of class. By the time I was en route from Florida, I was told the strategy with the final hotel was to pile in Saturday morning, reinforce ourselves with boxed lunches and bottled water, and not vacate until we were done. My family told the staff the event was a "family meeting," which didn't feel entirely untrue.

I was at the conference to speak about Stormfront's Internet radio, which still seemed to me like my biggest accomplishment within the movement, but winning my small election two months earlier had started to become dominant. David had held the same position in his parish GOP in Louisiana throughout the 1990s, and he had come to West Palm Beach to support me at a press meeting that fall. The ensuing national controversy that surrounded the process of being denied the seat by the party leaders had created a lot of press for the movement, and had elevated my public profile overnight.

In the wake of Obama's election, it felt like my thwarted victory was the most plausible political comeback available to the room of hundreds of White nationalists. They were almost in mourning, saying frequently during the breaks and in the halls that they didn't think there would ever be another White president. I came from a family that believed more firmly than anything else that their radical views could create popular political victories, and I repeatedly told everyone I talked to that the backlash to this election would prove that more than anything.

A few weeks before, I had taken a magazine writer for *Details*—a Condé Nast magazine marketed as a *GQ* for younger men—to my favorite fancy seafood restaurant near my grandparents' house on the water to discuss my views and my election. I always enjoyed meeting journalists at nice restaurants, because it meant tasty food on their company credit card. The magazine came out just before the Memphis conference with the title "Derek Black: The Great White Hope," with a picture of me next to a large shark hung up by its tail by the dock. I bought a bunch of copies and handed them out to friends.

A COUPLE WEEKS AFTER THE Memphis conference, the new members of the Republican Executive Committee were supposed to be seated. The night before, someone called our house and left repeated voicemails, which my dad kept for evidence. The caller addressed my dad and said he'd be waiting with a sniper rifle downtown the next night, ready to kill me if I tried to enter the building. It was an incredibly specific threat, which alarmed both of us. My dad took the unusual step of calling the police and making a report about it, and submitting the voicemails and blocked number as evidence.

He asked me whether I still wanted to go to the meeting, as it likely wouldn't make a difference in whether I was seated or not. I took a lot of confidence from the fact that the death threats had incorrectly described our house in one of the calls, which made me think the threat itself was probably fake. Either way, I didn't want to stay home on a night when national and international press would be waiting at the meeting for me to arrive.

My dad suggested we rent a driver for the night, rather than use my plan to park a block away and walk to the government building downtown. The black sedan would be harder to recognize if a sniper did know what my car looked like, and the driver could drop me off as close to the front doors as possible to limit how long I was exposed. I agreed, and a black Cadillac with leather seats and complimentary water showed up that evening to take me. My mother and sister and niece had gone separately, and were there when I arrived to sign in and talk to the reporters waiting for me.

Inside, the chairman, who had become my foil in the press that fall but who I'd never seen in person, ignored me except to comment that he was glad to see the press was taking such an interest in local politics at last. I sat in the front row for most of the proceedings, while people throughout the auditorium kept whispering and pointing at me.

When I realized there would be no opportunity for me to comment, I interrupted the proceedings and spoke to the room, telling them I had won the election and was more than happy to sign the loyalty oath. Some people booed and others clapped. Lots of photographers took pictures, and news networks tracked me with video cameras. I made my case and asked to be seated while the chairman told me over and over to sit down. Eventually, I finished my speech, and let the night go on.

The incumbent who lost was seated in my place, and eventually they gaveled the meeting to its conclusion and people started to mingle and file out. One of the reporters for the *New York Times* approached me, where I was talking to my family and local White nationalist supporters who had come out for me, to ask if I planned to do anything else or if it was safe for him to leave to write up his story to meet his deadline. I was slightly annoyed at the question, feeling like he was suggesting I hadn't done enough on a night during which I had been worried about being shot just by arriving. I asked him if he wanted me to do something else. He seemed surprised and said he obviously wouldn't tell me what to do or not do. Realizing I did need to enact one more piece of drama, I approached the chairman across the room, who seemed shaken and was talking with a group of his own supporters. I confronted him, accusing him of subverting a democratic election by denying me my seat. I didn't realize it at the time, but the candidate I'd beat, but who now had my seat, was in the group. The next morning, the headline photo of the *Times* story was a close-up of me engaged with the chairman, while everyone around us watched in shock.

AFTER I WON THE ELECTION but hadn't been seated, and had been publicly denounced for my family history, I realized I now had an opportunity and a platform to send out whatever messages I felt like. After giving an interview about my election to a local right-wing AM radio host, he told me on the way out of the studio that he'd heard I did my own show online. He told me the station would be willing to lease time to me in the slot before his show, and I was excited at the prospect of speaking directly to the local audience that had been so unsettled by me. Weeks earlier, friends had let me know that an FM station that usually played music was dedicating an afternoon to discussing my campaign. I called in to the show and the host proceeded to interview me for an hour. I knew that the White nationalist audience I could reach online was practically infinite, but that was an audience of movement people who had come to me. I wanted to reach my local community. So my dad agreed to buy me time at the AM station, and I began what I thought then would be only a temporary program, where I could explain my beliefs directly to the South Florida community. My dad, thrilled at my initiative, insisted that we expand the program into a permanent institution. He joined me as a co-host, and we started driving to the nearby neighborhood radio station every morning.

I was no longer being treated as a child of a movement leader, but as a rising leader in my own right. My quotes were sandwiched between those from Florida and national officials calling me "a rising Hitler" and a "stain on the state of Florida" who had to be stopped.

I joked about their quotes, but privately they stung. Trying to share snippets of my humanity, I took the opportunity to talk about personal details I knew would read like comedy. Shortly before the magazine writer for *Details* followed me around and featured me standing next to a shark, I had written in the movie reviews section of Stormfront, which I'd created several years before, how much I loved the first *Twilight* movie. I had taken my niece to the movies without knowing anything about it, and we'd both loved it. I'd subsequently read the books and took her back to the theater to see it two more times.

I had posted that I'd followed Taylor Swift's music since her first album came out in 2006, when we were both sixteen. When the glossy *Details* article came out, it mentioned that I raved about Taylor and *Twilight* both. I was embarrassingly proud of it, not necessarily because of my statements about "being opposed to discrimination against White people," or my fights with the chairman and state party leaders, but for the personal moments where people might know me for me.

Winning the election and the publicity around it felt like a triumph nonetheless. It was the first electoral victory by an avowed White nationalist in years. It felt like my full coming out as a trusted and charismatic leader within the future of the movement.

I ABSORBED DAVID'S MEDIA SAVVY as much by osmosis as from any formal lessons. When I entered the public sphere on my own as a political figure, rather than as the son of Don, I sounded more like David, whose political interviews I'd pored over in our VHS collection. As I began my own independent media campaigns, I saw my dad's ambivalence to condemn Nazism and the Klan as a mistake. I began to feel strongly that we needed to distance ourselves from both Nazis and the Klan if we wanted our White nationalist message to resonate with the broader White American public.

In 2008, when at my urging he finally banned swastika images from being used by Stormfront members, my dad gave an interview to an Italian newspaper that printed the full sequence of a mortifying anecdote: The interviewer asked my dad if Stormfront wasn't just the "new Ku Klux Klan," and my dad replied, "Yes, it's like that." I reacted in shock: "Next to Don Black is his son Derek, 19, Stormfront's internet radio organizer. From the beginning of our meeting he listens in silence, but now he interrupts his father: 'You never said it, you can't say it.' He gets agitated and tries to stop the speech with his hand: 'You know you can't say it.' The father remains still: 'I would never tell this to an American journalist, but you know it's true.'"

It felt like such a bizarre moment. I had suddenly felt confident or even arrogant enough to try to manage my dad's decades-long media strategy, and he had responded gently yet hadn't altered his statement at all. I understood immediately that he knew as well as I that being printed in another language wouldn't stop his statement from being translated back to English. The article went on to describe me: "Derek, always wearing an Australian cowboy leather hat, is the new face of White supremacy and has been elected to the Palm Beach County Republican Board." My dad went on to lay out the stakes of my campaign: "It is no longer time to try to create a third party destined for marginalization, we must present ourselves at every primary election within the Republican Party so as to impose our ideas in the debate, we must work to create our own interest group, to restore traditions and true White values."

What I considered strictly bad media tactics while I was waging my political campaign to be seated, he was using as part of his lifelong mission to both pull in the mainstream and draw in the hardliners and true believers who were the energy behind the movement. There had always been two channels, and using the media skillfully meant understanding how and where to signal any group you wanted. I had learned entirely from him, and yet thought I knew better. I realized I was taking for granted the White power community that gave me all my power.

The day that happened I felt like one of the self-possessed wine-and-cheese crowd among White nationalists who kept us at arm's length because they didn't want to be associated with the grungy reputation of our big White nationalist tent. As much as I wanted to moderate the rougher parts of our movement and attract a mainstream crowd of supporters, it was also clear that going too far into elitism, or too far into condemning the past of White nationalist organizing, might ultimately alienate too many people. It felt like a personal and activist paradox.

In the long arc of the movement in the twentieth century, there had never been true silos of militants, academics, elite politicians, rich or poor followers. They were all participants in one movement. Maintaining bridges between them was a tightrope walk, and more so while trying to also appeal to a mass audience beyond our supporters. My campaign was supposed to make a case that White nationalism was an ideology with broad enough support to claim a space in mainstream politics. My dad's decision at that same time to confirm that Stormfront was nevertheless the "new Ku Klux Klan" frustrated me. What I defended to him as only "good media strategy," in retrospect, paralleled my actual, unvoiced internal thoughts—my longstanding discomfort with Hitler and Nazis, and my recently growing discomfort with the Klan and its history.

When I came home after class one day to learn reporters had come to our house unannounced looking for me about some developing story, but that my dad had gone down the driveway to give an impromptu press conference on my behalf, I was openly frustrated and mad and told him I wanted to run my own media comments. He could speak to them, but doing so before I even knew someone was working on a story, was unacceptable. For the first time, I remember telling him that this was my campaign, not his.

CHAPTER 6

NEW COLLEGE

LATE ON A SUNDAY AFTERNOON in the early fall of 2010, I arrived after a three-and-a-half-hour drive from the Atlantic to the Gulf Coast at New College of Florida in Sarasota. After two years of community college, I was transferring to a four-year institution to finish a bachelor's degree. I had first heard about New College from my German professor in community college, who had taken me under his wing and became my unofficial academic advisor.

After finishing his German class sequence, I'd switched to serving as a teaching assistant for the course and founded a German studies club. Like most of the faculty, he knew about my infamous reputation, my politics, and my radio show. What made him different was that he actually acknowledged these things and talked with me about them. Before filing the paperwork to found a club on campus, I asked him if he was worried about being associated with me, and offered to recruit someone else to found it and just serve on their board. He told me he wouldn't support the application unless I put my name on it, and then explained that he'd already been asked to speak about me in a faculty meeting, where professors were worried about my presence on campus. It was the first time I'd known anyone in the administration of the school had even recognized that I was attending. I asked him what he thought about it all, momentarily wondering if he somehow agreed with my politics. He told me he thought that I was misguided, but that I was a good person, and that he'd told the faculty meeting that I'd more likely find my way by leaning into academic work than by being shunned from it. At twenty, I wasn't sure what I thought about that. One day while our students were taking an exam, we spoke on the balcony outside class. He asked me if I'd ever considered getting a PhD, and I told him genuinely the thought had never occurred to me. I asked how that worked, and he explained graduate stipends, teaching duties, comprehensive exams, and the dissertation. He told me I was already laying a good foundation of language study and the kind of research I'd need to do during the second half of my undergraduate work to be a good candidate.

One day, at one of our regular meetings, he asked me if I'd heard of New College. There had been a story about it on NPR that morning, he told me. My mom later confirmed she'd heard the segment during her morning drive. He suggested it might be a good fit for me. It was the state's public honors college, so it offered low tuition for in-state students but also the size, faculty relationships, and social life of a private liberal arts college. Most importantly, he said, they had a very solid set of medieval studies faculty members. There hadn't been any medieval studies courses at community college, so I'd leaned into German studies, but I was ready to start them.

The past two years had had their share of stressful moments, as I had been increasingly tying myself publicly to White nationalist advocacy. I took a lot of solace in knowing my White nationalist community had my back, but they were geographically scattered—they wouldn't be going with me to Sarasota. Leaving home felt exciting, but extremely uncertain.

I arrived in Sarasota alone, with a car full of suitcases, boxes, and my bike. Now, despite a long drive across the swamps and cane fields, I could still feel an unbreakable connection tethering me to where I'd grown up. For the first time, however, I could imagine somewhere else when I talked about where I lived and where I hung out. About to have my own space for the first time, I realized I now had the prospect of inviting people over to my place, even if that meant joining me in a shared fifteen-by-fifteen-foot dorm room.

I was late for orientation check-in because I'd taken too long packing the blue PT Cruiser my parents had gotten me to take to college. It was the nicest (and newest) vehicle I'd ever seen them buy. When I got it, I considered adding a new Confederate flag sticker to the window, like I'd done years before with our small red pickup truck. This time, adding a sticker felt adolescent and unnecessary. I didn't want to broadcast my opinions or commitments in this new place. Having my reputation precede me wherever I went was already draining. New College felt like an opportunity to learn without having to immediately defend myself.

I had visited the campus only once, several weeks earlier, for an "ice cream social" to let new students meet faculty. I drove through the previous night and day from Oklahoma, racing to complete a 9,000-mile cross-country road trip I'd taken with my twelve-year-old niece that summer. I met faculty that night without my parents—most other students had theirs accompanying them—and instead I had brought along my adolescent niece, and I happily explained that we were in the final leg of completing a transcontinental summer trip.

That fall afternoon, Google's navigation led me to the main administration building, which was closed on a Sunday and was on the wrong side of campus. The school was divided by Highway 41, the Tamiami Trail. Administrative buildings mostly took up the Bayshore half of campus, while the dorms, the fitness center, student green, and cafeteria were on the residential side adjacent to the regional Sarasota-Bradenton International Airport.

I wasn't the only one who went to the wrong place. That day, the first person I met was Juan, outside his car with his family, looking around at the locked doors of the pink marble facade of College Hall. Juan had grown up in Miami, and like me, had completed community college close to home. Neither of us knew where we were supposed to be, so we got back in our cars to drive the couple of minutes to the residential side of campus.

Nearly all first-years were assigned to one of the three dorms that surrounded Palm Court, an open-air square at the center of the residential side of campus, interlaced with royal palm trees and nicknamed the "Center of the Universe." The cubist dorms were designed by the architect I. M. Pei, who—anyone quickly learned if they didn't know already—later designed the glass Louvre Pyramid in Paris. The Pei dorms had a reputation as a slum for first-years. Each was made up of single-room studios with a private bathroom and a patio that two, sometimes three, students split. The doors of all the dorms opened onto outdoor courts, compelling students to pass each other as we came and went from the rest of campus.

In an email welcoming first-year students to life in the Pei dorms, an upper-year student commented that week, "Pei is a wonderful experience but there is much more to it than sweet nooks to hang out with your friends in and maybe play video games or do drugs or be really belligerent or cocoon." What court you lived in drove who you most frequently saw and shared intimate space with. I was assigned to First Court and Juan went to Third. He and I continued to see each other regularly, sharing an economics class and feeling a step outside our cohort, because we were both transfer students in a class of mostly eighteen-year-olds.

Whenever people visited my room in First Court that semester, they'd usually comment on how sparse my decorations were. The walls were bare, and my bedsheets were plain. I hadn't been sure what sentimental things to bring with me. As an adolescent, I heavily personalized my bedroom. I painted the ceiling dark blue and covered it in stars. I repaneled the walls with dark wood grain. I built matching bookshelves along the walls to hold my collection of fantasy novels and tchotchkes, like a set of bookends of Bilbo Baggins and Gandalf from *The Lord of the Rings*. I freely decorated the room with artifacts I'd collected from White nationalists over the years, including a Confederate battle flag, a decorative Viking battle axe that Danny Hawkins gave me when I was a kid, and a commemorative Confederate goblet with a pewter cover he also entrusted to me the first time I told him I also believed in White nationalism. I commandeered a plaster bust of the Confederate general and original founder of the Ku Klux Klan Nathan Bedford Forrest from my dad's office. He had owned it for years, a relic from when he ran the Klan; David Duke had a matching one at his home in Louisiana. I had picked an antique writing desk and, next to it, a curved glass antique cabinet filled with all the "treasures" I'd collected since I was little. By the time I left home, the collection varied from fossil shark teeth to crystals and minerals, antique coins, and snow globes I collected on road trips along with pressed souvenir pennies.

But I didn't bring many objects with me to represent myself at New College. What I did bring felt like private totems to anchor me. On my squat dorm bookshelf, I set a copy of Thomas Jefferson's autobiography and *Notes on the State of Virginia*, along with a tiny pewter statuette of him. I'd bought both years earlier when I visited Monticello in Charlottesville, Virginia. Jefferson had always seemed to both exemplify and normalize my family's beliefs, simultaneously affirming every facet of the White nationalist worldview while still being someone Americans refused to dismiss or condemn as nothing more than an irredeemable racist. Education and the university he founded were what he put on his gravestone, trying to establish how people should remember him. I wanted my legacy to mirror that. I saw my dreams for the future as radical and self-sacrificing, the way he saw his own, rooted in reading widely, expressing myself eloquently, and speaking up even when it felt dangerous.

Once I dropped off my bags in my First Court room on the ground floor that first day, I headed out again to find anyone out and about. I met David, another first-year student, sitting on the grass and we walked around together until we found some upper-years eating watermelon left over from the official welcome events. They offered us slices and then took us back to their dorms farther away from Palm Court, where we sat on plastic chairs on their second-floor balcony and talked for a while, before I went back to my room, unpacked my boxes, moved my clothes into the chest of drawers, and claimed part of the closet before my roommate showed up.

That first Sunday night, the parents who had helped move in many of my cohort were supposed to be off campus. Family welcomes were done, and the first day of administrative orientation was to begin the next morning. As the sun set, we gathered in our respective Pei courts to be greeted by our resident advisors. Standing in a gaggle in the middle of First Court, many of the people who would become my friends that fall stood together to take down the cell number of our RA, who said to call them if we had a noise complaint or if we or someone in our group ever got too intoxicated and needed help. In the distance, in one of the other courts, we could hear vuvuzelas, the long plastic horns used by World Cup soccer fans to produce a loud, obnoxious drone, accompanied by cheers and shouts. Suddenly into our midst came dozens of upper-year students who weren't meant to even be on campus yet. They were completely naked, streaking through the middle of the first night of formal introductions to our incoming cohort. They yelled out welcomes to us, blew horns, and sprinted through while we cheered.

After the streaking welcome party passed, we were dismissed and told to enjoy our first real night at New College. The sun had completely set, and I walked out of First Court slightly dazed but amazed at this place I had arrived at. I immediately ran into Juan, who had the same look of disbelief and enchantment. We went for a walk to reconnect and share how our first days had gone and who we'd met.

As we walked the lighted paths around the edges of the dorms, next to the dark area of trees that separate campus from the highways, we could hear party vibes coming from the pool in the distance. The upper-year streaking had turned into upper-year illegal skinny-dipping. Juan asked if I wanted to join. I said no, that it seemed like a bit more than I was ready for, and he said he was going for it. We parted ways as he passed the fence to join the naked revelers.

THE NEXT MORNING WAS THE first day of orientation week. After breakfast, we congregated in the conference center on the residential side of campus. Waiting in line to proceed into the room, I met several people who to this day are some of the most important people in my life. All I noticed then was how many of them seemed as worried of not fitting in as I was. I stood next to a guy who pulled out a pocket notebook to write down something we had quickly talked about. When I asked about it, he said he liked to write down new ideas during his day to make sure he didn't forget them later. Seemed like my kind of person.

When we filed in for the program to start, I sat next to a student who I learned was an out-of-state student. When they saw my name tag, my gut fell as my hope for anonymity seemed to crash around me in the first minutes of my first day. "Your name is Derek Black?" they asked, and I nodded yes. Maybe they'd seen my name in the early emails to our cohort and Googled it, which I had thought was unlikely because there were 202 names in that list, and nothing to distinguish any of us. It occurred to me I might be dealing with a class of people whose fastidious curiosity outstripped anything I'd dealt with before. It did only take one person to do that level of research and spread it to everyone. If anyone typed my name into Google, the entire first page of results was about me, my media interviews going back a decade, my kids' website promoting White nationalism, and my local election that had become a national news story.

When I tentatively inquired what about my name was interesting, they told me, "There was a kid named Derek Black in my high school. But he was an asshole." I stared back at them, unsure if this was a coded acknowledgement that they knew who I was. Before we could continue our conversation, a representative of the administration stepped onto the stage to begin the program. As everyone began to quiet down, they turned back to me and introduced themselves. "Well, it's nice to meet you, Derek Black. I'm Zoë." In the intervening years, they've begun using they/them pronouns.

When the morning's orientation ended, the administrators gave us maps and sent us to learn the layout of campus academic buildings. I was with my transfer student group, but Zoë's group was immediately behind mine. We kept exchanging glances, and I would make sure to run into them every time our groups overlapped. Eventually I joined their group at one of the last stops, which led to us walking off to go talk some more.

"Were you serious?" I remember asking about my name doppelgänger. Zoë said yeah and told me they'd grown up the child of professors in a college town in northwest Arkansas. Instead of reassuring me, this information only freaked me out more. I had just been in their area of Arkansas a few weeks earlier, where I'd stopped and had dinner with the co-host of my White nationalist radio show, and the third generation of the Robb family, who had taken over my dad's KKK group twenty years before. Unlike the older generations of that family who lived out in the holler around their church's land, in comfortable modern houses but a long drive to town on a dirt road, the younger generation lived in town and talked to locals all the time. They were trying to become more a part of the town and its community.

It occurred to me suddenly that I might not be talking to someone who wanted to expose me at New College before I even started. Maybe I was chatting with someone who'd have my back, who might understand my world, my experiences, and my beliefs, without me having to explain them. Maybe Zoë even knew the family I had gotten close to over the previous few years, who had made me realize how a Klan community could feel familial.

I said I'd just visited Arkansas on the way back from my summer road trip, but I didn't mention anything about who I visited. We were still in a group of other students, so maybe Zoë just didn't want to explicitly say they knew about me.

For a moment, I wondered if one of the first people I'd met had brought the same fears I had of being stigmatized and condemned, but could help me fit in at New College without what I then callously thought of as stirring up drama. My family had spent the spring and summer joking about New College's consistent rankings in *Princeton Review*'s top ten for colleges with the "Most Politically Active Students," "Most Liberal Students," "Most LGBT-Friendly," "Most Weed Friendly," and finally "Birkenstock-Wearing, Tree-Hugging, Clove-Smoking Vegetarians." None of those qualities boded well for my time there being comfortable or productive, at least from my perspective. I chose it for its status as the honors college, for the freedom it offered to steer my own education, and for the medieval history professors; I wasn't so worried, comparatively, about the *Princeton Review* lists. My parents and David all remembered their time at college as tumultuous yet formative. They had come into their own as White nationalist leaders then, where they'd been widely condemned by university communities with liberal sensibilities. At the same time, they'd also found the people who shared their worldviews and who had gone on to be their lifelong friends, allies, and members of the families they made. College had shaped the outcome of the rest of their lives. It had been the formative social moment that had defined their White nationalist careers ever afterward. I had been reluctant to even attend college, but I had discovered how much I liked research and crafting valid arguments. I didn't want to bring my activism to campus, so that this new home could be a respite for me. I was more curious how the people around me thought than I was ready to antagonize them. I thought my college degree would likely make me a better activist, but I had already had enough of conflict and being condemned to want to experience more of it while I was there.

Despite the public pronouncements that New College was a liberal hippie haven, I knew that whenever members of a community made outspoken declarations that they adhered to values against racism, hate, and bigotry—especially when that community was majority White—you could reliably find plenty of dissent in the ranks. The base of financial support for the White nationalist movement was made up largely of educated people afraid of being condemned as racist or called out for violating the liberal pieties of their social and professional communities, but who nevertheless had their own opinions and criticisms. It was rare that such people would risk being publicly branded as a racist. When they could become part of a larger community, they often behaved very differently.

It was one thing to declare you were not a racist, or that you didn't hate anyone. In many parts of America, "racist" is essentially synonymous with calling someone a "bad person." It was another thing to live out racially egalitarian ideals. For all the liberal bona fides New College projected into the world, its student population was whiter than other public schools in Florida. Its student body was almost 70 percent White, while the University of Florida, another very good Florida school, was just over half White. Who you chose to live with, to trust, to help, to care for and support, and to identify with said far more about your values than what you declared them to be.

Zoë and I realized we had been housed in rooms near each other in First Court, and we exchanged numbers and made plans to meet up later. I was super interested in what it had been like to have academic parents, to live in a couple different places growing up, and what growing up in Arkansas had been like. They loved Chick-fil-A, despite the anti-LGBT positions of the owners, and I agreed to drive a group of us to the one in Sarasota.

OUR COLLEGE HAD AN EMAIL forum that was student run, and all students were automatically subscribed. The next day, a student emailed out a PSA to all the first-years about the night before: "To whoever was taking photos last night during the RA court meetings, remember, stuff that you put on the internet (including stuff that you post to this forum) stays forever! If you have a picture of people in a compromising situation, get their permission before putting it anywhere." As someone raised in the public eye with a rigid list of rules on how to maintain data privacy and the risks of "compromising" things on the Internet, this had been exactly what I thought about in the moment. I had loved that they did what they wanted, but I was amazed that they also understood the importance of privacy and were actively making a choice to trust the New College community, even its newest members. That was the moment I realized I was in a space where people would show vulnerability and protect others, and that they expected me to do the same.

After the first day of orientation, I went back to First Court and found some people milling around, waiting for the first party of the year to start at 10 p.m. People could and did freely wander in and out of any of the courts, particularly on Friday and Saturday nights, when the open-air parties called "walls" were happening, because the parties happened in Palm Court, surrounded by the walls of First, Second, and Third Court dorms. They went late into the night every Friday and Saturday during the semester. Walls were the central part of social life, a reliable party every weekend. Students pushed at the beginning of the semester to host their favorite themes, among them Anything but Clothes Wall and Kiss Your Crush Wall, and equipment TAs managed audio/visual equipment that student government had purchased with student funds and owned for collective use.

My roommate had not yet arrived. I learned from an RA that he was a returning student who chose to live in these traditionally first-year dorms to save money. As I would quickly learn, his family didn't live far from Sarasota, so he always left town after his last class on Thursday to stay with them and didn't return until Monday morning. I'd have a private room for half the week for the entire semester, which was a pretty sweet deal. That first day, I took my guitar to the concrete table in the middle of First Court and started playing songs I'd practiced at open mics.

On road trips, my dad tuned to classic rock stations playing Crosby, Stills, Nash & Young, the Who, the Rolling Stones, Led Zeppelin, Pink Floyd, and Fleetwood Mac. Apparently at some point as a kid I called his music "degenerate," according to him, but by my mid-teens my best friend, also born into a White nationalist family, gave me a nudge toward the Beatles and I quickly absorbed all of the above.

As I sat on the table playing songs, a couple people came over and started singing along. We switched to old protest songs like Woody Guthrie's "This Land Is Your Land" and "Little Boxes," made famous by Pete Seeger. The girl closest to me on the table commented that she always felt bad about that song, because she'd always loved summer camp. The growing group sat for a minute and talked about how we'd all probably done our best to avoid getting put in boxes by coming to New College.

When I arrived at the party, I immediately recognized many of the people I'd met throughout the day. To make room in the cramped dance area, people spilled out onto the grass nearby. Nervous yet curious students lined the walls, just outside of the dance area. After meandering around and saying hi to people I'd met throughout the day, I wanted to join the main dance area, but I didn't quite have the nerve, so I ended up sitting down in front of one of the concrete walls near the DJ. Zoë had already started to meet and dance with the people who would become their friend group that semester. Zoë left the group to come up to sit next to me. I said I didn't know how to dance; they said no one else did either. I still begged off, and we walked away from the dance area to the quieter area under the trees. We talked about where they had moved from, what Arkansas was like, what honors classes had been like in high school, what kind of music they listened to, how Zoë had decided to come to New College instead of anywhere else.

The next song that came up was "Personal Jesus" by Depeche Mode. It felt like the anthem of loneliness and uncertainty. I told Zoë we had to join in, so we got up and ran over. I found myself jumping and dancing. I felt silly, and I felt worried, but I also felt welcomed. I already felt like a part of a place that I also knew couldn't last.

Afterward, we sat back on a block of concrete under the trees with a group of other students and started to talk about how our first days were going. I mentioned how much I liked and was impressed by all the people I was meeting. Other people said versions of the same thing. Zoë then volunteered that it was such a refreshing experience after coming from northwest Arkansas. People at New College were more experimental and open-minded, they said, and there was so much curiosity and exploration.

Then they added something that immediately ended my speculation that they might be familiar with the movement world I was coming from. "It's also nice," Zoë said, "that there are lots of other Jewish students here."

THE IDEA THAT ZOË WAS Jewish and from Arkansas hadn't even occurred to me, which I also immediately realized was exactly the stereotype Zoë had dealt with at home.

Oddly enough for one of the most well-known faces of the rising antisemitic White nationalist movement, I had known and been friendly with lots of Jewish kids throughout my life. When I was growing up, Palm Beach County boasted the densest Jewish population in the United States at over 20 percent of its 1.2 million people. At that same time, the Jewish population of metropolitan New York City was only 9.7 percent. The only places with a higher Jewish percentage in the world than Palm Beach County were in Israel. Before I left school, all my elementary school classes in our district public school had lots of Jewish kids, including some of my closest friends. Those relationships were always threatened by the fact that my family were some of the most famous antisemitic activists in the country. As a kid, I always held two things as simultaneously true: that many of my friends were Jewish, but also that my family believed it was trying to defend the world from a global conspiracy being enacted, presumably, by their parents.

During my homeschooled teenage years, none of my relationships developed as deeply or personally as they had before. I still encountered plenty of Jewish kids among the homeschoolers and after-school volunteers at the science museum. I never brought up my family's beliefs, although I grew more confident of my role in advocating them year by year. I remember one day when I was a tween—after explaining one of the brain teasers to a visitor, where the answer was to lay sticks in the same shape as a Star of David to produce the highest number of triangles—another friend piped up to explain the Jewish meaning of the symbol. After he explained it, I didn't reveal that I already knew it, not just because of my friends, but because my family had boxes of a book by David Duke called *Jewish Supremacism* whose cover depicted that star branding and setting the American flag on fire.

At that first wall at New College, sitting across from someone I was rapidly connecting with, it went through my mind that my family would be outraged if they learned I was developing my closest relationship at New College with someone who was Jewish. I imagined the potential blowback, and I also imagined the consequences of not telling Zoë about myself. I couldn't see any way to square either side. The previous two years, I'd experienced my life with my family and my reputation and responsibilities as the next leader of their movement closing in on every other part of my life. I was terrified by the idea that this New College space too would eventually slam shut on me. I felt selfish both for disrespecting what I knew my family would have demanded and for the impossible position in which I knew was putting everyone I was developing relationships with that night. I had no answer. For now, in the dark, while the music played in the background, I decided I could keep both by splitting myself in two and giving as much as I could to each of them as long as I could.

Later in the night, Zoë and I went back to our dorms in First Court, and ended up in my room, because my roommate wasn't back in town yet, so I had more space and quiet. We sat across the room from each other, on the two different beds that were raised up to their top-most positions like loft beds. I told Zoë this was the first time I had ever lived away from home, and they were surprised. They told me that I would probably find having a roommate annoying.

I told Zoë I was uncertain about college. That I had done well at community college, but that New College was the only four-year school I had applied to. They asked what I would have done if I hadn't gotten in, and I said I'd just have gone to build things for rich people in Palm Beach and quit academics. This school seemed like a good place to study German literature and I had learned they had medieval history and I liked that, too. I was frustrated that New College didn't accept associate degrees from community colleges as a full two years' worth of work, like most state schools did, which meant I would have to be there at least three years. That seemed like an insanely long time to me, but Zoë told me to think of it as a life-building experience instead of a race. They argued it took a long time to learn and grow, and we would all likely be different people after we grew up together for so many years.

We talked about past relationships. I told Zoë that I had had a summer fling before coming to New College, but that my only more serious relationships had been a couple years before. Zoë told me they had broken up with their boyfriend because they were both leaving for college and the idea of a long-distance relationship had seemed awful.

I was happy to meet them, already interested in them romantically, but mostly excited at this whole completely novel social situation. So many of us had come from all over the country, and in some cases around the world, to inhabit a few acres on the Gulf Coast of Florida for the next few years. We were all so different, yet I could already perceive a commonality. We all had lived much of our childhoods told by our communities and families that we were smart, and that our intelligence meant we had a responsibility to live up to our promise. It was the curse of honors kids everywhere. While the stakes felt high, it was also the first time most of us had ever been outside of the pressure cookers of our upbringings. We had come together and could make whatever we wanted of it, if we were brave enough to do it.

THE NEXT MORNING, I SAT down for the first time with my academic advisor, Dr. Glenn Cuomo, a professor of German literature and film. All new students who had been assigned to him met as a group. I had met him for the first time a few weeks earlier at the summer ice cream social, and I had immediately liked him as an advisor.

Faculty advisors were usually a professor in your area of concentration (AOC), New College's version of a major. The requirements for any AOC were subjective and flexible, so much so that many people at New College proposed their own AOC by cobbling together various classes and independent study projects. The role of an academic advisor was to be the ultimate sign-off each semester on your courses, tutorials, or independent study projects. In an email,

I told my mom, "As long as I've known him, he's struck me like an excellent lawyer. He always pursues my case and keeps my interests in mind (deadlines for financial aid and scholarships within the school, project proposals, etc.)."

That first day sitting down with him as an enrolled student, however, I didn't have many academic questions. The one that was plaguing me instead was about the firehose of hundreds of emails, headed at the beginning of their subjects [FORUM], that were filling my college email inbox. He said he didn't have any help to offer, because the Forum wasn't available to faculty, and he didn't really understand it or think it was a great thing. As a professor at New College since 1982, he'd seen all the versions of campus public discussion process over the decades. Before networked computers, discussions played out on sheets of eight-and-a-half-by-eleven-inch copy paper that people taped to the large glass windows of the cafeteria to declare an opinion, gripe, or argument. If it agitated someone, they'd write a response on the same sheet. If it attracted enough comments, someone would eventually paste a new sheet next to it to continue the argument. Sometimes the discussions could get heated, toxic, or ugly. Usually, it went on for only a few sheets, but sometimes it could cover ten, fifteen, or more. Etiquette demanded people sign their arguments. When they didn't, their comment would get trashed with arrows and harassment demanding "sign your name!"

In the early 1990s, students at New College set up an online bulletin board, using the same early Internet technology that my dad was using across the state to run the nascent Stormfront community. Personal computers were still rare and expensive, so discussion there was limited. A decade later, after college email addresses were issued to all students, an email forum was created almost by accident. In the early 2000s, the administration created an email listserv meant to update all students with announcements. Shortly afterward, as an older alum relayed, "Someone realized that anyone could send anything to the student listserv and, after a few days, the entire student body was getting film recommendations, recipes, etc. A separate, optional listserv for other stuff was then created, the Forum." The iteration of the Forum that existed when I arrived had been set up on a server in a student's dorm.

Student funds paid to keep it running outside official school servers and away from administrative control or oversight.

It's hard to imagine mentioning the Forum to a New College student or alum without eliciting strong feelings. All new students were automatically subscribed to it as soon as their addresses became available. Students' names were always attached to the messages they sent, which produced a measure of civility and personal responsibility in all discussions, though that wasn't guaranteed. The Forum was difficult for faculty or administrators to read, and forwarding threads to them—or to anyone outside the student body—was frowned upon. The intensity of the community was apparent from the moment its gates opened to first-years' inboxes a few weeks before we physically arrived on campus.

The deluge was immediate. Discussions among upper-years appeared in media res. Some of the first messages we received came out of a heated fight about racial profiling—one student's argument in response, that "Blacks are infinitely more likely to commit violent crime," was one I was familiar with.

When the upper-years realized the first-years were on the Forum, someone immediately sent out a satirical introduction: "Hello [FORUM]. Greetings! This is the [FORUM] for you if you're new to toking or you have questions about the herb. If you're new to the College, this forum might be for you, as well. Welcome!" The first member of my cohort to venture out posted a hesitant feeler: "Let me be a first-year and say that not only does the forum seem terrifying, but I am also all sorts of confused." Current students came in to reassure them: "The [FORUM] is the only place where you'll encounter any anti-first-year sentiment." Someone else then followed up: "The Forum is only for trolling, offensive opinions, and highbrow potty humor."

ON THE LAST DAY OF the orientation week, the administration organized buses to take us to see the white sand beach in Sarasota. Writers for the student newspaper, the *Catalyst*, interviewed us on that outing. I was one of the few students who gave them a quote. I remember at the time wondering whether it was a bad idea to risk having my name in print, because it might bring too much attention to me. I decided I wasn't going to make myself small or hold myself off from experiencing campus life and connecting with people. Giving them a quote, which I was presumably the most practiced at of anyone in our cohort even if no one knew it, felt like a choice to lean as much into being my full self as I could. The quick line they printed encapsulated my restrained eagerness: "Derek Black, a transfer and first-year student, told the *Catalyst* that his class is an 'interesting group of people' and that he feels 'enriched by meeting a new person each day.'"

Just as legendary as New College's culture of communal information sharing was its party culture. The student newspaper bemoaned, "One aspect of New College history that administration has been known to diminish is New College's vibrant drug and party culture—although perhaps this is no surprise, so as to preserve the college's reputation for prospective students and their families." A representative of our student government sent out a PSA early in the week warning against trying to host any "unauthorized" parties: "There is nothing worse than planning for a spectacular wall to have it shut down instantly by the cops because it was unauthorized/they didn't know it was going on." They signed off, warning, "Bear in mind that as an event sponsor you take responsibility for everything that happens at your event" and then the wisdom that "New College is New College. Deal with it. Just make sure we all use some tact when it comes to drinking, nudity and parents. Those three don't usually mix."

OVER THE COURSE OF THE semester, Zoë and I kept hanging out. Zoë lived above me in the dorm and kept their MacBook music drive open for people to listen wirelessly. That first weekend, I went through their MP3 collection and listened to tons of new songs.

I asked Zoë about their family. They told me occasionally about Jewish community things, but much more about how quirky their dad had been for doing things like listening to sea shanties, how their mom had married a funny Jewish guy, or about their brother. I told Zoë about my niece, who sent me a care package at one point with a drawing of me in my hat. When I played Zoë some of my favorite country songs, they often told me I had conservative taste. Nevertheless, Zoë was not always comfortable with feminism, and, being from Arkansas, was familiar with country music. I had some of my earliest and most thoughtful conversations about both the good and bad qualities of conservatism in those months. They described how the beauty standards at New College were very different from their high school. At New College, it felt like women didn't need to wear makeup for social approval, and body hair was accepted.

I often felt uncomfortable in the new (to me) social context of campus. I was used to having my own space, my isolated family house where I went back at night and none of the people I'd got to know that day would be around. On campus, it felt like I could never fully drop my guard, or get away. Once, late at night when I left the group to go sit in my car, annoyed or uncomfortable with something, Zoë somehow knew where I had gone and came to find me. We talked about whatever had been upsetting me and then decided to drive nowhere in particular. We went north on the interstate for exit after exit, until we eventually got off and made our way back down the local highway that led eventually back to school. Along the way, we saw a twenty-four-hour diner and stopped for breakfast around 2 a.m. We talked about classes, our past relationships, our worries about not being good enough to accomplish our goals.

I told Zoë about my experience of being homeschooled in West Palm Beach, going to the beach whenever I wanted. They were surprised to realize I hadn't worked as hard in the traditional academic way as most people in our cohort. Over time, they noted some of my academic gaps, such as how I read too slowly and too thoroughly for many school assignments, that I needed to learn to skim. I confessed my math was abysmal, and this confession became the basis for our getting together later on in the semester, when they spent their time walking me through many of the assignments for our shared economics class, explaining the meaning of formulas.

WHEN CLASSES STARTED THE NEXT week, the semester began to take on a predictable cadence. Looking back, it's hard to believe that it was only about three months, because in retrospect it felt like an entire era of change and growth. As the weeks proceeded, I felt a slight distance from my friend group of other first-years. I never really overcame my hesitation about going to walls, although I usually made an appearance and navigated through them at the beginning of the night. On weekend nights the gap just felt larger. When none of them woke up early one Saturday morning to ride bikes with me to the farmer's market, I went alone and passed them walking groggily to breakfast when I returned to campus a couple hours later. The only time I've ever bought alcohol for minors was when they asked if I'd go with them to the liquor store. I annoyed the clerk by bringing the whole group in with me, not even trying to hide the fact that they were picking out what they wanted and handing it to me. He looked at me, exasperated, at the register and said I could buy what I wanted, but they needed to wait outside.

I took multiple medieval history classes that semester. I began to study Latin, and I kept up the German language and culture courses that had initially coaxed me into enrolling in community college. That first semester, I asked to be let into an advanced seminar on the Carolingian Empire, the ninth-century sprawling political domain of Charlemagne that established the bounds of what would become Western Europe. That class set me on the research focus that I followed in my graduate training for the decade after New College. In that course, both Theodoric and Roland—the early medieval historical figures that my dad had named me after—fell out of the hazy legends I'd understood them through and into the documented history we read and parsed as a group.

My dad had given me each of my three legal names. His family name, Black, traced back to Scotland and, from the road, through a large 1980s cell phone he'd been using for David's campaign, he convinced my mother to agree to Derek Roland as he drove home while she was in labor.

He'd always tell people he picked them because when you said them "you can almost hear the clash of Viking steel." Derek was the shortened form of Theodoric, which I later chose as my username on Stormfront. Roland was the semihistorical, self-sacrificing hero of the wildly popular medieval epic poem, *The Song of Roland*. I knew the vague outlines of both men's stories, because I was curious what had inspired my dad's choice, but I didn't dig into their actual history or read contemporary medieval accounts of them until I arrived at New College.

My professor not only shared their life stories in that seminar, but he also addressed the myths that modern White supremacists attached to that history. I didn't realize anyone outside my own insular world was even aware that White nationalists talked about medieval history, much less took the time in an unrelated class to debunk it. He directly addressed the ways White supremacists misunderstood the conflicts these early medieval kings had with early Islamic raids into Europe. Without knowing anything about my background, he lectured about the irresponsibility of ascribing even a desire to "defend" Christianity to these territorial conflicts, much less any idea of Europeanness or Whiteness, which no one had yet developed. I felt called out, but no one looked in my direction. Like everything else we were studying in that class, we turned directly to the accounts people at the time wrote down and we deciphered what they were saying rather than what we were glomming onto because we knew what happened later.

They had different languages and religions, and they identified by different ethnic names that seemed to pop up and then disappear again in the sources in ways that suggested they often had more political than personal meaning. It was only centuries later that their descendants retrospectively interpreted that earlier history as a defense of Europe, Christianity, or Christendom.

That was my first moment engaging with the distant past of Europe, which I had always assumed shared an ideological continuity with my own beliefs. The foremost White nationalist organization publishing supposedly scientific and educational material for the movement was, and still is, an American nonprofit named after Charles Martell, the grandfather of Charlemagne (also called Charles the Great). The Carolingian era that we were studying was named after these two Charleses. Realizing their interpretation was modern, not ancient, left me with a sense of embarrassment.

TO THIS DAY, THE ONLY time I've ever fired a handgun was with New College students. It happened when the group of first-years I was hanging out with all decided they wanted to try out going to a gun range down the road from campus. I was also curious. My dad had been legally prohibited from owning guns, and despite the reputation for violence in the White nationalist movement—or maybe because of it—none of the leaders or movement members I knew kept guns around them. Despite all this, personal gun ownership was common in Florida. One afternoon, a conversation in First Court revealed that one of our friends had grown up in a family that kept guns, and his dad had taken him to practice at the gun range his whole life. He was the definition of gentle and soft-spoken, and we were surprised. The five of us realized none of the rest of us had ever fired a gun or been to a gun range, and we'd like to see what it was like. I volunteered to drive, and we all shuffled into my PT Cruiser to drive less than ten minutes to the nearest shooting range. Our friend took the lead on getting us checked in and taught us how to load and aim a handgun. As you might expect, the rest of us could barely hit a target, while he reliably hit bull's-eyes and headshots. We joked that we now knew who to stick with when the zombie apocalypse hit.

On the drive back, one of our group, who was Jewish, asked if any of us had noticed the tattoos on the clerk behind the counter. They weren't fully visible sticking out of his sleeves, but she had been worried they were Nazi symbols. No one else had noticed, but I let her know I'd seen it too. I didn't tell her that our fears had been different—I had been worried about the off chance this guy might be tied into the movement enough to recognize me. If he did, he had had enough self-awareness not to say anything, and we'd left without anything notable happening. Driving my friends back, I sat with the weird knowledge that we had been the only two to notice, but for such vastly different reasons.

LATE ONE NIGHT EARLY IN the semester, several of us ended up sitting cross-legged on the floor of Zoë's dorm. The conversation turned to people's experiences of discrimination and how the world had felt to them at home before they came to New College. Someone mentioned what it was like coming out as gay in high school or staying closeted. Zoë described growing up as one of the only Jewish kids in their high school in northwest Arkansas. The negative experiences from that ranged from outright hostility to the invisibility that comes from ignorance.

I remember trying to explain that some of those people probably didn't know how it had felt. I had been quietly thankful all semester that I had chosen not to put a Confederate flag sticker on my car before coming to New College, even though I believed it was the most innocuous White power symbol. When I got my driver's license a few years before I left for college, I adopted our small red pickup truck as mine. Learning to drive on a manual transmission was one of my prouder moments, though early on I had stalled the engine turning left in the middle of a sixteen-lane intersection in suburban Palm Beach County while oncoming traffic bore down on me. Another time, as I was accelerating too slowly onto Interstate 95, a group of angry teenagers sped up from behind me to drive close on my left while we went down the freeway. They launched a full gallon of water at my door that landed like a bomb. It was only in the dorm that night, when I mentioned that I had driven a truck with a Confederate flag sticker and saw the looks of shock on everyone's faces, that I realized the somewhat obvious fact that that sticker may have been the cause of their anger.

What struck me, sitting in the dorm trying to keep those two domains separate, was how they suddenly overlapped in personal ways I couldn't deny or dismiss. Zoë mentioned offhandedly that there was also a Klan group that had a headquarters not far away. Knowing the Klan was there, and that they had events and caused uproars constantly, made Zoë feel worried and threatened.

The blood rushed to my head because I knew the exact people Zoë was talking about. Although no one turned to me or expected I'd have any thoughts besides sympathy, I felt put on the spot and I wanted to be able to say something. There were many KKK groups I would have been happy to disavow. "The Klan" is not a trademarked term. Anyone can call their organization the KKK, and many of them were persona non grata within at least my circles of the White nationalist movement. But not this group.

I wanted badly to be able to denounce the group in Arkansas, even if I couldn't dare say it. Instead, it felt too close, and the hypocrisy and duality that I could usually ignore and avoid rose to the surface and felt like it was crawling all over my skin. Zoë was describing people I knew intimately. I had stayed with them less than two months earlier and over the previous couple years, I'd come to know them in a way I didn't know any other group like them. I considered them some of my closest friends and allies.

Sitting in that dorm, emotionally reaching out to this new community, I knew I couldn't keep my identity—or my new relationships—a secret forever. I knew I was violating the trust of my new friends and acting in bad faith, especially for my Jewish friends and friends of color, who were the targets of my ideology. While friendships in the past had been fine, these new friendships, and this new community, was more intimate, and I felt like I was engaged in a terrible deception in a way I never had before. All my public connections were as a White nationalist. Before coming to New College, I had asked my dad not to mention where I was going to school because there was nothing good for my education that could come from mobilizing movement power. Sitting in that dorm late at night, I only felt more confident I needed to keep my presence there away from the public and from the rest of the movement as long as I could. I was now holding the vulnerable truths of my friends, and selfishly, I wanted to stay there with them, as one of them. I knew that I would only hurt them when the bubble burst, but if I held my breath and didn't step too loudly, maybe I could keep pretending forever.

I KNEW MY FAMILY FELT like they had been demonized in the press and misunderstood by the public. I still agreed and empathized with them, but I also knew the kind of fear my family felt wasn't the same as what I was hearing from my classmates. My family were afraid of being attacked at events by Antifa, certainly, but that was political violence. They were afraid of being harassed, sued, disdained, and ostracized. Yet all these outcomes were consequences of political activism, which everyone knew could come with a cost—a cost that was a major part of their identity. But when violence is against your identity, your person-hood, it follows you. No matter how much my family tried to adopt the language of persecution for White people broadly, there was no equivalent to living your life in fear because a Klan group that called you satanic regularly put on marches in your area.

The fear and guilt of what it would be like when my New College friends realized what I was keeping from them grew by the day. I had been accepted to a study abroad program in Munich, Germany, for the second half of the academic year, which meant I'd be off campus that spring. Soon after the conversation in the dorm, I got an email asking me to confirm whether I would still be coming. I wrote back that I was excited to join the program in Germany, instead of spending the full academic year on campus at New College. I wanted to attend the program, but there was also a small part of me that hoped that maybe by being out of sight, I could be out of mind. Maybe I could stave off the explosion I knew would come at some point and stay a part of my New College community for longer.

I'm not proud of the level to which I was committed to maintaining the opposing levels of my life. I did not cease White nationalist activism when I was accepted into my New College community. I continued to wake up early Monday through Friday mornings to dial in and join my dad for an hour as he kept up our AM radio show, which I had started in order to share my White nationalist message directly after being rejected from the GOP committee. My dad took over managing the show, changing the name from *The Derek Black Show* to *The Don and Derek Black Show*. My friends thought my hour-long morning "family call" was weird, but they were accepting of weird.

My dad and I continued to correspond on the ins and outs of White nationalist activism. Things were relatively quiet, and he told most journalists that I had moved on from my campaign to be seated on the Republican Executive Committee to focus on my studies for now. As always, strange offers and inquiries continued to come in. One morning, he forwarded me a message from an academic philosophy magazine in the Netherlands, asking for an interview with me for an edition on evil. I replied privately to my dad, "What do they want to know about evil?" He replied, "You know as much as I do. When I first saw the email, I thought they wanted to interview us as representatives of Evil." I asked him to turn down the interview on my behalf and jokingly responded, "Did they want me to read a philosophy book first? Or can I just say I'm beyond good and evil?"

My life as a leader-in-waiting continued and I tried to put it to the back of my mind. Miraculously, I successfully navigated all the potential pitfalls that first fall semester. One morning when I gave Zoë a ride to an early doctor's appointment, the appointment ran long. Driving back, the time came to call in to join my dad on the radio. Incredibly, I somehow decided I couldn't miss a day of the show. I told Zoë I needed to make a regular call home and I proceeded to make enough innocuous chitchat on my end of the call that nothing seemed unusual. I still feel baffled and sorry for that choice—for having them sit shotgun, clueless, while I listened to guests on the radio show spout antisemitism. Another time, in the library, our study group somehow landed on the procrastinating task of googling each of our names. I don't remember what I said that got me out of that situation, but somehow they got distracted and changed the subject before typing *all* our names in one by one. I do remember the terror.

Another bizarre, out-of-body moment came at the beginning of a campus talk on the female orgasm. My friends and I filed into the teaching auditorium and sat together in a row. A guy I knew peripherally was sitting in front of us, and he turned toward me and asked if he could tell me something weird: he had been mistaken about me earlier in the semester. I asked what he meant, and he said he had thought I was a White supremacist. He explained he knew better now, but that when he had gone into my room once, he had noticed my copy of Thomas Jefferson's autobiography, and assumed I must subscribe to Jefferson's racist worldview.

I didn't even have to say anything, because my friends jumped in to tell him that was a rude thing to say, and that his reasoning didn't make any sense. Jefferson was a major founding father, and we all could read historical books without identifying with everything they said. I let the subject drop, but I couldn't believe how closely he'd come to exactly the right and most unexpected conclusion.

As the hypocrisy, guilt, and fear of being found out rose in me, I reveled in the moments when I *was* aligned politically with my friends. I had always been loosely pro–gender equality and pro-choice, although my understanding of both issues certainly increased in college. My parents had protested the Iraq war in the weeks before both Desert Storm and Operation Iraqi Freedom more than a decade later. When I mentioned those protests to leftists on campus, we were in total agreement. I left out the part about how my family also thought Israel and Jews broadly were controlling American foreign policy. The line between omission and directly lying to my friends became finer and finer, and the ice I skated across seemed increasingly thin, even with how hard I was working to maintain it. One time in the cafeteria, talking with a student about our shared love of *The Lord of the Rings* and J. R. R. Tolkien, he told me how outrageous it was that the White supremacist website Stormfront had a *Lord of the Rings* section. For a moment, I wondered if he was trolling me, trying to get me to admit what he had already figured out. I responded by asking him what Stormfront was, and he explained the cultural weight of the largest White power community to me. I couldn't possibly tell him that I was the one who had created and led that *Lord of the Rings* section.

IN THE FINAL MONTH OF the fall semester, after talking about it several times and saying that I didn't want to date, I asked Zoë to talk, and we sat on a bench in front of the library. I said I had changed my mind, that I had obviously wanted to date them, but that I had tried to convince myself to just be friends. I asked if they'd consider it, at least until winter break, when we all went home. I wouldn't be returning in the spring, and they said they didn't want another long-distance relationship. I said honestly that I was okay with that, and we'd stay friends after. We didn't make any promises about ever getting back together later, but enjoyed those last few weeks. In retrospect, I did a massive amount of mental gymnastics to rationalize this to myself.

When the semester ended, I cried in my dorm with Zoë the night before we had to vacate for the winter break. I cried in response to having to say goodbye to this person I had grown to care for so deeply; I cried in response to my guilt for lying, both explicitly and by omission, and thus having effectively stripped their autonomy to make fully informed decisions about me; and I cried in anticipation of the future version of them that would—and should—inevitably feel betrayed by me. I walked them to their car and went back to my room alone to finish packing. Unlike most people, I wasn't going to return soon after the winter break. Going back and forth to my car carrying boxes, I passed other First Courters who asked, "Wow, you're really leaving?" but I kept cheerily responding, "But I'll come back!" The weight of keeping so much from people I had gotten closer to than I'd ever expected to was pressing down heavy.

For a long time, a small candle of hope inside of me had stayed lit for the idea that I might be able to get through my years at New College without anyone learning what I was keeping secret. Too many close calls and unbearable moments told me that was impossible. By semester's end, I didn't know if I even wanted to keep that secret. I knew I was betraying people who had gone from interesting personalities to friends and relationships that were becoming some of the most important in my life. I didn't know what would happen when they learned about my life and activism, or the ways that I directly helped build and support ideas and movements that scared them and didn't see them as fully, equally human. I didn't know how to tell them, and the impossibility of saying something only grew as the semester went on. For better or worse, avoidance and compartmentalization had always been my strong suit.

Every time I imagined returning to campus the next fall and rekindling those relationships, I couldn't bear again living with the knowledge that every moment of intimacy would only deepen the hurt of what was to come. But I also didn't know how to actually tell anyone. I never had initiated a conversation about my beliefs with anyone outside of the movement before. It felt as impossible to me as breathing underwater. So I made an odd choice, maybe a coward's choice, to try to force the issue and make someone else speak instead. I took out the copy of *Details* magazine that had been published the previous year. I had been proud then to see the multipage spread with glossy photos and a profile of me covering several pages, and I had brought a copy back to campus from home after Thanksgiving a couple of weeks earlier. Over the final month of the semester, it sat deep in a folder under my bed, where I felt confident no one would stumble on it. On that last day, I carried it to the gym to stash among other magazines.

My picture wasn't on the cover but, a few pages in, a full-page photo of me wearing the same leather hat I often wore on campus led into the headline, "Derek Black: The Great White Hope," with the subtitle, "On the surface, he's just another baby-faced fan of Taylor Swift and *Twilight*, but underneath lurks the next David Duke." The article went through my biography, including "the eventful childhood he's barely out of. There's the HBO documentary, *Hate.com*, that he appeared in when he was 12; the *USA Today* article the next year that cast him as half-Huck Finn, half-Damien." It described an ominous version of the student many people on campus would recognize: "Beneath a broad-brimmed black leather hat, he's gaunt and pale with shoulder-length red hair, knoblike cheekbones, and pond-water-colored eyes." I left the gym, and hoped the custodians wouldn't clear out the magazines over the winter break, so it would still be there when students started to return in a few weeks.

INSTEAD OF LEAVING IMMEDIATELY FOR Germany, I spent that January back at my parents' house in West Palm Beach, free from academic work. I happily reverted to the homeschooled schedule I'd missed ever since I started community college a couple years before. A sound-mixing board took up much of my desk that I'd used for years to run live Internet radio each night. I'd also use it to record demos of songs I wrote. After my parents went to sleep down the hall, I used the bulky studio headphones to lean back in my chair and listen to music late into the night until the twilight glow began to lighten outside my window and remind me it was time to go to sleep for a few hours. I'd drag myself out of bed several hours later to join my dad in the studio for our 9 a.m. radio show.

During my last year of school when I was eight or nine, I distinctly remember riding the bus home one afternoon and realizing that, despite my best mental efforts, I couldn't convince myself not to like a rap song that an elementary school classmate was playing. I remember telling myself I needed to change my opinion. My parents railed against hip-hop and rap as inherently bad and "not music." But I liked the song. I remember thinking when I left school that year that being able to avoid getting to know someone or something that I couldn't allow myself to love would be the best way to make sure I never did.

When I showed up at New College, the version of me that had ridden on the bus as a nine-year-old felt very far away. I had spent the decade since then using my access to the Net to pore over tens of thousands of songs and albums from the dawn of recorded music, and I had still managed to uphold my childhood commitment never to enjoy music that would make my parents ashamed of me. My niece hadn't followed any such restraint, and she'd covertly ask me to download albums for her without our family knowing. I'd listen to the mainstream pop, hip-hop, and occasional country she asked me to get for her, and I liked some of them, so I added them to my own collection. I decided I had outgrown being afraid to admit I liked something for the sake of upholding the ideological demands of my community. At least with myself, I decided, I wanted to be open to new experiences and passions. Trying to close off a new feeling before I could even understand what it was, to filter anything new through the lens of whether it was appropriate, I decided, was a sign of hesitation in my beliefs, not of confidence.

After doing the radio show, on days we didn't stop for breakfast on the way home, I'd drop my dad off at the house and then drive the few minutes past Mar-a-Lago to the ocean to swim freely or to paddle my kayak in the waves before the sun got too hot.

Like many kids who were taught to swim in the South Florida ocean, I knew how to tread water and float to conserve energy. The beaches there are notorious for rip currents, pressure built up by waves near the shore that releases suddenly back out to sea. Swimmers often get caught and pulled into deeper water. Tourists often panicked when they found themselves out too deep. Rip currents could be surprising, but they were very predictable, and the solution was not to fight it. You just needed to keep your head above water, and wait until it was over.

Signs on all the beaches declared, "Break the Grip of the Rip!" and told swimmers to let the current pull them out in the short run to conserve their strength for when the pull stopped. Fighting it tires you out, and you'll usually be dragged away regardless, all my mentors told me. But rip currents don't pull you out forever; experience teaches that you're never too far to get back to where you came from eventually. Swim parallel to the shore, out of the rip current, until you escape the undertow. On those mornings, I accepted that I couldn't control what pulled me where, but I could choose my battles, and take the long way around to get home.

IN EARLY FEBRUARY, AS THE spring semester began in Sarasota, I prepared to travel to Europe for my study abroad experience. Except for a short video call after Christmas, I hadn't spoken to Zoë in the month since I'd left New College. A big part of me thought it was best to continue keeping my distance, knowing that we had shared wonderful moments together, and that we had walked away mutually and fondly. But I didn't opt for that practical and reasonable decision. Before I left for Europe, I mailed them a letter and a couple burned CDs—this was the era before streaming music made sharing playlists easy.

Because my academic semester in Munich wouldn't begin until the end of April, I filled my time the next two months exploring the medieval places I'd learned about in classes at New College. A few days before my mid-February birthday, Zoë wrote me an email saying they'd gotten my package, updating me on what was happening at New College and our friends, and making fun of me for still reading the Forum. I responded, "I read the Forum so much more than I did when I was in person. I actually checked it from a Starbucks in Leicester Square in London while I was laid over. It's my anchor so I don't lose touch." Zoë responded, "That makes sense, though the Forum doesn't seem like it'd be the best anchor." Over the next couple months, we kept up regular correspondence about classes, worries, new relationships, and conflicts we had with family or friends. Our emails were certainly a better anchor to New College than the Forum had been.

Even factoring out the behemoth elephant of White nationalism, which I worked hard to avoid thinking about even as my anxiety rose, we had left a lot unsaid. Communicating about emotions was not something I was ever good at; transparent vulnerability was not a skill I had. So instead, we sometimes communicated in song lyrics, with all the angst, earnestness, and plausible deniability of young adulthood.

"Never should have called, but my head's to the wall and I'm lonely," I signed one message. "Older brother, restless soul lie down," Zoë responded, "You'll hear your sister sleeptalking, say your hair is long but not long enough to reach home to me." Zoë wrote me, "You've got too much to wear on your sleeve," and I responded, "But your memory is here, and I'd like it to stay."

In the afternoons in Europe, I kept up my responsibilities to call in to the radio show my dad continued to run. In the evenings, I wrote Zoë about the turmoil I felt through cryptic lyrics. This was not going to end well, I thought. I was born into my place among my White nationalist community, but I had gone above and beyond to become their representative. I publicly championed their moral right to segregate themselves and send everyone away, while I privately cherished my own relationships with the people they wanted to drive out. I was split between the community that had raised me, told me every day that we were hated by the world, and one that I loved privately, but expected to reject me as soon as they learned who I really was. I knew that they were justified to do it for the harms I and those around me had caused, even if at that point I didn't see those harms the same way.

One day I sent a photo that a passing photographer had taken of me playing guitar in a park in southwest Germany and described it to Zoë: "I felt very nervous about playing on the street on Saturday for the first time. It took me hours to get up the nerve. Then I did it and I got people who stopped and clapped, got to see hundreds of people walk by, and I made 30 euros in two hours. Let this be a lesson to you to let your ambitions fly." The same day, I wrote my regular travelogue to my mom, describing the same event, with noticeably fewer emotions on display: "I played music in the park for an hour and a half and received an incredible response. Little kids stopped and danced and by the end I had a real audience of families sitting on benches waiting for the end of the 'show.'" I had finally gotten up the nerve to perform in public just before all the lead-up came to an end. I had enjoyed my long reprieve, but it was soon time to begin the next era of my life.

CHAPTER 7

DUDE YOU'RE FAMOUS ON THE FORUM NOW

I TOOK A TRAIN TO Munich to finally begin the academic semester in late April, while my friends in Florida were about to prepare for their final exams. The American study abroad program housed us in a large multistory dorm complex in northern Munich constructed in the late 1960s and early '70s. Called Studentenstadt, meaning "student city," the complex of dorms housed over 2,500 students from all over the world. Nearly everything was available within the complex itself: a shop for essentials, a sauna, a beer garden on the roof, a pub, and sports organized by the students. Adjacent to the northernmost point of the English Garden, one of the largest urban parks in the world, there were wide-open green areas and fields, places to grill or lay out, tables to play games, and courtyards where people hung out. Studentenstadt was largely self-governed by the student residents, including an annual music festival at the end of every spring. The most common language between students was English when they didn't have to speak German.

Despite the ample opportunities for socializing, it was also easy to find privacy. All housing was single occupancy in self-contained spaces. All the people in my building were assigned to hundreds of standardized, 129-square-foot rooms, each with its own single cot, a desk, a window, a kitchenette with two electric burners, a wardrobe, and a shower and toilet set apart by plastic walls in the corner. I was assigned a room near the ground floor, overlooking the dumpsters and the bike ramp into the English Garden. My window offered me reliable people-watching, often more than I might have liked.

I arrived excited for the stability the semester offered. It was the oldest study abroad program that placed American students at a German university, called Junior Year in Munich, or JYM, run by Wayne State University in Detroit, Michigan. Established in 1953, the program was meant to reintegrate Germans and Americans after World War II. Unlike many study abroad programs run by other universities that manage their own classes and experiences, JYM was an affiliated academic institution at the Ludwig Maximilian University in Munich, founded in 1472, and was treated as an official course of study. All instruction was done in German, and we were permitted to take any courses we chose. That semester, I took a large lecture class on the German Middle Ages, and several smaller seminars. My language ability never felt sufficient, but it was a sink or swim situation and, starting on the first day of our classes, we introduced ourselves, wrote seminar papers, gave presentations, and navigated the administration and library bureaucracies over the next few months entirely in German.

The orientation week reminded me of meeting people at New College the previous fall. They showed us Munich, gave us a scavenger hunt list and transit passes, and sent us out into the city to learn to get around in it and find all the hidden treasures. My cohort were all Americans, from universities across the country, mostly in their third year of college. I felt calmer about my new German cohort than about the New College friends I had left behind. I think I never expected to get close to these new classmates, because we were all only here for a semester. It soothed my nerves.

They took us to the city registration office to comply with the formality of German bureaucracy. We had an hour over lunch to wait for our paperwork and photos to be processed and given back to us as proper licenses. I wandered away from the group and found myself in a large field in the middle of the city, expanding out in every direction, with a sixty-foot-high bronze statue of the personification of Bavaria overlooking it all. I walked to the statue and found an unguarded passage inside that led up a cramped spiral staircase. It ended inside the head with viewing holes overlooking the city. I read the history of the field and realized I was on the grounds that hosted Oktoberfest every year. In late April, no one was around while I explored alone. I went to a beer garden and sent a note to Zoë.

Later that day, I got a blunt email from a family friend: "Your father is in the hospital. He will be ok. He is in the ER." I asked for more information and didn't get a response. I spent the weekend calling home, following up, with little else to do. My dad's health had sometimes been precarious since recovering from his stroke three years earlier. My family eventually confirmed the email, that he was stable and recovering, and that he would be home soon, although he was restarting physical therapy.

The Internet connection to the Studentenstadt internal network was not yet working on my laptop, and it wouldn't be until the end of the coming week. Cafes and public Wi-Fi in the city were the only places I could connect either with my home or with New College. The office that managed the study abroad program had a sitting room with antique chairs and couches and Wi-Fi, but the office closed at 5 p.m. Several times I was the only person left there, sitting at one of the desks, when the head of the office came to lock up. We'd chitchat about how I was getting along and how my travels had gone before I arrived in Munich.

Monday went well and consisted of meeting professors and other students. Tuesday after lunch I sat down in the JYM sitting room and my stomach dropped. I hadn't yet responded to Zoë's message from the day before. It was still early in the morning in Florida, but Zoë had preempted my reply to our normal thread: "Oh woah dude you're famous on the Forum now. Well, that was an early morning surprise. I feel the need to defend you on the Forum, but I am too tired. Later. This is um weird. I feel very confused."

The Internet connection hadn't yet been turned on in my dorm, and the JYM office closed in a few hours. Some of the other American students were going to get food and coffee to get to know each other. They invited me to come along, but I told them I'd discovered I had a lot of work to do, so I'd see them another day, as my heart pounded.

I opened the folder where my email forwarded the constant stream of Forum messages. Under the subject line, "this week just keeps getting better [stormfront]," an upper-year who was graduating that semester had sent a message to the entire school with a photo of me from the *Details* magazine article and a question in large font that asked, "Have you seen this man? Derek Black: White supremacist radio host . . . New College student???"

He quoted the Southern Poverty Law Center (SPLC) profile about me: "By age 12, Derek Black had created a children's page on Stormfront, complete with White pride songs and anti-Martin

Luther King Jr. bedtime stories. As early as 10, he was accompanying his father to White supremacist meetings. His involvement in the movement drew enough attention that he was the subject of a *USA Today* article and appeared in an HBO documentary, *Hate.com*, before he was a teenager." He quoted from *Details* magazine, the issue I had placed in the gym a few months earlier: "David Duke flew to Florida and lent his support and enthusiastically endorsed Black as the face of the next generation of race hate in America, 'We're so privileged to be in your presence here, Derek,' he gushed, and predicted that Black would have 'a much more extensive national and international career than I've had.'"

The student provided a link to a video of my dad talking about my admission to New College months earlier on our radio show where he called it the "third-highest graded academically of any public school in the country and the third-most liberal!" Ominously—and, of course, setting up such a dramatic moment had been my dad's intention at the time—my dad had added, "Soon enough the whole faculty and student body are gonna know who they have in their midst!"

It's telling now that I'd chastised him that same day, surprised he hadn't naturally assumed I wanted to keep my school life private. He knew I liked to keep different spheres of my life separate, and I had ever since I was nine years old. Hearing him talk on the radio the previous summer about a school I hadn't even arrived at yet felt like a selfish betrayal. When I told him I didn't want that part of my life taken over by White nationalism, like so many other parts had been, he consented and didn't mention it anymore.

The posting student, who planned to go into journalism after school, further reported, "Multiple people have confirmed that they have seen an individual who looks exactly like this guy on campus with the same name, even wearing the same hat. One person knew him fairly well and had no idea of his very outspoken political views. His name appears on the publicly available email list."

His final call to action was to ask, "How did this get past admissions? How do we as a community respond to this?" In a smaller font at the bottom of his 2 a.m. email blast, he added, "Note: in the incredibly unlikely event that you happen to be a ginger kid named

Derek Black who is not, in fact, the one described in this thread but merely look eerily similar to him . . . um sorry for alienating you from all of your friends." A couple messages later, when people asked him how he'd discovered all this, he said, "Another student sent me a link to the *Details* article saying, 'I think I know this guy!'" I never did get confirmation of whether the magazine I'd placed in the gym was what ultimately burst the surface tension of the bubble I could no longer live in.

Even though the message had gone out at 2 a.m. in Florida and had only been up for a few hours by the time Zoë pointed it out to me at 8 a.m. Florida time, there were already nearly sixty messages about it. Students were waking up and the number of responses was growing by the minute. Looking back on that thread now, it's remarkable to see each of the opinions, predictions, and responses that would define the rest of my experience at New College appear in just those first few hours. Over the next week, the discussion ran to nearly a thousand messages, still the largest discussion thread in the Forum's history.

Each of the four lines of thought that would dominate my life over the next few years appeared in the first half hour. The first reaction anyone voiced was annoyance at calling out a fellow student, calling it inappropriate: "He does have the right to have whatever opinion he wants. Even though most people rightly think this opinion is despicable. I also don't think new college students should flip their shit and ostracize the crap out of him." Others immediately added to this idea: "Is he disrupting student life, academic or personal? People are entitled to their opinions, no matter how disgusting or misguided others might find them to be." This first line of thought—that my opinions were my own, so long as I wasn't engaged in sharing or enacting them directly on campus—continued to be restated in different ways for the next several years.

The second reaction was hope for change based on the transformative power of New College: "To be honest, I came into New College as a very different person from who I am now. Being at New College exposed me to several new avenues of thought. Maybe what this kid needs isn't to be called out on things he's done in the past, but to be given a chance to open his mind." And, "I believe the best and the only appropriate way to handle this is to first accept that it makes us uncomfortable, and second attempt to move past the discomfort to reach out to him as a friend and a peer with kindness and acceptance. This could allow him to reassess his professed beliefs without fear of judgment for his past actions that we can clearly see are manipulated by his position of birth."

The third was a call for the campus community to mount a defense of its values by excluding me: "I disagree about the efficacy of ostracizing him—we are talking about a kid who grew up surrounded by White power enthusiasts—social rejection might be exactly what he needs to realize how fucked up his ideas are." And, "I think it's kind of silly to think that we can change him, 'He's so wrong that if we only engage in intellectual discourse with him, he will somehow come to understand our enlightened ways.' He thinks we're as brainwashed as we think he is. I don't get the impression he wants to engage with us. I don't think there's anything wrong with us saying to him that as a community we'd appreciate it if he left."

The final reaction that appeared in those first responses spoke to the marginalized experiences of people on campus and an awareness of the world beyond our bubble: "Well . . . New College is mostly a White school. Might be one reason he CAME here." And, "Maybe he hasn't been acting like a dick on campus because you're all White." Another pointed out, "It is really telling how only White people are defending this guy." One asked, "Why does it even matter whether or not he has seemed racist in person, because he is affecting a lot more than his small encounters with New College kids." Another said, "It doesn't matter if he's racist to you. It matters because he actively promotes White nationalism." They were speaking up for people for whom White nationalism was not an abstract idea: "The fact that he can hide being a hateful White supremacist doesn't detract from the fact that he's a hateful White supremacist." In retrospect, looking back, these are the responses that gave me pause the most. I had no good response, because it cut to the heart of how I saw myself. They knew me personally, and that didn't overcome what they thought about how I acted publicly.

A student summarized the options: "So what should we do, oh Forum denizens? Ostracize him? This will not help change his mind or open up his point of view to a more accepting and open opinion. This might only serve to solidify his ideas. Treat him with kindness and acceptance? This might actually work to disarm him and to expose him to the kindness and acceptance we hope for him to possess." To that another student responded, "No one here is 'clever' enough to change my political ideology—it is almost as if that isn't how politics works most of the time." Reading all this in Germany, I couldn't agree more with that dismissal of what seemed to me like ridiculous dreams about how they were going to change my mind.

Initially, all the messages were posted by people I didn't know personally. In my life to that point, I had learned how to deal with the anonymous aggression and contempt I'd receive online. This, however, was rapidly becoming more personal, and my usual internal mantras about how *these people don't know me* and *they're just talking about an idea of me* felt weaker than ever. Then people who had met me started to post. They began to share anecdotal accounts about my behavior on campus—that I had not been prejudiced or harmful in my relationships on campus, that I had even been a good friend to people, including Jewish students and people who weren't White. It was momentarily gratifying to see my personal character validated, but it turned to shame quickly when I thought about what these people who I'd supposedly been such a good friend to would think now that they knew that I'd lied to them. My mind quickly went to Zoë and my friends, none of whom had posted anything in those initial hours, likely confused and holding off, like Zoë had said. My list of guilty, culpable anxieties flashed through my mind—that I had led them into positions to be harassed or judged because of me; that at best people would treat them as naïve and at worst believe that they had known and were White nationalist supporters; that I would lose them; and, the part I had most avoided thinking about, that I would *hurt* them.

Eventually, people I had known personally, but who weren't especially close, began to post, clearly confused and uncertain: "He was actually a decent friend of mine. Yeah, it's a shock finding out. I mean at first, I was all 'lolololol wtf,' but then that quickly turned into 'well, fuck. my friend's a racist.'" The student who had asked me if I was really leaving campus when I was moving boxes to my car posted: "Derek has never done anything racist on campus. I have only seen him be reserved, perfectly polite, and a little strange for wearing the same hat every day." She added, "Derek Black probably hasn't responded to this thread because he is in Germany. (Not kidding.)" Then someone else hit too close for comfort: "I'm not threatened by him because I've talked to him. Also, he hangs out with a Black dude and (apparently?) dated a Jewish person."

I knew Zoë was reading these responses in real time just as I was, in a place that felt like home after living there for only a few months. "Thanks for letting me know," I responded to Zoë directly, not having any idea what to say to the person who had kept me grounded for so long, and not knowing how to be vulnerable in the best of times. "I don't at this point intend to respond though. I suppose I'm glad that I'm not there and also that the semester is nearly over, so people have finals to focus on. I hope no one outside of the group is aware that you know me well."

It was midafternoon, I had homework assignments already, and the JYM office was closing in a couple of hours. I ended my message, "I don't have internet in my dorm yet, but later in the week I'll video call you." I thought I would feel better being away and not having to face anyone. As I sat alone in Munich, I realized that wasn't true. As the thread ballooned, and I began to worry that Zoë would become a major part of the discussion, I sent another message: "I'll actually try to get on again tonight somehow. I'm sure you can handle yourself if anyone does bother you because of me." Zoë wouldn't be available until after class, which would be 10 p.m. in Germany.

I stayed at JYM for the next few hours, obsessively reading the thread about me as it expanded into hundreds of replies. I decided I wouldn't respond to it, even to the vague threats and wishes for me to get hurt which appeared as the thread ballooned: "I just want this guy to die a painful death along with his entire family; is that so much to ask?" I was used to not responding or giving my enemies more energy, and I was used to assessing threats, to protecting myself. I was not used to seeing people I knew and cared about recoiling from me. It was painful to know that the people I cared about weren't weathering the accusations right along with me, coming together into a shared defensive crouch, bonding like my family and White nationalist community always did. My friends this time bore the brunt not only of the denunciations that I was receiving, but also of the abuse I had put out in the world. It was unbearable how alone I felt, unable to reach out for support because this moment when I felt at my lowest was simultaneously a betrayal of the people I wanted to go to for comfort.

Friends emailed me, confused. "I kind of assume you know but if not, I didn't want to leave you in the dark about what is going around campus. Basically, considering you are at a pretty liberal school, people are getting pretty upset about your identification as a White supremacist." I responded, "I have, unfortunately, read the (what I believe to be) record breaking forum thread. In spite of my pride at being so interesting, I am glad to see it losing steam. Honestly, if people must riot anyway, it's best that I be abroad and come back in the fall. I'm fine and I've got a thick skin." I added, "I'm sorry if this affected you at all." I didn't know how to explain myself in any way that could actually make them feel better; it's not like what I was being accused of wasn't accurate. Because it was the only stance I knew how to take at the time, I struck a dismissive, nonchalant, cool tone in my replies. I had only ever tried to keep my White nationalist world separate from the rest of my life. Watching them integrate like a public high-speed car crash was making me face the reality that underlay that choice throughout my whole life: White nationalism was antithetical to most every other community and way of life. Choosing it meant turning my back on everyone else.

Another friend wrote, "While I don't know anything about your political beliefs, I do know that you were one of the kindest and most thoughtful people who I met this year. I hope that you will be able to integrate back into the New College community next fall, and I think that if anyone has the stability to be able to handle that kind of crossfire with equanimity it would be you. There are definitely people on campus who respect you as a person, and I think that was reflected in many of the forum posts urging people to look beyond the surface and not judge so quickly. If you feel like sharing, I would be interested to hear what you think about the accusations about you being a 'White supremacist.'"

I wrote back, fumbling for words, to this friend who was one of the kindest people I'd ever met, "I am no White supremacist. Every life has a purpose, and everyone has something redeeming. The term itself seems to me to show people who consider themselves supreme. I don't want to go into great detail here about my motivation for putting myself out there, but my core belief boils down to the maxim that mental and physical violence against White people is the inevitable result of the common parlance of terms like 'White supremacism.' While trying to be careful, at the same time I've made myself an individual example of that." I was hedging. I couldn't even claim what I believed to his face. Instead, I retreated to the easy territory that "the people who advocated violence against me in that thread showed themselves to be very unstable and bigoted." I wasn't ready to claim my own instability or bigotry.

When 5 p.m. arrived, the program director came to let me know she was shutting the building down. Something about my demeanor tipped her off that I wasn't having a great afternoon, although I was trying to hide it, and she asked me if I needed to keep using the building. She told me I could stay there as late as I needed to use their Internet connection and she let me know how to lock up after I left. I thanked her, once again gave the vague excuse about having some unexpected work coming up at the last minute, and I went back to obsessively watching my worlds collide as emails continued to mount. Late in the evening, my time, Zoë logged on. The room was mostly dark, and I was bleary eyed. I'd spent the last seven hours reading the Forum.

Zoë was in their dorm. All our old friends were in the background. When I asked why, Zoë said they were there for moral support. Since that first week, we'd had many one-on-one conversations, many in that room, but now talking to me no longer felt safe. Zoë was painting their nails, and I made small talk about it, and they cut me off saying they needed something to do with their hands. They asked abruptly, "So, what the fuck?" I asked what they wanted to know, and they said, "Are you a White supremacist?" I sputtered some version of what I'd been trying to form all afternoon, some way to connect these two worlds.

They had emailed me that morning, "I knew you were Conservative and not in line with the GOP, but I just thought you were like a

Ron Paul Libertarian." I said I had been inspired by that campaign, and I had met him, and that I did agree with some of the Libertarian movement. I didn't tell Zoë that the picture Paul had unknowingly taken with me and my dad had been one of the big controversies that dogged him in his campaign. I tried the talking points I'd learned to use when talking to journalists: that I wasn't a "White supremacist" but a "White nationalist," that I thought race was biological and that those groupings were the most important category for understanding humanity, that I didn't hate anyone else, as Zoë knew from knowing me, but that I just wanted to protect White people. I confirmed that I didn't support my family's antisemitism anymore, although I had believed in it when I was younger. Eventually Zoë needed to end the call and we said goodbye.

Suddenly alone again, I packed up my things and left the JYM office, locking the door on my way out, and quietly biked the four miles in the dark through the forests and fields of the English Garden to my dorm. Along the way, at 3:36 a.m., I stopped outside a shuttered cafe and connected to the Wi-Fi to send one more message. I apologized to Zoë for keeping my background from them, and concluded, "When we became friends, I just wanted things to stay the way they were. There's a time from last semester that I could live over again happily."

After a week of no response, I sent a pleading song lyric; Zoë responded with a firm denial in song lyric form. I sent another sorrowful song lyric, and Zoë responded in prose: "I can't talk to you right now it's too much." I responded, "That's fair. Sorry to become an issue in your life instead of a reliable thing." My closing lyric, which selfishly centered my own despair rather than the confusion and hurt I had caused them, went, "And the days went by like paper in the wind. Everything changed, then changed again. It's hard to find a friend."

THE INTERNET BEGAN TO WORK in my German dorm, and so I spent the next few days alone in my room, stocked up with food, reading the Forum and watching movies and listening to lonely songs on loop. I watched the park outside and I didn't find a good reason to leave. When I told my family about being outed, they congratulated me. A few days later, my mom wrote me, asking, "Any more news from Sarasota?" I responded, "They are winding down the huge email discussion now, and I assume the administration is having its own huge email thread right now." I told her I'd decided to stay in the dorms, even though I suspected I could get late permission to live off campus now that this had happened, "but it would seem like running away." She gave me an update on my dad, and added, "I can't imagine them trying to get rid of you now. That isn't very tolerant!" I wrote back, "My next semester there will certainly be different from my last. It's nice when everybody knows your name, like at Cheers." The end of the week was Easter weekend, and I left my room for the first time to go to the mountains to camp along with some other students. I spent Easter morning at the foot of the Alps before returning to Munich.

That next week, David Duke drove up from his home in Austria to visit me for the day. I met him at a beer garden, and he gave me an impromptu tour of the highlights of the early Nazi movement. Hitler had first organized the Nazi Party in Munich, and it was there that he was arrested for trying to stage a coup in 1923. During his imprisonment in Bavaria, he had written *Mein Kampf.* While walking with David through the city, stopping to have lunch and then dinner along the way before he headed home, I shared the broad strokes of the Forum thread. He reassured me that the same thing had happened to him in college. It had been for the best, he said, because afterward he became free to fully lean into his White nationalist activism. Facing the outrage of your fellow students was the forge I needed to really become the most effective activist. I should really embrace the opportunity to learn how the enemy thinks, and how intolerant they can be, he told me.

The Forum thread quieted down when final exams, senior thesis defenses, and the time to finally clean up and move out of the dorms loomed in Florida. I stopped hearing from people at New College, and I didn't know if I still had friends there. Within a couple weeks, the time to draw for roommates for the next academic year arrived. All students were required to participate in room draw, with very few granted off-campus exceptions.

I messaged Juan: "I'm sure you're aware of the massive forum thread. Would you be interested in rooming with me next year? I'd like to room with you partly because we've got the same community college background and partly because I know you're a chill person." He wrote back a couple hours later, "Hey dude. I have two possible roommates so I was looking for one. I'll talk to the others to see if they confirm. Hope everything is well in Germany, looking forward to seeing you next semester." It was a huge relief to see his response, because I hadn't been sure how he'd take my request. Juan wasn't White; his family had come from Peru when he was little, and White nationalism, at its root, was predicated on aggressive opposition to immigration of anyone who was not White.

Looking back, rooming with him—or even feeling close enough to think he'd be willing to decide to room with me—should have felt like more of a personal challenge to calling myself a White nationalist. I knew Juan from our first moments on campus, and we had gone on to take a difficult economics course together that first semester. In retrospect, maybe I shouldn't have bothered him, but I knew him. I trusted him, and he knew me well enough to trust me in his living space.

A few days later, he told me one of his prospective roommates "didn't feel comfortable about it since he doesn't know you (he only knows you by the thread that has been going on). I don't think it will be that complicated to find roommates though." Not only had he agreed to room with me, but he was sticking with me even if it meant losing someone else. I didn't thank him for that loyalty. I only responded, "I presume I'm not too much baggage to bring into the roommate negotiations." He found a new match, and we got the dorm we wanted.

At the end of July, a few weeks before we were all set to return to campus, and just a few days before I flew back to the United States from Munich, the residential housing office emailed me, months after the deadline and decisions had passed, to ask if I would still like to be off campus for the fall semester.

I asked my old community college German professor what he thought, and I separately forwarded the offer to my mother. Both of them asked me what *I* wanted, and I said I wanted to get away from the campus. On the one hand, I was clinging to the idea that I'd still have friends there when I got back, and I was worried that being off campus would let the administration tell me to stay off the residential side. More powerfully than that, however, I didn't want to live some-where I'd be hated all the time.

I felt bad about abandoning Juan after he'd stuck with me and lost a different roommate. I accepted the offer to live off campus, and the housing office emailed him, informing him who his new roommate would be before I had a chance to email him, or maybe I was dragging my feet. He wrote me, saying "I just received a message that leads me to think you got out of campus housing or that you will not be returning to New College. I just want you to know that whatever decision you made I'm cool with it. Will you be returning to New College next semester?" When I confirmed that I would be returning but accepted their last-minute offer to live off campus, he replied, "No problem, Derek, glad you are indeed coming back. NCF can learn a lot from you, and you can learn a lot from it as well. I will see you in a couple of weeks, good luck!" I certainly didn't deserve the level of kindness and solidarity Juan showed to me, but it felt grounding, like I had something solid I could hold on to. I appreciated it then, but looking back now, I can't imagine making the same wild, selfless, generous, and perplexing choice.

I WAS HURT BY THE ridicule and blame I had read from so many people I felt connected to, and I understood that the pillars of White nationalism hurt people I cared for, but I still thought that the ideol-ogy—although emotionally unpleasant—was factually correct. I wanted to return to my White nationalist community, to be around people who would reassure me. I needed to talk about ways to convince other people we were right.

As the months wore on toward the looming date when I would return to New College, an idea formed in my head to organize a new kind of White nationalist event. I had become obsessed with the concept of teaching White nationalist activists better ways to talk to the press and conduct interviews, and how to argue the ideology of the movement. For the previous two years, so many White nationalist events had been canceled after vendors learned who they were or after Antifa protested, and it had started to demoralize movement regulars. A month before I came back home, I asked my dad if he'd want to finally put on his own Stormfront event. I wanted to frame it as an educational seminar for activists, loosely modeled on the Highlander Folk School, a progressive leadership training school. Just as so many tenets of White nationalism are stolen from Black nationalism, here I was again stealing the premise of a social justice training program for our purposes. I proposed we host it near where Highlander was located, in East Tennessee, where my family had long wanted to create a physical Stormfront headquarters. I had good relationships with leaders across the White nationalist movement spectrum. I wanted to finally call in those relationships and bring together the people who had taught me everything I knew and have them share their activist knowledge with a new generation. I was self-conscious that I was alone in Germany, and that I would soon be on a hostile campus. I wanted to feel secure in my movement community. I was putting together a seminar, ostensibly for the benefit of other people—but if we're being honest, it was for the benefit of me, so that I could be fortified by all the older leaders I had admired and modeled myself on. I was twenty-two.

The letter I wrote that summer and sent to every White nationalist I invited read, "A seminar on verbal tactics will convene in East Tennessee on the third weekend of September. This seminar will address the simple verbal tactics that crumble the facade of anti-Whites and give our people the offensive. All attendees will leave with the tools to turn any curse word, such as 'racist,' on its head and leave their antagonist retreating." We called it the Practical Politics Seminar: Non-Voting Politics and 21st Century Verbal Tactics for Anyone White and Normal.

A Stormfront volunteer began coordinating with me to secure a location. I wrote my mom, "It seems that the SF seminar/conference will go forward. I've started talking to people whom I'd like to present but I haven't heard from David. I hope he'll be in the US at that time." We were having trouble finding a suitable location, which was made doubly difficult by the need for secrecy so the event hosts wouldn't cancel it. I had initially wanted to book it for September 10, but some of the people I wanted to attend were already going to the National Policy Institute (NPI) conference in Washington, DC, that weekend. NPI had been taken over by Richard Spencer earlier that year. Spencer,

I heard, was revamping the organization and they were hosting their first conference the weekend before mine.

Because of the looming fall semester at New College, for the most part I kept my distance from my fellow study abroad students. I wasn't ready to deal with another unmasking, much less while I was in a country with hate speech laws. But I did still have a full summer outside classwork. One day, riding through the English Garden on my bike, I stumbled on the standing wave on the Eisbach river. Surfers lined up day and night to ride the wave as long as they could until they fell off and got washed down the swift river. At that point the next rider would throw their board out and jump on. I got excited enough that I bought a used surfboard from an online listing along with a wetsuit and started going down each morning to learn to surf. I didn't completely avoid getting to know people, but I kept things mostly surface level and activity-based; I went hiking, camping, to open-air movies in the park, and art galleries by night.

When the semester ended, I used the last week I had left in Europe to hitchhike across the Alps to Italy. I visited Verona, Ravenna, and Venice, more major medieval and Renaissance cities I'd only read about in books. I ended the trip on Lake Garda in Northern Italy, where thousands of German and Swiss families had come to camp along the beautiful lake with their families. I didn't have a tent, so I went from campground to campground until I found one that would let me sleep in the open under the stars for a few euros.

The next day, I took a train north and arrived in Munich late on the night before my flight back to Florida. I had already returned the keys to my dorm, so I covered myself in a jacket and slept in the grass out in the open on the early August night. The next morning, I went to the airport and began the journey back to Florida and to New College. Eight months after I had left the campus tearfully, I was returning to a place that felt wholly changed, and I was terrified.

CHAPTER 8

MIDDLE FINGERS, MURMURS, AND THREATENING EMAILS

THE FIRST SIGN THAT THINGS were different back at New College was that no one would respond to my calls or emails about off-campus apartment options, which were largely coordinated by New College students and alumni. I suppose this shouldn't have been surprising, but I hadn't anticipated this part of it. I showed up a few days before the semester without housing, and for the first few nights, I stayed in a motel near campus while I kept sending out housing requests.

I also was coming to realize that I wasn't fully a pariah on campus. Some relationships had survived, though they tended to be ones that had been less intense, less rapidly intimate. For them, the Forum thread had hit as a shock, and then as a curiosity, and less like a personal betrayal. Another common feature was that non-Jewish White people tended to keep their distance, while Jewish people and students of color were more likely, in those early weeks, to approach me. I've since mulled over why that was. Maybe White students didn't want to be seen as supporting White nationalist sympathies, and so long as they didn't interact with me, their job was done; maybe those who were the targets of my ideology felt like they had to bear the brunt of responsibility and the emotional labor of doing something about my presence. Shortly after I landed back in the US, I got a text from Matthew Stevenson.

Matthew had lived adjacent to my dorm in First Court that first fall semester, and he had come down the stairs to my stoop to sing old folk songs with me when he heard me playing in the evenings. On Halloween, I had invited him over to my dorm to watch *Zombieland* with a few other friends. I knew he was Jewish because he wore a kippah. We had exchanged cell numbers because we took the same class in medieval history that first semester, and he, Zoë, and I had shared study guides. One afternoon that first semester, I'd passed him sitting in the cafeteria and he told me he'd heard that Zoë and

I were dating. When I said yes, he gave me a hearty, "Mazel tov!" I remember that moment especially clearly because of how worried I'd been about the fact that people were clearly gossiping about us, which would make things worse for Zoë when my background eventually came out.

When Matthew messaged me shortly after I landed back in the United States, asking where I'd be staying this academic year, I immediately knew he'd talked to Juan. I didn't know it yet, but the roommate Juan had paired us with before I'd moved off campus, Moshe Ash, was also one of Matthew's close friends. On Friday nights they hosted Shabbat dinners in Matthew's dorm, the weekly meals eaten after sunset by observant Jews to begin the sabbath. I responded to Matthew that I was still looking for a room, and asked if he knew anyone with a space. He told me he hadn't heard anything, but that he'd be on the lookout, and like Juan, Matthew welcomed me back to campus.

On my third night in an offensively bland motel room that was beginning to eat into my bank account and was never going to feel like a home, I was starting to get worried. I sent out another round of messages to Craigslist at 10:45 p.m. One of them texted me back immediately, telling me the location in the Newtown neighborhood about three miles south of the New College campus. Having only lived on the New College campus, I wasn't very familiar with Sarasota neighborhoods. I did know that, a few months earlier, there had been an international news story when the bodies of two drunken British tourists had been found in Newtown. The neighborhood was 60 percent Black, and news stories about the murders called it "plagued by crime." I asked the landlord, Maynard Hiss, about safety in the neighborhood, and he told me I should come over right then. Seeing the neighborhood at 11:30 p.m. should give me as good a sense of whether I felt safe there as I could get. I saw the logic, so I got in my car and drove to Newtown.

When I got there, I loved the big backyard. I imagined finally having the vegetable garden and chickens I'd been dreaming about, and he told me I was welcome to use his kayaks to paddle out into Sarasota Bay. Maynard introduced himself as the son of Philip Hanson

Hiss, the man who, more than any other individual, conceived and created New College in 1960. Hiss, a philanthropist and architect of early Sarasota, had been the largest donor for the fledgling school and had been elected the first chairman of the board of trustees that shepherded the school into existence.

Maynard's dad had dreamed of New College to "fill a need long felt in the South of liberal arts institutions of very high academic standing" and he had described the educational program of independent study periods and narrative evaluations instead of grades. His father had even been the one to select and reach out to famed architect I. M. Pei, becoming friends and contracting him to build the dorms where I had met all my friends the previous year. Hiss had described how the student population of New College "would not be allowed to exceed 1,200 students," and that it "was to be a close community that encouraged communication between students and faculty. Thus, its architecture was extremely important—not just the style of its buildings, but the situations they were intended to stimulate." Hiss ultimately walked away from the school frustrated, but the vision he and Pei created shaped my life.

Maynard was the youngest of Philip's kids. I learned over the next few years that Maynard was known throughout the city for his environmental activism around land use. He despised how local media portrayed him as "an often-barefoot minimalist who's been known to show up for dinner parties carrying his own granola mix," or "a wild-eyed socialist for suggesting that estuaries and rivers were as vital to land use as schools and highways."

That night at his house in Newtown, Maynard joked to me that he wasn't smart enough to attend New College, so he loved to rent rooms to us so he could pick our brains. I accepted his offer that night, and I moved my things in the next morning. We spent a lot of time together those first few weeks, and I hoped that his connection to current students might be distant enough that he wouldn't find out about my reputation. That hope burst one afternoon within a couple weeks, when he'd gone to the grocery store and mentioned to a cashier, upon finding out she was a current New College student, that he was renting to another student named Derek Black.

He came back in the house carrying bags of groceries, crestfallen. Visions of being kicked out of his house flashed before my eyes as we sat down in the front room. Once again, I tried to explain my ideology like I had to my New College friends four months earlier. Maynard took it differently than they had, much to my relief. Years later, he wrote in an email, remembering, "I got to know him very well before I found out about his specific interest in the White nationalist movement. To tell you the truth, when I found out about Derek's involvement, he was really straightforward and was honest about telling me anything I asked." Looking back on our conversation that afternoon, he remembered, "I did inquire about Derek's White nationalist policies and found his arguments spurious compared to his other logic. The White genocide concepts were sort of silly. He seemed to have no problem living in a mixed-race community. Something a lot of people are not willing to do, including some of my friends." Maybe because he was older than the young leftists at New College, maybe because his personality swung more laissez-faire than hardline, maybe because he had been through decades of environmental activism, maybe because my ideology was not one that attacked his identity, and maybe because we were able to come together instantly on being against the Iraq and Afghanistan wars, Maynard thankfully decided to give me the benefit of the doubt. I lived at his place for the rest of my time at New College.

STUDENTS DON'T LOSE THEIR NEW College emails when they graduate, and they don't lose access to the Forum; to this day, more than a decade later, I receive Forum emails to a subfolder in my inbox. While it was usually considered gauche and intrusive for alumni to get involved in campus conversations, many alumni had certainly read the campus conversation about me. Some of those alumni had gone into careers in journalism.

A few days after the first Forum thread that previous spring, an alum who was working for NPR wrote me on my student email: "I heard that people have been criticizing you on the student email forum, and I'd be interested to hear your side of the story." I responded by trying to shut down the story as well as I could: "At the moment I don't plan to talk to any press. The issue is strictly a New College one, and, in such a small school, it would be high-handed to go outside of the community."

They reached out again just before the beginning of the fall semester, pushing the story, but trying a different angle: "The debate that popped up on campus during your time abroad is more of a jumping-off point than it is the central focus of what I'm looking to do." I still had no interest, but I was surprised—and felt oddly protected—to learn that my New College community also, apparently, did not want to participate in stories about me; the journalist shared in a follow-up email, "After talking with several New College students, what I'm hearing is that you're not the problem." I don't think that was ever true, as I was clearly the problem, or at the very least *a* problem. But the fact that my New College community had opted to continue to recognize me as part of it and told the journalist not to write the story—considering it to be something to be dealt with internally, rather than expelling me as an outside organism—left me with soft feelings I didn't know quite how to handle. The journalist said they were still coming to campus to do a story and left it to me whether I wanted to have my own side heard. They wouldn't be on campus for several weeks, so I postponed my decision and put off responding.

I DIDN'T KNOW IF I had a place on campus, although I wanted to find out how much the vitriol on the Forum translated to real-world personal confrontations. The previous spring, I'd watched as students openly discussed the ethics of physically fighting racists (i.e., me), a question that years later would become known as the "punch a Nazi" debate when it centered on a viral video of someone sucker punching Richard Spencer in the face on the streets of DC after Donald Trump was inaugurated. On campus, I was the personified figure of that debate.

I had sat in Germany reading as they debated whether "violence against White supremacism will send a message that White supremacists will get beat up. Or, in slightly more nuanced terms, that White supremacy is not acceptable. I think that's *very* productive. Not that I'm *going* to fight this kid, but you guys' prerogatives are all kinds of messed up." Someone immediately challenged that: "If you want to use the word 'fighting' in a non-violent sense, go right ahead. But when you move beyond that and on to 'beating up,' you've crossed a line which he has not."

Seeing the discussion branch into calls for violence against me, students pushed back: "Regardless of how you feel, and regardless of if you're being serious or just talking a bunch of bullshit, DISCUSS-ING or ADVOCATING VIOLENCE against another New College student on the Forum, EVEN IF you think they're wholly undeserving of sympathy, has SERIOUS LEGAL REPERCUSSIONS. Not to mention the fact that the man himself is, as far as we all know, STILL RECEIVING FORUM EMAILS. What's to stop him and his family from collecting your statements and using them against you in court later?"

Watching this conversation play out while I sat alone in my single room in Germany, which I was affectionately describing as "the cell," had been unnerving. There was nothing that more clearly encapsulated the sense that this community did not want me than seeing calls for violence against me met with cautionary warnings that there might be legal repercussions for saying that so publicly.

Here was a familiar fear that had always justified my defensiveness and distance from people. I didn't mention the violent rhetoric at New College to my family or to any White nationalist friends. I knew that telling anyone in my family that students had talked about hurting me would escalate the situation beyond the campus and beyond my control. I had learned long ago that, as long as I compartmentalized and contained my fears, I could rationalize them, minimize them, and get through them myself. My family would not have let me just vent. If I'd told anyone in my family that I did worry about getting hurt, they'd have intervened, threatened the administration with litigation, and taken the story public.

The irony was that I didn't think many students on campus were actually taking the potential for violence or harassment from members of my movement seriously enough. I knew that neither I nor my family had control over our own followers. Our community was atomized, and explicit calls for violence and intimidation against enemies of White nationalism appeared daily as quickly as moderators could delete them on Stormfront. Our movement was one that praised murderers as martyrs, which justified the most horrific attacks as self-defense and justified political violence. The designation of "lone wolf" attackers wasn't at all accurate for a movement that named its enemies and eschewed traditional membership organizations specifically to avoid legal responsibility for that violence.

I knew there were racist skinhead and Nazi groups all across Florida who might have considered it a generous favor to intimidate students online or even physically come to campus in the name of protecting me, protecting their own. The only way to keep them away was to keep the problem within our New College walls. After years of receiving constant threats online, I had a good sense of when one rose to the point that I needed to take action. For now, I recognized more fear among my fellow students than rage, and I trusted them more than the unseen members of my supposed movement.

TRYING TO REINTEGRATE INTO CAMPUS did not go well that first week. My application to write for the student newspaper, the *Catalyst*, got the response one might have expected—they said they did not have a position available for me at the time. When I inquired about student-led tutorials or about joining student organizations, I didn't get any responses. Student clubs took me off their email lists. When I signed up for a jiujitsu class, the class roster was publicly posted, and someone responded, "Derek Black made it on the roster for jiujitsu. I hope you all have fun wrestling with a Neo-Nazi." I withdrew from jiujitsu. The risk of being in a class where accidental injuries happened seemed like tempting fate. I sent a group email to people I knew who liked to go hiking about organizing a trip to Myakka River State Park to hike, and I ended up driving alone that Saturday morning.

The morning I moved my boxes into Maynard's house, I got an email from one of the roommates Juan had originally arranged. Moshe Ash introduced himself and said he was surprised to learn when he arrived that day that I wasn't going to be staying with them: "So I just got to New College to find that you are no longer living with us. Did you get off-campus housing? Please let me know! Feel free to drop

by anytime for conversation or one of Juan's beers." I replied saying
it was nice to meet him, apologizing, and reassuring him, "I definitely
didn't jump ship because I wasn't looking forward to rooming with
you. You guys are very cool. I've still got doubts about the fact that
I'm not in there." I took him up on his offer immediately: "Will you
all be around tonight? Juan's beer sounds good." I drove to campus,
met up with all of them for the first time, and we decided to walk to
the nearest bar on Tamiami Trail, the highway that ran past campus.

While walking, the three of them expressed some level of bewil-
derment that they were hanging out with me. Moshe was Jewish, and
so was their third roommate; it was my first time meeting them. As
the night went on, I remember Juan asking, "You don't really think
interracial marriage is wrong, right? You know I'm mixed, right?" I
responded to the second question but not the first; I told him I of
course knew that, and that I thought he was a great guy, and I had his
back. One of his other roommates asked, "You don't really believe
that Nazi stuff, right?" I told him I wasn't a Nazi, and I also wasn't
antisemitic. I remember one of them asking, "Since when?" but I just
wanted to move on. Potentially to the detriment of anyone who ever
wanted to have a tough conversation with me at that time, I was quite
adept at non-responses and quick subject changes. It was a nice night.
When we got back to campus close to midnight, I left the dorm and
the roommates that could have been mine.

Instead of heading directly home to unpack, however, I made the
mistake of trying to attend the first wall of the year, attracted to music
I could hear just around the corner from the neighboring dorms.
Attending campus parties hadn't been a big part of my time on campus
even when I wasn't notorious, but I did usually stop in early in the
night and say hi to people. It was a space where everyone could enjoy
dancing together under the stars regardless of whether they'd gone to
parties in high school. It was the center of campus life, and joining in
even for a moment felt like a powerful chance to feel like I was still a
part of the community. I hadn't been there long when several students
I didn't know cornered me. Backed up against one of the walls of Palm
Court, they yelled in my face and formed a semicircle around me. A

student from my year, Blair Sapp, who I'd shared a class with, intervened, and he and I walked away to one of the dorm lounges to talk.

Compartmentalizing my fear about what had just happened, I answered my classmate's questions about White nationalism. I knew how to argue for this ideology, and I did so with him quietly and calmly, repeating a script I'd followed in countless media interviews. It didn't feel personal. I felt detached. I said that I supported the White nationalist movement because it had all the biological facts about humanity on its side. We parted, and I went home to my new apartment off campus, realizing I no longer had a place on campus.

I felt shaken by the physical confrontation, isolated from campus, and worried about how things might escalate. I wanted to speak up for myself, to tell them how callous and hurtful they were. I wanted to demonstrate why my arguments were correct. I was too in my head, scared and hurt and defensive, to consider perspectives that weren't mine, like the perspectives of the students of color who saw a White nationalist at their party and may well have been trying to stand up for themselves, their identities, their rights, and their community.

I was up late sending various innocuous messages, offering to buy textbooks from someone, sending a message to the sailing club asking to schedule a time to get certified to take out boats. I fell asleep at Maynard's house for the first time that night around 4 a.m., all of my things in boxes on the floor around my bed.

When I woke up the next morning, I emailed back the alumni journalist who wanted to write a story about my presence on campus. It had been ten days since their last message to me. If they were going to write about me as a threat on campus, I decided, I didn't want to let my silence look like acceptance. I responded only, "Sorry to take so long to get back to you. I would be willing to give an interview. Give me a call when you want to set up a time or place."

I immediately regretted it.

ZOË AND I HAD PLANNED to meet up that afternoon in their new dorm for the first time since I'd gotten back. It was a cold, distant meeting, as I should have expected, sitting in their common room, but I was grateful for the chance to see them at all. They asked me how things were going. All that morning, I had lied to everyone I'd spoken to, not telling them how uncomfortable or anxious I felt on campus. I talked to my mother about co-signing a loan for tuition and when she asked how things seemed after that forum thread, I told her I thought everything was going to be fine.

Zoë was the only person with whom I could even name any negative feelings at all, which for me felt like Herculean levels of vulnerability. I thought Zoë's responses to me were harsh at the time, but looking back, their responses to my self-centered angst were admirable, even as I felt like the victim. I shared what had happened the previous night, and they were sympathetic, but also told me it seemed stupid to have shown up at the party. They mentioned that they'd heard from a friend who worked on the student newspaper that I had applied, and they told me the staff had had a meeting to decide what to do about it. I said I was disappointed that they'd turned me down. Zoë asked me, wary but incredulously, if I really didn't understand why the editors had to turn me down.

Protecting the New College community from White nationalists felt more important to me than I wanted to admit, but I was feeling petulant, emotional, and kind of like I wanted to throw a tantrum to get a reaction. I didn't mean it, but I told Zoë that I was considering inviting Jared Taylor to come speak. He was the White nationalist who ran *American Renaissance*, the most academic White nationalist publication, whose group had first introduced me to professors and academia. I claimed I wanted him to explain to the school how much evidence there was for my beliefs, and to debate people who challenged it. I'd seen YouTube videos of him doing that at other campuses over the years. Zoë looked stricken and told me that hosting an event like that would be awful, and that they couldn't believe I would consider doing that to the community. I quickly backtracked, and I told them they were right, that I wouldn't do anything inside the school, that I was just hurt.

Zoë and I had another shared class that semester. While we talked, I half-jokingly asked if we should sit together, and they told me they didn't want me to speak to them anymore, and it was probably time that I leave their dorm and go home. It wasn't my best showing as a human being. I didn't know how to talk to them, and I hadn't yet even begun to learn how to be open. I didn't even apologize. I didn't know what I could say.

LATER THAT FIRST WEEK, THE controversy of my presence was introduced to the brand-new first-years with another post on the Forum: "Healthy reminder, the host of this radio show goes to your school." I was indeed still calling in to *The Don and Derek Black Show* each morning. The responses were varied, from "This shit is way too corrosive. Aren't we supposed to be a community? I mean, if someone wants to be somewhere so badly that they'll stay even though everyone hates them, can't we just leave them alone?" to "If you found out some guy you knew privately held racist views, by all means, ignore him. Act like he doesn't exist. Passively exclude him from your life. But Derek Black is a public figure who espouses his opinions on the radio."

Reading the comments, I realized this new thread was inspired by what had happened at the party. Apparently, the official hosts and safety patrol hadn't been willing to kick me out themselves, although they had been asked. "Fuck anyone that wants to stick up for the neo-nazi," one person stated: "To all of the palm court patrollers who would not confront Derek Black because the person making the complaint was 'too White,' fuck off you fucking collaborators." Another posted, "I'm sure more than a few people would be proud to say they were arrested for arguing with the poster child for White nationalism." Someone else reacted with "In my experience White nationalists don't listen to we people of color when we talk. Physically forcing them out of PoC safe spaces and anarchist conferences has been pretty effective in my experience. It certainly doesn't change their minds, but it does make nearly everyone else feel a hell of a lot safer."

By 4 a.m., the discussion was going back and forth between arguments for ostracism and persuasion, how to deal with the first week of having me back on campus. At the same time, two students posted their own manifestos, trying to summarize the situation. The first began, "What is this bickering on the forum doing?" He continued, "He isn't reading this, and if he is, he either doesn't care, or is just

being more solidified in his views . . . If you truly care, understand
how people work. Reason isn't always the answer. Attacking someone
for their views isn't always the answer. Empathy with persuasiveness
is a much better tool than telling someone they're an asshole. When
someone trusts you, and feels that you are actually listening to them,
they are way more likely to listen back to you."

The other student delivered his own lengthy assessment: "If you, as
one who identifies as someone who is anti-hate, are thrust into a situation in which you are actually face to face with those people who say
the things you abhor, how do you react? It's not surprising that there
isn't consensus on this, because, really, how many White nationalists
have any of us met in person?" He continued, "If you believe that he
can change or that he might not be comfortable with what he is, then
he has already had every opportunity to fix it. More are happening
every second. He hasn't made that choice yet and until he does, he is
the rising leader of the White nationalist movement and will have to
face everything that comes with it. I literally can't believe it took the
longest forum post I have ever written to convince NCF students not
to defend a White nationalist. Not even how to go about addressing
his beliefs, but just not to defend him."

I emailed the head of the pluralism committee, a student group
advocating campus inclusion, asking if I'd be welcome at their events
like I had the previous year. He invited me to his dorm to talk. There,
I once again tried to explain my ideology, that I wasn't racist, that I
didn't hate people. I shared that I thought racial groups biologically
determined crime and IQ on a large scale, but that I didn't think it
applied on individual levels. He told me he thought the students would
be uncomfortable with me being there, and I didn't attend.

The next morning, as I walked to the library and class, still wearing
my black leather hat, random people I didn't know gave me the middle
finger, as they'd continue to do for months. I mixed up my schedule and
walked into a classroom for what I thought would be the first class of
my course on postwar integration in Germany. Instead, a different class
filled the room, and the instructor was in the middle of explaining the
syllabus. Seeing the look on the professor's face, many of the students

turned around to look at me. Trying to seem less awkward, I sat down in the back for a few minutes, instead of leaving instantly. After ten or fifteen minutes, I got up to quietly leave. Weeks later, a student who had been in that class asked me what message I'd meant to convey that day, and he let me know the professor had asked the class as soon as I left if everyone felt okay about what had just happened. I explained to him I'd just mixed up my schedule and hadn't wanted to be rude. He couldn't believe how inane my answer was for what had unnerved all of them and taken away time from their class so pointlessly.

I SPENT A LOT OF time alone that fall, and I started exploring Sarasota and the region. My landlord, Maynard, regularly attended contra dance nights in St. Petersburg, an hour north, near Tampa. Contra dancing, an eighteenth-century form of the word "country dancing," I learned, is a mixed style of New England and Appalachian social folk dance. Participants pick partners and form long lines up and down a dance hall with a stage at one end. A dance caller explains what combination steps the next dance will involve, usually combining different moves from a basic list of common ones everyone knows. Regular events run for about four hours, with a break in the middle for hydration, snacks, and waltzing. The social scene can be involved, with people traveling across the country for larger weekend or weeklong events that sell out quickly, and with hundreds of skilled dancers coming together to see popular callers and bands.

As Maynard was heading out one Friday evening early in the semester, he saw me in the front room playing my guitar and asked me what my plans were. I said I was going to stay at home and watch a movie, so he invited me to join him at a contra dance. I ended up spending a lot of weekends over the next two years at contra dances with him, receiving gas money to drive us and other local enthusiasts across Florida and as far away as Atlanta.

Other times I went on drives to the beach at sunset, on hikes to state parks, and to local restaurants. A frequent destination was Yoder's, the famous restaurant run by members of the Sarasota Amish community known for their pies. When I was leaving Yoder's one afternoon, I discovered my car wouldn't start. While I waited the couple of lonely hours for AAA to come and tow me, I listened to music, thinking about how much I had lost at New College.

AS I WITHDREW FROM CAMPUS social life, however, things seemed to still be on edge and activated, even with me at a distance. The counseling and wellness center had put up a poster asking people to write what they "own," giving examples like "my voice," "my body," and "my right to say no." Someone anonymously added the n-word to the list and "ten slaves," which sparked a horrified Forum thread. A Black first-year student replied, "Wow, honestly this is kind of why I'm trying to transfer from here. There are some people who just ruin the school as a whole for me." An upper-year replied, "I don't care if this shit was posted as a joke, as a piece of art, or to prove a point. It's clear the person who posted it did not care about how it would affect me or the dozen or so Black people here." A student jumped in with "I blame your resident neo-Nazi," and another replied, "I think automatically blaming Derek Black reinforces this weird idea that New College is an otherwise prejudice-free institution that has been invaded by a single openly racist person." .

A mutual friend of Zoë's and mine the previous year messaged me asking, "In terms of whoever wrote the thing on the poster, that was not you. For what I know of you, I would never, ever expect you to do that. Can you affirm this?" I wrote back, "I absolutely did not write anything at all there, and I'm offended by the nasty sentiments from whoever did."

NOW, WITH THE DISTANCE AND licked wounds of a decade, I can admit that the New College community judged me pretty accurately and responded to me in ways that were, in fact, often far more generous and graceful than I deserved, with more attention often paid to my comfort than the comfort of the students of color and Jewish students on campus. But at the time, I resented the loss of a community that I thought had misjudged me and misunderstood me, and that feeling of mourning made me retreat to the only other community I'd ever been known and loved. Even had I wanted to tell my lost friends that I didn't hate anyone, that I didn't want them to be afraid of me or what I represented, I wasn't willing to deny my beliefs. And I was willfully pretending to myself, when I thought about those friends, that I was just one person whose opinions didn't carry broader implications for a social movement, as if I weren't someone whose invitation could bring racist activists together.

In September, I traveled to Tennessee to emcee the first-ever Stormfront conference. I didn't speak or coach the audience at that seminar. Instead, I introduced all the White nationalist luminaries who had taught me how to be an outspoken activist, how to conduct an effective interview. I had been occupying myself by micromanaging the planning. I argued with the other facilitators about the color of the signage (I preferred a blue logo to a green one) and I was very annoyed at the incorrect Latin someone had proposed for the slogan, but because I was only starting Latin at New College, I didn't know how to correct it. I messaged my Latin teacher, trying to seem as casual as possible, asking how one might say something like "victory through words." He thought it was a strange phrase, but suggested something like, "*victoria in disputatione*," which I then had a volunteer emblazon on a shield crest image to print on the program.

Traveling to Tennessee a couple weeks into my isolating return to New College was a deeply symbolic reconnection with the community that had raised me. From listening to the elders of White nationalism who had directly tried to work against the civil rights movement of the 1960s, I learned that our activism needed to be thoughtful, organized, and strategic. Most of all it needed to be communal.

White nationalists often talked about the Highlander Folk School in Knoxville, Tennessee, like it was a nefarious and shadowy underground, funded by a global Jewish conspiracy, operating behind the scenes and "staging" activism. It seemed clear to me, however, that a school that introduced prospective social justice leaders to each other and shared best practices was clearly a model to be emulated. White nationalist leaders put a lot of emphasis on media training, presenting the movement in the best light to gain followers and sympathy, and discussing how to organize events, rallies, or boycotts so that they best highlighted the movement's strengths. It seemed very hypocritical to me to despise the Highlander school—I believed we should be studying their methods and reproducing them, not grumbling about conspiracy theories. I devoted myself to trying to re-create their best practices within the White power movement.

Rosa Parks, who sparked the Montgomery bus boycott that initiated the civil rights movement, talked throughout her life about how inspiring her experience at Highlander had been. Yet, to my frustration at the time, she didn't praise any particular, brilliant strategy she learned there. Instead, she spent the rest of her life talking about the simple fact that the people at Highlander lived out their egalitarian ideals in their own lives. "It was one of the few times in my life up to that point," she later said, "when I did not feel any hostility from White people [and] I felt I could express myself honestly." Highlander hosted nearly every leader in the civil rights movement and had almost a summer camp atmosphere. They were successful at turning out effective leaders not so much because they imposed lessons on them or had excellent strategies or even funding, but because they brought inspiring people together in a space that affirmed their ideals. Living out their visions of equality and cross-racial friendship helped activists like Parks make the personal sacrifices she embraced soon after her first experience there.

The inversion of living those ideals to inspire the White nationalist community would presumably be going to ever more racially isolated places, I figured, but I also knew how much less inspiring it felt to find ways to keep people apart. Paradoxically, we could achieve that by going to the same region of the country Highlander had set up its grounds. In the mountains of East Tennessee, my dad was fond of pointing out, even the hotel housekeeping staff were White. Even then, I had to admit that discouraging our followers from being socially close to people who weren't White wasn't quite as uplifting as the idea of an island community of togetherness like Highlander. It struck me then that, despite my discomfort there, it was New College that embodied the spirit of Highlander more than the seminar of isolation and fear I was organizing.

Nevertheless, I drove with my family north, and we orchestrated one long day of camaraderie, organizing, and speechwriting training.

To prevent Antifa from finding out the location and getting the venue to cancel our booking, we had the idea of telling people to meet first at a third location. (Antifa certainly does not get enough popular credit for the myriad ways they are a constant thorn in the side of White nationalists, in daily ways that law enforcement agencies and social justice nonprofits never are.) Once attendees arrived at the gas station near the venue, we confirmed they were attendees and then gave them the direct address down the street. Walking into the small convention center, which we had already stocked with enough water and food to keep everyone in the building for the day, I orchestrated a parade of speakers to talk not only about the rightness of our cause, but also the most effective ways to argue it. By the end of that day, I felt refreshed, and I finally felt connected. Heading back at the end of the weekend so I could return to the loneliness of New College felt physically painful.

En route, I received another text from Matthew Stevenson. I hadn't heard from him since I'd arrived. He wanted to know if I had any plans that coming Friday night, because he hosted a Shabbat dinner in his dorm, and he wanted to invite me to attend.

CHAPTER 9

WE WANT HIM TO COME BACK

AT THE BEGINNING OF MY first semester back on campus, I started volunteering every Saturday for Habitat for Humanity through a campus-coordinated program. It felt good to get back to home construction projects, and back to feeling like a part of the community in a way that I wouldn't be excluded. In retrospect it was probably self-centered to force my way into community space where I knew I wasn't wanted. One friend, who I'd spent a lot of time with first year, also joined the weekly group and rode in my carpool. A year earlier, he had approached me at a party to ask whether I wanted to date Zoë, and asked me what my hesitation was. He had done it in German, because we were the only two in the group who understood it. I told him no over and over, we were just friends, but he said my answer just didn't really make sense. A year later, as we commuted in relative silence every Saturday morning, the reasons that I had been so avoidant were clearer, and it seemed like there weren't many reasons left to keep asking me anything, so we just listened to the radio or my MP3 player.

Some of the people I'd interacted with back then, but who I didn't know as intimately, did make public posts about their thoughts on me. Their comments tended to hit me hardest: "His radio show is disgusting, as are all his speeches that you can watch if you look him up on YouTube, but he's been surrounded and homeschooled by people like fucking David Duke his whole life. One of his first friends at New College was a gay person of color and he dated someone of Jewish descent. Maybe he's trying to slowly break away from his parents?"

Every time they revealed something about my time and friends on campus a year before, I was horrified that they were spotlighting the people who I was most afraid to hurt further. I had always been afraid of the gravity of my public identity sucking in my friends, who had no idea what could be in store. I had spent my entire adult life and my later teenage years avoiding being in pictures with people I cared about so I wouldn't cause a controversy. When I founded clubs or initiatives among homeschooling groups, the science museum, or in community college, I tried to keep my name off the leadership records or public announcements, so they'd be able to avoid my baggage.

It was a fundamental part of my identity that the people and things closest to me would be better off if they weren't publicly associated with me, or if they could at least maintain a plausible distance if anyone asked. Despite a family and community of White nationalists whose praise reinforced me, it always felt shameful to know that what I said and did in the world had made me into someone so many people felt guilty for being friends with. That first fall semester on campus, I had usually ducked out of photos, so the pictures couldn't become weapons against my friends later, trying to proactively create the distance I suspected they would later wish they'd chosen. I didn't post on the Forum supporting people I liked when they ran for student government or announced an event, because I knew that one day those endorsements might get picked over by people trying to figure out if I had any ideological allies.

In so many ways, I hated the vortex of my public role, the feeling of duty to uphold the expectations of my community and my family. Individual relationships seemed like something that could only survive in private, and my life was one that didn't allow for privacy. It didn't occur to me then that this was the result of active choices I had made, and choices I was continuing to make; it felt inevitable, the only possible reality. The only thing that felt like it could make this worse was the spotlight of mass media following me to New College, because it would make me choose between the movement I felt called to lead—the community that I had felt responsible for my entire life—and the fragile friendships I saw already withering around me. But, a few weeks into the semester, no one had forwarded the story to journalists or seemed to be working with the few alum journalists who I knew had read the discussion. The experience of media privacy was entirely novel.

Being known personally, however, removed one of my primary defenses against the vilification I'd dismissed my whole life. They thought what I was saying and doing was cruel and stupid while also knowing that I could be a good friend. They didn't think I was a villain. They thought I was some combination of naïve, avoidant, confusingly opaque, dangerous, or deceptive. In retrospect, all of those characterizations were accurate, and the truth of them crawled under my skin, even as I tried to deny them to myself under the guise of being "misunderstood." It would've been simpler to be the villain.

Meanwhile, the Forum discussion continued, vacillating between attacking the White supremacy I represented and hoping to persuade me. Many people kept jumping into the discussion, hoping that my presence on campus and how I had acted thus far showed that I was at least questioning my beliefs. It was a level of good-faith belief in me, and the belief in how flexible someone's identity could be, that I think would be difficult to find outside of college kids. It also continued to prioritize me front and center rather than the students on campus who were frightened of me and my White nationalist community. Some of those posts even gamed out different future worlds where I might change my mind due to the intervention of the community. Others pushed back: "Why on earth do you think I would be so preoccupied with 'changing the views' of a White supremacist leader?"

Students in the civil discourse camp countered that organizing could only work if persuasion were possible: "If it's arrogant to think we can change one person's mind, then why are you so hopeful that organizing will do anything? Racism is a mental process. Changing people's minds is the only way to fight racism. . . . If we can't change one serious racist, then we can't change any serious racists. Yes, New College would be safer for people of color. But trying to help this person see things differently will have a profound effect on other racists. He's influential outside of New College, remember? That's why this blew up to begin with."

Reading from the sidelines, I thought it was ridiculous for them to assume that "changing my mind" would be a matter of arguing with me until I saw that they were right. I had spent my life seeking out all the authorities who endorsed the worldview I'd grown up with. While those figures were driven to the margins, there were still plenty of them scattered about the halls of academia, and they had given lectures and answered my questions throughout my adolescence. Looking back, I wince at how I scoffed at my classmates, and I admire them; while I think the youth of college was very much on display, their passion and investment and wanting to do *right* by this community was breathtaking. Their discussions, antagonistic though they were, felt more familial, tight-knit, and invested in one another's views than the White nationalist community discussions I had grown up around.

And while I thought I was academically, loftily correct in my ideology, I had no satisfactory response, at night, in my room, to their charge that, "If you're dark, Jewish, or gay, he's actively working to undermine your rights."

It started to become clear that the answer to "what the community should do" would always, in practice, come down to the decisions of individuals: "Possible inherent arrogance of the strategy aside for a second—if people want to have dialogue with this kid with the intent of affecting his beliefs, go for it, I say. Fine with me. But do not think this is somehow better than those of us who instead decide to ostracize him. As a person of color, I am not comfortable having a one-on-one talk with the guy—have you considered that maybe that's the case with other people here too?"

Those who wondered whether I was secretly already doubting my convictions were in fact wrong, for the most part. It didn't feel like I had changed anything at the time. But in retrospect, by that point I had done some odd picking and choosing of what those convictions actually were. No antisemitism or global Jewish conspiracies, no pro-Hitler, no pro-Nazi, no current or future violence toward or disruption of the lives of any Jewish person or person of color, no belief that race could predict anything about a person on an individual level, no (explicit) belief that White people were superior to any other race of person. Maybe these pieces of White nationalism were always the weakest and most poised to crumble, but it's difficult to argue that my New College community relationships weren't their nail in the coffin.

The core belief I did maintain, which felt like the most critical, central pillar, was that on a group level, race meant something, and that White people were under attack and needed to be protected, ideally by having their own country. If I were being honest, my version of the ideology at that point would have been enough to gain the side-eye of my family and White nationalists, if I had ever been so open as to share it plainly. But when you're the heir to the movement and a leader in it, your offbeat differences in stances, strategy, and beliefs feel like they can be visionary, can have the power to steer the ship in the "right" direction, rather than marking you for exclusion. It was never going to feel like the movement wasn't right for me—I would just make the movement into what I believed was right. I had the power to do it—a few weeks earlier I had summoned White nationalists from around the world to Tennessee with a few emails to teach them the message I wanted. I made my version of White nationalism into something that felt clean enough, felt harmless enough, felt academic and ivory-tower enough that I could keep believing in it. I worked hard to ignore just how destructive, brutal, and cruel my beliefs still were, or how much more destructive a sanitized version of this movement could be. Making it more palatable for a (perhaps larger) portion of the mainstream right that was receptive to it, I knew, was the most powerful future for this movement.

I COULDN'T UNDERSTAND THE CONCLUSIONS of people who doubted that I meant what I said or did, even if many of my actions at New College didn't seem to align with my activism. I was friends with people of color and Jewish students, people my ideology clearly excluded. It was convenient that I had structured my beliefs such that groups and populations, not individuals, were the problem.

Matthew Stevenson knew that I had befriended Jewish students, which I suspected was the reason he had invited me to attend the Shabbat dinner he hosted in the common area of his dorm suite. He told me we would be joined by several other of our friends. Juan would be there, as would Moshe Ash, who would also have been one of my roommates had I stayed on campus. Notably, none of them could plausibly be accused of being White supremacists themselves, because they either were students of color or were Jewish. I accepted the invitation with some trepidation, worried it would be an ambush where I'd have to defend my beliefs, but if it was, I felt like I could handle it fine. I had just come back from feeling reinforced at the Tennessee Stormfront conference, but I was clearly still craving campus community connections.

I arrived at his room in the early evening before sunset. I brought kosher wine; I didn't want to be rude. We sat at his common-room table, around a nice meal that Matthew had cooked that afternoon. After he gave the opening prayer, we started to serve ourselves. I didn't find out until later that the small attendance was unusual for Matthew's dinners, which usually attracted more students who came for a home-cooked meal and nice conversation before heading out to the Friday wall. When they heard he had invited me, most of them, especially his own roommates, who were White, insisted he uninvite me. When he refused, they told him they wouldn't be there. The people who I didn't break bread with at my first Shabbat dinner, it turned out, were making as conscious a choice as the ones who I sat down with.

One of those conscientious objectors arrived back to the common room as the rest of us were about to begin the meal. She came in wearing athletic clothes, her boyfriend trailing, both returning from playing soccer on the tennis courts, a weekly tradition on campus. I remember Matthew greeting her: "Hey, Allison, would you like to join us?" He turned to me to introduce us: "Derek, this is Allison Gornik, one of my roommates. Allison, this is Derek Black." I started to tell her it was nice to meet her, but it quickly became clear she wasn't interested. She greeted Matthew, Moshe, and Juan, but refused to make eye contact with me or acknowledge me, and made a show of passing the table on the way toward her own room. Her boyfriend followed her lead. I realized I was experiencing one of the approaches that I'd read on the Forum a couple weeks earlier: "The best tactic, in my opinion, is to completely ignore people like Derek Black. Their ideas merit zero consideration. Thankfully, if he never changes, at least he, and his racist comrades, will be dead one day."

Matthew, Juan, and Moshe noticed as well—somebody made a quick comment that she must not be hungry—and we continued our meal. Even at that point in the conversation, I was braced for the moment when somebody would bring up the unspoken tension in the room. I knew, obviously, that they had read the Forum threads, but I didn't yet know that Matthew and Moshe had also spent hours reading thousands of my posts on Stormfront going back to when I was twelve years old, listening to my radio show, and reading other mass media publications about me in order to prepare for the dinner. I had years of practice avoiding any reference to my reputation, acting oblivious to even bold references to racism or antisemitism. At this dinner, however, nobody went there. Years later, I learned that Matthew's initial hope had been that we'd all get a bit drunk and talk about my beliefs under the pliancy of alcohol. At that point, however, I rarely drank, much less at a dinner where I wanted to put my best foot forward.

Matthew, I also learned later, had instructed Juan and Moshe before I arrived that he didn't want us to get into a big argument. "We want him to come back," he told them. Instead, they leaned into our personal relationships. We talked about the start of classes, our schedules, how our summers had gone, my experience studying in Germany, the new building that had finally opened on campus after months of construction, and various campus gossip. Matthew and I remembered that we'd shared a passion for religious history, not just my academic focus on medieval monasticism but the particulars of any and all religions and theology. Having grown up in an atheist household, I'd had a particular interest in learning about where and how religious ideology had tracked through time and what it meant to different communities across the world. We discussed historical movements within Buddhism, Hinduism, Jainism, Islam, Judaism, Zoroastrianism, Bahá'í, and Christianity.

The closest anyone came to breaking the act was when Matthew and I were discussing ancient Christian heresies. Talking about a particular early Christian theologian, Matthew turned to me and asked, "Wasn't he an Arian?" The others stared at Matthew for a moment, caught off guard, before he clarified he'd meant the ancient Christian heresy of Arianism, a different view of the Trinity named after an ancient Christian priest named Arius, not Aryanism, the ideology of the Nazis. I answered the question and we moved on.

I didn't make it home until late, logging online and sending a few emails before I headed to bed. I had genuinely enjoyed the dinner. While I had expected them to confront me, it had been a surprising relief to not talk about it at all. Every chance I'd had so far to explain my ideology had only left me cold and further from the friend I was trying to reassure. It was a wildly avoidant choice that led to lots of awkward moments, but it was the best I knew at the time.

I sent a message to another New College student I'd met unexpectedly at the first contra dance that I'd attended a couple weeks earlier with Maynard: "I plan to attend all the dances I can up in St. Pete and Tampa this semester." She was a first-year that semester, and I didn't want to bring down my reputation on her, but she was already fast becoming known as an active organizer on campus for queer issues, students for Obama, and antiracist causes. Like most people who decided to talk to me despite everything, she'd met me before hearing about me from anyone else. After clarifying that she knew what everyone on campus thought of me, I offered, "If you ever need a ride, feel free to come along and Maynard can regale you with stories during the entire drive." I didn't know how I'd reintegrate myself into campus, but the prospect of having at least a few friends made the next couple years seem tolerable, and so I tried.

LOOKING BACK, I'M SURPRISED AT how few accusations of hypocrisy I heard. Anyone would have been right to accuse me of being a hypocrite for being friends with—and genuinely caring about—people who my ideology marginalized and stigmatized. I was on record advocating for rigid immigration restriction, while being privately good friends with non-White immigrants. I had espoused obscene antisemitism in mass media, but had numerous Jewish friends on campus. This conflict between my vociferous advocacy for White nationalism in the press and my personal life on campus was hard to square, even for me. The one question no one seemed to ask was whether my loyalties were being split between my two communities; I worked hard to avoid the question, too.

My commitment to the White nationalist community was constantly shaken by the clearly evil outcomes of our ideology in brutal violence, in hatred, or in persecution. It was impossible to deny the accusations of anti-hate groups: "These forums have to be watched very carefully within whatever the legal bounds are. This is where these people live.

This is where our domestic terrorism is coming from." My dad constantly reassured me (and himself) that "the kind of people that are more likely to go out and do something and go on a shooting spree are by themselves typically. If they become part of our community they are less likely to do something because they have a support group." As if being racist needs a support group, or as if the statement wasn't self-refuting by the number of members who committed attacks. Antiracist SPLC researchers countered with the obvious truth, grounded in the fact that this was a movement that did not just attract members with the same beliefs, but reinforced them: "It is a myth that racist killers hide in the shadows. Investigators find that most offenders openly advocated their ideology online, often posting on racist forums and blogs for hours every day." The spree of murderers over the years was so clearly motivated by our ideology to the letter, insofar as they often cited our websites, books, and organizations as their inspiration.

On July 22, 2011, less than a month before I arrived back at New College, and less than two months before my seminar in Tennessee, a White nationalist terrorist in Norway murdered seventy-seven people, thirty-three of whom were teenagers. He first detonated a car bomb at a government building in Oslo that killed eight people and wounded hundreds more, and then, during the confusion that followed, took a ferry to an island near the city where the center-left Labour Party had an annual summer camp for kids. He dressed as a police officer and spent hours on the island shooting everyone he came across while adults and children hid, ran, climbed onto the dangerous rock outcroppings around the island, or tried desperately to swim to the mainland.

At that moment, I was a thousand miles south, taking final exams and completing the semester in Munich, selling my surfboard and guitar, and preparing to come back to New College for the first time since I had been outed on campus earlier that spring. I don't remember how I reacted immediately to hearing about the Norway attack. Mass violence in the name of White nationalism wasn't rare, but the scale of this attack, and the fact that he had targeted children, made it particularly horrific.

News of mass murder in the name of White nationalist ideology happened enough that we had a callous, cold routine for them. Our

first response in the early hours after any violent attack was to hope
the attacker wasn't White, then to hope they weren't a right-winger.
If both turned out to be true, as was obviously often the case, the
next step was to quickly check to see if they were a known poster on
Stormfront. If they had posted, we would hope we'd already banned
them before the attack for some predictably horrific post, calling for
violence or something else that violated the law or our rules. My dad
usually didn't talk to the press about it, dismissing the murders as the
acts of lone psychopaths.

It turned out the Norway killer had posted on Stormfront, and he
hadn't been banned. He had never said anything directly violent. His
rage had been generic, not advocating for specific violence. He had
fit right in. He had talked about Muslims "flooding" Norway, and he
had complained about feminism and liberal academia. When he was
arrested after the attack, he told the police he had done it in retribu-
tion against the Labour Party for allowing Muslim immigration into
Norway. Immigration is exactly the issue that primarily motivated
White nationalists, and the way they most justified their positions and
activism, and their violence. I had framed everything at the Tennessee seminar around immigration as an existential genocide of White
people, which raised the stakes to unbearable levels.

While studying abroad in Europe, I was still calling in to co-host
the radio show, although my dad had begun taking over more of my
hosting responsibilities. We spent the hour interpreting the news to
help listeners frame the world through the lens of White nationalism. It came naturally on the radio, because I'd spent my adolescence
learning to do it for myself.

When the Norway news broke, I had no response. We condemned
him, of course, as we always did. We called him a psychopath. In
his manifesto, he explicitly claimed that he had been banned from
Stormfront, which helped my family argue that Stormfront and their
movement weren't responsible or connected, but the distancing itself
was disconcertingly close. Years later, however, he admitted from
prison, "I was never kicked out of Stormfront. Instead, I attacked
them in the compendium in order to protect them . . . [as] an army
of leftist journalists otherwise would strike hard." I didn't know then

that the murderer had emailed the manifesto to one of the main speakers promoting the message of "White genocide" headlining my Tennessee seminar.

But I also remember my dad and our guest hosts directing the blame for what drove him insane on the politicians who had told him to accept the "genocide" of his race, reiterating exactly the justification he gave to the public when he surrendered himself after hunting children along the cliffside of a summer camp.

In the years after the Norway attack, my dad increased his efforts to distance himself from violence and to explain how he saw his community. He gave many different explanations and dismissals to the constant, inarguably correct accusation that he and his movement produced violence. Years earlier he told a reporter, "You can accuse any movement of eliciting the same violence. What about Zionism? What about the violence during the civil rights movement?" He argued that violence was inevitable, and his movement was in fact the best shot society had at preventing the apocalyptic future he anticipated. In that same interview, "busy bickering with his son, who's barefoot and wearing a long Spider-Man T-shirt, playing pinball on a nearby computer," he said, "We want to take America back. We know a multicultural Yugoslav nation can't hold up for too long. Whites won't have any choice but to take military action. It's our children whose interests we have to defend."

When I was at college, privately wrestling with my own beliefs and the harm I had caused, my dad awoke on the morning the Norwegian terrorist was sentenced to a thread on Stormfront praising the murderer. He responded, "Unfortunately, I happened upon this thread this morning, just before our radio show. This makes me want to pull the plug on this place and never look back. We attract too many sociopaths."

The reality, of course, was that White nationalism is an ideology that demands conformity of belief around the threat of its enemies. No matter how the contours of its strategy might change, or what philosophy or branding could be incorporated to widen its lens, it could never move beyond its obsession with drawing the lines between in-group and out, and perceiving anyone outside as a threat.

A researcher for the anti-hate organization SPLC commented: "I don't see the race war that they want so much. The threat is against individuals. And I think it's entirely likely we'll see another Oklahoma City. It doesn't take much to motivate someone who's been talking about revolution for years. The more people mouth rhetoric, the more likely it is someone will act on it."

AS THE SEMESTER WORE ON, I settled into a routine of coursework, contra dances, and attending Matthew's Shabbat dinners whenever he was in town. The rest of the campus seemed to be trying to move on from the drama my return had caused. People continued to reach out, occasionally, approaching me and asking to hear more about what I really believed: "I know you probably hate talking about all of this stuff where a bunch of campus is against you, but I like you, and . . . I've wanted to talk to you about it for awhile just to hear your side." I'd generally reply, saying the truth as far as I could muster it when they pressed me: that I didn't hate people, I tried to judge people on an individual basis, but that I did consider myself a White nationalist and an advocate for that community. But, self-protectively, I preferred to try to avoid talking about it as much as I could.

Zoë and I messaged back and forth a bit. When I sent them another song lyric, they replied simply, "I think it is time to stop with the song lyrics." I replied ten minutes later, "It's probably time to stop with the whole thing." A couple of hours later they replied, "Yeah." In retrospect I should have stopped bothering them long before.

After agreeing to an interview at the peak of my anxiety on campus, I'd stopped communicating with the journalist pursuing the story. When they sent me an email in October finally canceling the story, I was relieved. My instinct to outlast an angry crowd, to wait for them to get bored or move on, felt like it had worked, in a sense. I kept being invited to and attending Matthew's dinners, while recognizing how bewildering it was that a known White nationalist was one of the most reliable attendees at his traditional Jewish Friday nights.

I had even outlasted the will of his roommate, Allison, who one week without preamble sat down with the group. Matthew welcomed her, and she said she wasn't going to keep missing her weekly dinner with friends. She still didn't talk much with me, and it was clear I wasn't her friend, but she wasn't ignoring me anymore. I'd usually stay with Matthew late into the night, when everyone else went to the wall, including Allison. When they returned around 2 or 3 a.m., Matthew and I would often still be up, sitting in the common room talking about philosophy, religion, or whatever else we'd landed on that night.

Near the end of the semester, Allison posted an innocuous thread on the Forum: "Greetings, lovely [FORUM] dwellers, I've been craving some new acoustic-y type music. So you, with all of your wonderful music tastes, should recommend some. Please?" The thread that unfolded while everyone procrastinated on their final exams was a beautiful collection of great recommendations. I made the bold move of publicly adding my own favorite artists to the list, worrying I was going to derail Allison's thread, but people mostly moved past my post. One student privately messaged both her and me, "This thread is beautiful and has restored my faith in humanity." Another criticized me for including Mumford & Sons in my list of "Americana" acts as, he reminded me, they were from England, and "I also wouldn't call anything they did innovative." I had listed several other artists, so the fact that I only took flack for one of them felt like huge validation.

One afternoon later that week, I saw Matthew and Moshe sitting on a bench outside the library; they called out, and I stopped to talk to them. Allison walked by, saw us, and joined. I felt my fear growing that I was messing with all their reputations by being seen with them, but I reminded myself that I knew they were making an intentional choice, even if none of us were naming it. Allison asked the group what we planned to do for ISP, the upcoming January interterm independent study period. As a result of sending cold emails to places that interested her, she had created her own internship at a nonprofit children's crisis clinic in Cleveland, where she had grown up and could commute with her mother every day from the suburbs.

Matthew also had an internship planned. Clearly the slackers of the group, Moshe and I admitted we hadn't fully fleshed out our ISPs yet, although it was already late November. I knew I'd write a research paper on some topic in medieval German literature and submit it to my advisor, but I hadn't landed on what exactly I was going to write about. Allison, who had never really spoken much directly to me, now made it clear she was unimpressed with me. I was squandering an opportunity to actually do something unique, she told me. New College even had sources of funding for well-planned ISPs, so I really had no excuse to not use the time wisely.

I told her I didn't have anything else I wanted to do more than go home and swim in the ocean, maybe go sailing. At that moment, I was on my way, in fact, to the sailing club to take a boat out before the semester wrapped up. She mentioned offhand that she wished she knew how to sail. I said I'd be happy to teach her in the spring, once we were all back. She told me she'd believe it when she saw it, and the four of us parted ways for the long winter break. I didn't expect I'd hear much more from her, but I liked her, as well as her brash honesty.

I SPENT CHRISTMAS AT HOME, but then, in part to avoid joining my dad daily in person at the radio station, I drove restlessly north to Gainesville, where the first-year student I'd met at contra dances was from. She had invited me to stay with her friends for a weekend dance on New Year's Eve. Like I had on a summer road trip preceding my first semester at New College, I took my niece on the road. Whereas before, it had been the wider White nationalist community who welcomed us at every stop, this time it was a group of contra dancing liberals. At contra dances, men often wore skirts, the twirlier the better, and progressive politics were almost the rule, although these spaces still tended to be mostly White. My niece and I slept that night on blankets on the floor with my New College friend's Unitarian Universalist youth group friends, mostly queer and trans kids, and it was nice to feel accepted by them. While there, I met up with a White nationalist friend attending the University of Florida, who I'd known for several years. He took me to a bonfire party in the woods being held by the law school, and we talked about my fraught experience that last semester. I realized that the only part of the story that fit the narrative everyone expected was my campus-wide ostracism, and I told him in private that that was what I had experienced. I didn't—I couldn't—describe the friends I'd made, because I knew that friendships required privacy. I wondered whether I'd found some kind of new truce, a space on campus where my friends knew all about my White nationalist activism, where the worst of the condemnation I'd feel had already happened. What I didn't know was how much they were privately doubting their choices in order to make me feel comfortable.

AFTER ALLISON HAD GOTTEN TO know me attending Matthew's Shabbat dinners, she'd been surprised to realize that none of our conversations at those dinners actually involved my racist ideology. Privately she asked Matthew if I had ever talked about my ideology, and he told her that he didn't think anyone on campus was having that conversation with me. When she challenged him to be the one to confront me, arguing that by having me coming to their dorm every week it seemed like he was the obvious person, he rebuffed her. The dinners themselves, he argued, challenged my ideology. Even if I had rejected antisemitism, my community certainly hadn't, and beyond that most of the attendees each week were either Jewish or students of color. He guessed I had never been in a social scene like that, and if he confronted me now, I'd immediately become defensive. Furthermore, while he was confident that my beliefs were ludicrous, he hadn't spent his entire life arguing against White nationalism the way that I had spent my life learning to argue for it. He was doing more, he told her, by just being an ear for me. He encouraged her to talk to me directly if she wanted to.

Allison asked Matthew and their mutual roommate what they thought about her asking to talk to me privately, if that was a risky decision or even unsafe. They had each known me for quite a while, and they told her that how I was at the dinners was basically how I always was: quiet, avoidant if you tried to talk about my ideology, thoughtful, and kind. Because I hadn't brought up my beliefs with them, they only knew what they read online, which didn't seem to connect with how I acted around them, or even the fact that I *was* hanging out with them. They were as curious as she was, but they weren't going to be asking. Allison felt confident I wasn't a personal threat to her, but she knew the world I represented, and apparently wielded a lot of power in, was very dangerous. Beyond that, she knew that my being on campus deeply hurt many of her other friends, like one who was a leader in Hillel, a Jewish student life organization, who had canceled their meetings when I first returned to campus.

Like synagogues across the country who pay private security, keep their doors locked, and meet in community only under strict protection, Allison's friend knew that a publicly announced meeting of Jewish students always brought some level of a risk to their safety. New College had always felt welcoming. Now they knew that I, a central representative of the movement that had been responsible for nearly all of the violence perpetrated against Jewish communities over the decades, was receiving their announcements on the Forum and the students' list. The members didn't feel safe declaring their meetings and coming together, and so at first they had stopped meeting. Allison knew how much fear and pain I was causing, even if she was not Jewish; and she was White, which meant that she didn't feel personally threatened by my ideology.

She decided that maybe that meant her responsibility was to use her access. She had the future leader of the White nationalist movement coming over to her dorm every week, sitting at a Shabbat table, but never being confronted with the discomfort, fear, and consequences of that ideology. The worst that would come from talking to me privately, she thought, would be reminding herself of what kept coming up on the Forum—specifically, that I was dangerous because I seemed innocuous and "normal," while my advocacy had so much more of an impact on the world. Despite herself, she liked me, and didn't understand how my openness and quirky interests fit the story she heard about me from everyone else. She wanted to get closer to me, but she wasn't sure if that was a good idea. If I was willing to talk about my ideology and my movement, then maybe that discussion could lead somewhere. She decided when she saw me in the spring that she'd follow up on my invitation to teach her to sail, and she'd ask me to explain to her what I believed and how I could justify causing so much pain.

CHAPTER 10

THAT'S YOUR POISON

AS THE JANUARY ISP PERIOD ended, I returned to a tense campus for the spring semester. Nothing had seemed to come from the endless debates on the Forum. The administration didn't seem to listen to or do anything to address student concerns. I had been afraid that the administration might take some kind of action, but their approach stayed hands-off.

Our school president was stepping down soon. I had heard that students had met with him, not only about my presence and student fears around this direct connection to the White nationalist movement, but also about the series of racist acts that had happened on campus in recent months. Students of color had long expressed their feeling that this mostly White campus community, which outwardly prided itself on its commitment to diversity and inclusion, was often a very uncomfortable place. Even if White students could be oblivious to it, campus police regularly stopped the few Black male students on campus and asked for their IDs. Discussion on the Forum repeatedly shared racist comments or jokes to the inbox of every student on campus. It was always White students who defended or minimized these posts, reminded students to give them the benefit of the doubt, rushed everyone to consider how painful being publicly shamed felt, or outrightly defended each occurrence individually, calling students of color who called it out oversensitive and even at times suggesting that those students of color should be the ones to leave the school. I was the biggest beneficiary of that Herculean effort at minimizing racism on campus. As much as I felt ostracized or hurt, never acknowledging my own responsibility, even I had been shocked at the outpouring of defense for me that had appeared in every thread calling me out.

Within days of returning for the spring semester, we all received an announcement that the faculty had voted to support a student motion by unanimous consent that would shut down normal operations for one day when everyone, including faculty and staff, could come together for a campus-wide teach-in. New College's president sent out a notification, which mostly dealt with the logistics. The reason he gave for the faculty vote and such an unusual and largely unprecedented school shutdown was simply "deepening concern about issues of mutual tolerance and respect at New College."

The motion had been put together quickly over just a few days by a collection of about thirty student social justice activists, many of whom had been talking to faculty, organizing workshops about their discomfort on campus, and yet felt like nothing was changing. In their motion calling for the faculty vote, they cited specific offenses, including when someone had written the n-word on a poster in the student union the previous semester, and the fact that, just days before, a student had flown a Confederate flag from his dorm balcony for days, refusing at first to take it down. The organizers of the teach-in didn't name me, but I couldn't help but feel some level of culpability even then, wondering if the fact that I was still there, and seemed resolved to stay, was empowering the racism of others.

For the teach-in, the students had invited a representative from the SPLC, one of the foremost anti-hate organizations in the country, one that often focused their publishing and watchdog operations on my family, to lead a full day of workshops. In the days leading up to the event, responses on the Forum ranged widely, but there was much more criticism than I had anticipated. One student wrote, "Not going to lie, I don't like the fact that what I feel is a minority of students can decide for the rest of us whether or not we have the right to go to class and stay caught up with our studies." The hostility was sometimes striking and uncomfortable; common White nationalist talking points I'd taught members of the movement to use were also emerging as pressure points at New College, a place I sometimes thought of as being immune to our messaging. At the Stormfront seminar, we instructed people to chastise Whites who argued for social justice and antiracist positions, to describe them as virtue signaling instead of acting out of genuine conviction. Being called out like that was a more subtle version of the caustic cries of violent movement extremists who targeted antiracist activists as "race traitors." In either case, the goal was to alienate Whites from antiracist work and embarrass them into being quiet.

Someone on the Forum asked, "Is this event spearheaded by White privileged hipsters who want to flex their community-organizing muscle and just want to be part of the 'movement'?" This tangent felt familiar to me in my own activism. An organizer jumped in to bring things back to the point: "The teach-in is not meant to reprimand anyone, rather it is presenting an opportunity for members of the community to join together, share their stories if they wish, ask for the changes they would like to see."

This new thread wasn't directly about me, so it didn't raise my defensive hackles in the same way. I was able to engage in perspective-taking, which at the time was embarrassingly hard for me to do. Because I wasn't so busy insisting to myself that I was still a good person and working hard to convince myself that my activism and my friendships were separate things, reading the rationale for the teach-in made me reflect more personally on my effect on the world in a way that I hadn't before. I thought the teach-in was a potentially powerful statement, and I admired the boldness of activists putting it together. If I'd shared their ideology at that point, I would have supported the action as the first bold and effective move to change the campus. Juan, who I regularly saw but with whom I'd continued to stubbornly refuse to talk about my beliefs, posted why we as a community needed this day to hear each other: "I have never felt ostracized, discriminated, or alienated from the New College family (and those who know me understand this), but I have friends who have felt this way, and that makes this issue my fight." His closing comment hit close to home: "If you feel comfortable with having your friends feeling alienated, then that's your poison."

Even if I wasn't flying a Confederate flag, even if I wasn't writing hate on posters on campus, even if I could see the pain caused by minimizing America's history of violence on the faces of people who still faced the aftermath of it, I was perpetuating a movement that did and defended all those things. I had stood for all those things, and I continued to endorse them on the radio, even if I did so increasingly by saying nothing while my co-hosts did the work in my name. I claimed to support my friends, but I refused to do so in the part of my life where it most mattered, where I had the most power.

Instead, seeing the community organize so we could hear the students I was affecting most scared me, because I saw no place for myself in it. No matter how much I tried to avoid reality, I knew that I had more power than almost anyone at the school to change things outside our walls. It would require, however, breaking with my family, telling them I thought they were wrong, and that I regretted what I had done. I was hurting my college community, avoiding substantive conversations about my ideology, asking for them to ignore what I was doing and accept me anyway.

When the day of the teach-in came, I approached it briefly, and I had a mix of reactions seeing hundreds of students, faculty, and staff gathered on the green, coming together to discuss their experiences. Looking out on the field, I saw no way to join. Coming to sit down would cause every head to turn toward me. I could only imagine stifling the conversations, and I couldn't imagine anything productive coming from sharing myself. As much as I didn't like to admit it, I liked that, for once, my voice—real or imagined—wasn't the focus. And the focus could actually be on the experiences of those who had legitimately experienced that ostracism, discrimination, and alienation Juan had highlighted. Before I left, I snapped a quick photo, one of the few I ever took while at New College. I turned away to walk back to my car, and I saw Moshe running toward me from the crowd. He had been attending the workshops all morning and came to ask me my plans. I said I was going to lunch, and he offered to come with me. Over burgers, he told me what he'd experienced there.

A couple days later was my birthday, and Matthew invited me to his dorm for a special midweek get together of the Shabbat crew. That night, Juan let me know he was applying to become a resident advisor the next year, and wondered if I'd be willing to write a peer recommendation on his behalf. I agreed wholeheartedly, happy although surprised he thought my endorsement was a benefit. Allison approached me afterward and reminded me I'd promised to teach her to sail this semester. I told her I was still down, that she just needed to name the time.

ALLISON HAD STARTED AT NEW College the same time as I had the year before, and had arrived in a serious relationship. We had just missed each other constantly over orientation week, attending the same events a few rows away from each other, being assigned to different scavenger hunt groups, standing in different places at the walls that week. In the group photo of the incoming class taken at the beach that week, we were standing about six or seven students apart from each other. She remembered me tipping my hat to her like an old-timey cowboy one day as we passed.

I liked Allison. She seemed to puzzle over problems with an intensity and attention to detail I sometimes didn't muster for even major problems in my life. The things she said were so often completely different from what I had expected, and it made me want to understand her. She was well-liked, social, friendly, and affectionate. Getting to know her had been a surprise, but once we started talking, I started seizing opportunities to ask more about her. She seemed committed to balancing how seriously she took her academics with attending walls. I admired the fact that she often was the only person in a room willing to ask an obvious question that everyone else was afraid of looking stupid for asking. As someone often quite closed off and self-protective, it was refreshing to see how forthright she was in her interpersonal curiosity, almost to the point of being intrusive. I was intimidated because she often wouldn't let things go. For someone like me, who had mastered changing the subject, giving off-putting body language to say I didn't want to talk about something, Allison struck me for her persistence. It was deeply charming how she thought seriously about both big and little things, but usually things different than those I focused on. It made me curious to understand her. I thought I recognized in her a perspective that made her stand slightly apart from a lot of the community, a world-wariness and a subtle sense of being an outsider that I assumed was borne from the precarity and struggle she'd had to execute perfectly to get there.

Allison grew up in the suburbs of Cleveland, and as a high school senior, she was stubbornly fixated on the idea of attending a small, academically rigorous liberal arts college. She thought that place would be in Ohio, like Oberlin or Kenyon, but she applied broadly, trying to focus on schools that were on the more affordable side. She had hoped that high grades and high performances on standardized tests would make a difference, and while they were enough for admission to most colleges, they weren't enough for the level of financial aid she would need. Her family had limited ability to contribute and did not feel comfortable cosigning loans. The only school that could be reasonably covered with Pell grants and government Stafford loans, in addition to the offered scholarships, was New College—but that was only going to be true if she were an in-state student, not an out-of-state student. New College had the unique feature of being a *public* liberal arts honors college, and had the associated public school cost. In a move that felt radical but necessary, she requested to delay her admission by one year and moved to Florida the month after graduating high school to jump through the hoops of establishing residency. In that time, she needed to find a job that would let her make enough money to meet legal guidelines to switch residency under educational regulations, but she had no prior work experience. If she didn't find an entry-level job in the finicky, tourist-based Florida economy, or if she didn't make the minimum income requirements, she wouldn't qualify for the in-state tuition rate that was key to her plan.

After floundering at first, as summer was the low point in Florida hiring, when most tourists left and many businesses reduced their workforce, she got a job at a fancy grocery store in Sarasota. She studied it like she had studied every other challenge in her life, memorizing the number codes for everything in the produce section. She spent that year earning just above minimum wage, and the pull of employment and her new life slowly drew her away from her academic goals, acclimating her to the shift schedule, monthly rent due, and the long-term plans of her local romantic relationship. When Allison matriculated at New College the same semester as I did, successfully considered an in-state student, she was given an on-campus dorm like every other first-year, but she wasn't there often that fall. She often went home at night to the apartment she shared with her boyfriend, who asked her what she could possibly be experiencing at school that meant she needed to sleep away from him. Unlike Zoë and Matthew, she wasn't in the big medieval history class on the history of the Norman conquests that united most of our common friends. When I left for Germany that fall, we hadn't met.

Over the course of the first semester, Allison came to grapple with how toxic and controlling she felt her relationship had become. She broke up with the boy in early January of our first year, about a month after turning twenty, and moved to campus, where she made friends with many of the same people I'd left a good impression on. In the end, Allison was the only person at New College who I became close to who knew everything about my public persona before we met.

ONE AFTERNOON, WHILE I WAS walking to the library, our gregarious student body president, who'd won election as a first-year and gone on to a string of "youngest ever" offices as a student representative in the state university system, rode by me in his golf cart. It was already laden with too many people, but he brought the cart to a halt and yelled out, "Derek!" I turned and he told me to climb on. They were going to the sailing club to take his sailboat out in the bay. I joined the group and, as usual, dealt with the glares from all the students who'd really have preferred I not be there.

When we arrived at the sailing club, even more students were already there waiting to get on the boat. The student president had made a public announcement on the Forum and was determined to fit as many of us together as possible. Clearly making several students uncomfortable, who simply and quite reasonably didn't want to be on the deck of a small sailboat with an infamous racist, I was relieved to see that Allison was among them, a familiar and more friendly face. Throwing my usual caution to the wind when she gave a head-nod of acknowledgement, I sat on the boat next to her, forced by the overcrowding to sit so closely our legs were touching. Once we embarked, she teased me that I hadn't taught her how to sail yet, and I told her to name a date. She accepted the challenge and we exchanged phone numbers.

A few weeks later, she and I were back at the sailing club, where I was to teach her how to control a sunfish, a small two-passenger sit-on-top sailboat that my grandfather and mother had taught me to sail. I taught Allison what my grandfather had taught me, that you were fine in the water as long as you stayed calm. The worst thing that could happen was capsizing the boat, called turtling, but you could easily flip it back over if that happened. The only way to get confident with that fact was to intentionally flip the boat out in deep water, tossing each of us off. I warned her and we did it, flipped it back over, and then turtled again. One time when the wind caught the sail a little more forcefully than I expected, the boat flipped faster than I expected and the mast hit her as we tumbled. I jumped toward her, worried I was about to find her unconscious or injured, but she was fine and said she appreciated my concern.

When we came back to shore, we made plans to launch a day-long sailing trip in a few weeks. I didn't presume it was a date, because I knew she had trepidation about my ideology and outsize reputation on campus. She surprised me, however, by how explicit she was about wanting to know more about this whole part of my life that everyone knew, but most people didn't feel comfortable bringing up with me. She requested that we have a conversation about White nationalism that she'd been wanting to have with me for a while. Looking back, I admire this mix of making plans but winging it, this balance of getting what she wanted—a sailing lesson—while also rapidly setting the tone that she wasn't going to ignore my ideology.

Allison's proposal for the location of that conversation was entirely unexpected but couldn't have been more appropriate. She asked if I wanted to see a secret way she'd found to get onto the roof of a dorm, where she sometimes went to get away from things or have private conversations without leaving campus. At community college, I'd decided that I would show that I'd conquered the school before I graduated by walking on the roofs of every building on campus. Some proved harder than others to access, but I eventually accomplished it without being spotted by security. Allison's way up was a relatively safe passage that ended in a patch of roof with rails that felt like a secret rooftop patio.

The evening we planned to meet, she led me up the stairs and off along the railings, guiding me along the edges of roofs and rain gutters, around corners, and ultimately into our own private pocket right in the middle of campus. Up there, looking at the stars above us and the students walking below, she reaffirmed that she wanted to talk about my White nationalist beliefs. It was a romantic setting for an inquiry. She asked directly if I was willing to talk to her about that subject, because she knew I never did at Matthew's Shabbat dinners. I said I was, which is what I always said when directly asked. Allison asked if I could explain to her what exactly it was that I believed, because she'd heard so many stories from other students, and done a lot of her own reading online, and she couldn't square the hateful rhetoric with the kid who would come weekly to Shabbat.

I proceeded to explain what I believed: that race was the foremost division of humanity. She interrupted, surprised, and then apologized and asked me to go on with my explanation. I said I had seen convincing evidence that racial groupings predicted intelligence and criminality, with East Asian people having the highest IQ and lowest violent crime rates, White people next, then a spectrum of racial groups like Middle Easterners and Native Americans, with Black people having the highest propensity to crime and lowest IQ as a group. I said this didn't mean I hated anyone. Allison asked how it was, if I believed that race decided so much about people's characteristics, that that belief didn't seem to affect my personal relationships. I told her I thought these racial qualities only applied in the aggregate, when you talked about millions of people, not on an individual level. Individual people could be anything.

I said this was how I'd been raised, but that was a lie—my family had never really given me this wiggle room. My parents talked about Latin American immigrants as violent and unintelligent, about Black neighborhoods as dangerous because the people there were dangerous, and they didn't withhold judgment about any particular people. This distinction between individuals and groups was a lifeline I had rationalized for myself. It was one of many hypocrisies I clung to so that the dissonance wouldn't be so loud in my head. My openness to my friends, my curiosity about their lives and their choices, desperately needed to feel compatible with the White nationalist framework so that I could keep on being their spokesperson.

I told Allison that I didn't think these racial qualities should be treated like they were morally good or bad, hateful or kind, or even respectful or condescending. Instead, I said I accepted them as an unfortunate reality. The consequence of them was that people would be happier if nations were divided along racial groups, which I said was proved by how Whites separated themselves so intentionally in suburbs exactly like where Allison had grown up. It was government intervention that created integration, I had been taught, and I argued that White nationalism was less a movement hoping to force people apart and more one that would let White people make their own choices without being called racist or prejudiced.

I HADN'T YET LEARNED HOW ironic this view of history was, as the forms of segregated neighborhoods, schools, and businesses I knew in the twenty-first century had in fact been created by explicit government intervention, by elaborate legal systems, and had only been accepted and justified by regular people after the fact.

In the first couple centuries of British colonization of Indian territories in North America, the colonies contained large numbers of Native Americans as well as people from Europe and Africa. European colonists began to use skin color and ethnic origin in letters and legal statements as shorthand, at first primarily to specify their hatred of and distance from the indigenous population, who initially were in the majority. Throughout the sixteenth century, colonists had waged brutal wars against Indians in Virginia, Maryland, and New England. Those shorthands and stereotypes, however, were not identities that rigidly dictated who could be enslaved or for how long, and they didn't answer questions about the morality of enslavement of people. People expected their rights to be tied to class, education, and their skills, not where their ancestors came from. That reality only began to change slowly over a few decades, when the Virginia Assembly, a body controlled by wealthy English colonists, became the first North American colonial government to decide that "race" was a legal category that described a person, and meant something as to their rights.

In 1662, leading up to that eventual decision, the Virginia Assembly passed a law that declared any children would inherit their mother's legal status, whether she was free or enslaved. That act established the idea that enslavement could be inherited, that it had something to do with blood, rather than the understanding until that point that it was a condition inflicted on an individual because they been captured in war. In 1667, the assembly passed another law, this time declaring that baptism as a Christian could no longer be used as a legal argument to end a person's enslavement. This ended complaints among Christian missionaries that slavery was incentivizing planters to keep them from teaching Christianity to enslaved people. It legally demolished a boundary, doing away with the idea that Christians couldn't enslave other Christians. It did so by a new justification that the qualities of "race" took priority over culture or religion, because this new legal category was an inherited, biological one that could be seen on people's faces. "Race" was not a legal category before this. But if "race" justified slavery, and enslavement could be inherited, then wealthy planters no longer needed to defend their practices on moral grounds. People descended from Europeans, categorized as "White," had no reason to argue against this new system, which increasingly apportioned rights and wages away from the people they worked next to.

In 1975, the historian Edmund Morgan published a book that argued the axiom that has become a foundation for the policy-focused theory of change in the modern antiracist movement: "If Negro slavery came to Virginia without anyone having to decide upon it as a matter of public policy, the same is not true of racism." Morgan argued that, over the last decades of the 1600s, the governments of the British American colonies in Maryland and Virginia created legal categories of "race" by granting or withholding rights to ethnic and cultural identities that would have gone on having only minor social significance without the meaning these new laws gave them.

Furthermore, as my future self would learn, racial segregation was an even more tenuous fiction I had rested many of my arguments on. It had not been imposed in America, particularly in the South, until after the Civil War. When it had, the rules had come down from governments just as much invested in maintaining their system of labor and low wages as in centuries before through the same violent suppression and social enforcement of racial categories. Once again, Whites largely accepted the system, because it made them feel protected and superior. Over a century later, I was the next generation of a group of people fighting to maintain their sense of superiority by mounting tenuous justifications about nature, behavior, and inheritance.

I TOLD ALLISON THAT NIGHT on the roof that I believed these things because I'd spent years attending conferences of tenured professors who had shown me the statistics and data underlying it; I didn't admit that my understanding of math and statistics had always been poor, and I did little questioning, because their evidence fit within my family's worldview and it sounded convincing. I told her that White national- ists, almost as a rule, ascribed the rise of multiracialism and integration to a conspiracy of international Jewish power, exactly like Hitler and the Nazis believed. I said I'd ascribed to this too when I was younger, but that I had abandoned that belief, because it required too many ridiculous assumptions to maintain. I knew too many Jewish people, and I always had, to be able to maintain the belief that they or their parents were secretly ruling the world. The common attendant of belief in a Jewish conspiracy was Holocaust denial, which I'd entertained as a teenager, but had had to accept was ridiculous as soon as I looked at the historical records myself. I instead no longer believed these policies were being promoted by a Jewish conspiracy, but rather by capitalist needs for exploitable labor, a social hatred of White people, and a desire to end "White supremacy" by ending White people through interracial dating and immigration from predominantly non-White countries. I told her the "White genocide" talking point I'd been converted to several years earlier and had made myself central to promoting.

Allison was quiet for a bit. Much later, she told me that some of what I was saying sounded like a significantly more extreme version of the mainstream racism she'd seen growing up in Republican, heavily White, northeast Ohio; anti-Black and anti-immigrant rhetoric in particular was not unfamiliar to her. Other parts sounded especially out of left field, particularly as it related to Judaism. Her understand- ing of racism and the agenda of racists was fully disconnected from

Hitler, Nazis, and Jewish conspiracies. She thought of Judaism solely as a religious identity, not a racial one, and it was perplexing to her to hear me talk about an ideology that considered it impossible for "White people" and "Jewish people" to be overlapping categories.

It seemed to her, she later told me, that I was presenting supposed facts as the reasons to advocate for White nationalism, rather than expressing some kind of gut feeling of discomfort about people of color. Statistics, she reasoned, she could argue about. She also knew that she likely had quite a bit of unlearning to do herself, having grown up in a segregated suburb, and she wanted to be the kind of person who had good, persuasive, evidence-based arguments against racism. She could find and read research papers, and she was partway through a series of statistics courses. She felt reasonably confident that if this came down to an argument of facts, she could make better arguments than the old men who had instructed me all those years. The question, however, was whether I was willing to listen and to genuinely engage in these types of discussions with her.

Allison asked me if I'd be willing to keep talking about this, in private, without any particular goals other than that she felt very confidently that I was wrong but wanted to research how I was wrong, and show me. I told her I was up for those conversations, and I was excited about the chance to spend more time with her. I was used to people who decided they wanted to be close to me also choosing to avoid talking about my life in White nationalism. The idea of finally explaining my beliefs to someone at New College who I trusted, who I knew would argue against them, was interesting. I saw myself as someone who believed things because I could show they were true, because there was evidence for them. If any piece of the elaborate arguments I'd drawn from lectures by professors were false, I didn't want to keep using bad evidence. More than that, I trusted Allison was sincere when she said our conversations were private. She wasn't trying to catch me in some outrageous statement she'd post on the Forum to embarrass me. She wasn't spying on me to gossip about my beliefs behind my back.

I agreed, with the condition that not every one of our conversations be about White nationalism. We agreed that roughly every five times we had a conversation, it could be an opportunity for her to challenge some of my supposedly intellectual arguments for racism. She'd need time, anyway, to research and build up her case. And I was looking forward to finding excursions off campus for us to explore together.

AS THE SPRING SEMESTER WOUND on, Allison and I stayed in touch outside of Matthew's weekly dinners, which we continued to attend. She didn't have a car, so we planned adventures around Sarasota. We were clear that we weren't dating, just hanging out a lot. I'd gotten used to planning solo adventures, so having a partner was a welcome change. She'd broken up with her boyfriend months earlier, and she had started filling her time with social activities, sports, and get-togethers with her friends. As part of that semester of activities she wanted, she and I visited museums, aquariums, hidden beaches, Tampa and St. Petersburg, and we bought tickets to local food festivals. As promised, Allison began sending me different research articles, asking me what was and wasn't persuasive about them, and thus began the pattern of the next year of often very heated arguments.

We planned our long sailing trip for the end of the semester, the day before final move-out. We packed fruit in waterproof tubs and brought bottles of water. Neither of our phones were waterproof, so we left them behind. Because the boat didn't have anywhere to keep things dry, we wore only our bathing suits. The plan was to sail out across the bay to the mouth of the Big Sarasota Pass inlet. The day went perfectly right to the end. We sat on Lido Beach's white sugar sand, shot each other with a water pistol we found on the beach, and ate our fruit picnic.

The problem arose when we realized the sun would be setting in the next couple hours. Packing up, trying to sail back, the wind abruptly died, leaving us stranded on the beach. We wanted to prevent a rescue operation from being launched when we failed to return by sunset, but the only phone numbers either of us knew by heart were our parents'. We borrowed a cell phone and I got my mother and explained the situation. I asked her to call the school to let the sailing club know that we wouldn't be back that night, but that we were okay, and we'd return in the morning. Allison had the idea to walk a block or so up the beach road, barefoot, to one of the resorts to ask to borrow towels we could use to cover ourselves. The attendant said she'd look the other way, but asked that we bring them back in the morning.

Sleeping on the sand next to the boat got cold quickly, and the towels only kept the wind and bugs out to an extent. Allison slept in her contacts. At dawn the next morning, we set out again and slowly made our way back across the bay toward New College. The hours to clear Allison's dorm were ticking away while we puttered through the water.

When we arrived, she bolted toward campus while I locked up the boat. All my clothes were at Maynard's off campus, so I went into the "free store," a corner of the student union where people donated clothes, and grabbed a pair of shorts and a T-shirt. Then I helped Allison scrub down the common area where Matthew had hosted so many dinners that last year. He and her other roommates had already left town, leaving notes hoping she was okay and telling her to call them.

When she checked her messages again, she learned that the message my mother had called to convey to the sailing club had made its way to the campus police, who entered us as "LAS"—lost at sea. When one of Allison's closest friends, wondering where in the world she was, became concerned enough to contact campus police, they duly told her that there was nothing to worry about. Allison Gornik was safe, she was just LAS with another student, Derek Black.

CHAPTER 11

A COMMITMENT TO THEM, AND THEM TO YOU

AFTER OUR SAILING MISADVENTURE, ALLISON headed back to Ohio for the summer and I returned home to West Palm Beach, but again only briefly. Within a week, I was headed north, driving through North Carolina, seeing the mountains and anticipating going to concerts I liked. I was again avoiding doing the daily radio show my dad expected me to join him in.

Allison and I had once sat in her dorm room and took an online quiz about attachment style. Perhaps unsurprisingly, I got the result that I was avoidantly attached, which had the handy definition that I was uncomfortable with emotional closeness, that I tended to suppress and hide my feelings, and that I deal with rejection by distancing myself from the source of that rejection. True to form, although I didn't recognize it at the time, I became embarrassed about this result and internally resolved to not speak to Allison for three weeks.

A couple days later, Allison and I were messaging on Facebook. In response to how short my responses were, she gently asked if I was feeling bad about the attachment quiz. I said that I might be, but it wasn't a big deal. She said I was allowed to be, and then gave me a list of four to five options of how we could move forward; one of them was "coming over and talking about it" and another was "coming over and not talking about it," along with some choices that didn't involve coming over. I ended up choosing to come over and talk about it, but it was a totally newfangled, brilliant concept that I could proactively communicate about not wanting to communicate.

It was the very first time I can remember someone coaxing me to communicate when I'd shut down. My family were never open communicators, preferring more often to stew and avoid confrontation, which was an ironic feature of life in such a publicly outspoken family.

It was exciting to take steps into new ways of being, and I enjoyed building new patterns with Allison.

IN LATE JUNE, I GOT a message from home about my dad's health. He had fallen and was in the hospital again, preparing for a new round of physical therapy, and they needed me home. When I got there, he was briefly incapacitated, and Stormfront had been taken down by an antiracist attack on its server. That wasn't unusual, but it was up to my dad to manually intervene to get things back online. I had never been very hands-on during those times, but I was the only other person who he trusted with the administrator passwords. He wouldn't write them down anywhere, because those passwords let you do anything, including wipe the server. While he was unconscious for the day, I went home and logged into his laptop. The solution was relatively simple, just requiring logging in, talking to an operator at the server host, resetting some parts of the server, and rerouting traffic.

After a year back at New College, however, the weight of my role in his absence hung on me. I had not posted on Stormfront that year, and I no longer logged in. There were more days of the week I didn't call in to co-host *The Don and Derek Black Show* than days I did. For a moment, now, I was the central figure at the nexus of all White nationalist communication. Although I had been increasingly absent, all the senior moderators knew I was next in line with the keys to the kingdom. My phone was overwhelmed with calls and texts keeping me informed about back channels, places online the community was trying to reform in Stormfront's absence, and messages people were sending asking for more information. My dad's chief of staff tried to keep many of the questions at bay, but he wanted to know the state of my dad's health, and how seriously we needed to be planning to transition leadership.

The doctors soon told us my dad would be fine, but the single night when I was the most senior person responsible for Stormfront, a night when I dutifully brought back a server that hosted a community who hated my friends, grounded me in the truth of what it meant to be the heir. I was not one actor among many. I was not a child looking up to their parent. I was not the second name on a byline for a radio show that I constantly complained about hosting. I was the person that an entire movement expected to facilitate their sense of connection and make choices about the best way forward. When my dad woke up, I told him what had happened, and that I didn't want that responsibility. He had always expected to bequeath Stormfront to me, although he hadn't expected to do it so soon, and he had expected me to want it. I told him he needed to find someone else he could trust with the logins, someone else who people could turn to if the worst happened to him. I didn't tell him why, and he didn't ask.

ALL SUMMER, ALLISON AND I fell into a rhythm of early-morning calls while she waited at the bus stop in Cleveland where her mother dropped her on their morning commute downtown. Allison had parlayed her January ISP into a part-time paid summer internship at the children's crisis center, but she wasn't expected until 10 a.m. I often dragged our calls past the 9 a.m. hour, preferring to talk to her rather than to join the radio show that felt less like my own project and more like a millstone drawing me away from the world I wanted to inhabit, asking me to make sacrifices I was no longer sure I could make. I was finding refuge and seeing the possibilities of a new world in our conversations, and I was never really ready to hang up.

My dad got increasingly frustrated at me for missing showtimes, but when he asked me who I was talking to, I deflected the question. I told Allison about it, and she replied by telling me she didn't want to be my excuse for not doing the radio show. I wanted to maintain privacy from my family while we talked. I was worried that once that privacy broke, the relationship that we weren't trying yet to define would as well. The show had become an expectation to our community, my dad reminded me regularly, and he often told me on air that it was selfish of me to have started a radio program only to lose interest. I leaned on my conversations with Allison that summer, to avoid owning up to what I really wanted, which was getting away from being the heir and spokesman for this cause.

As promised, every five or so conversations between Allison and me were about White nationalism. She pursued two main lines of argument: first, that the scientific "evidence" behind White nationalism was either fabricated or misinterpreted, and second, that White nationalism—racism—was actively damaging to people. Put another way, as she often said to me when she got frustrated, not only was I wrong, but I was also doing harm.

Allison sent me articles on racial bias, the effects of discrimination on health, the overwhelming consequences of the differences in average racial wealth and resources, blind studies that showed persistent discrimination in hiring against the same resumes that varied only by having stereotypically White versus Black names. We talked about crime statistics. I was aware of the classic antiracist argument that a person's race does not produce crime, but rather intergenerational poverty and lack of resources generates crime. Much like the other popular antiracist line—that race is a social construct—White nationalists knew this sentence, but dismissed it immediately.

I had never thought that deeply about what those arguments actually meant. Being asked to explain why I didn't think they held water was challenging—of course exclusionary social policies reinforced poverty. White nationalists dismiss all the social inequalities people are born with, willfully choosing to believe it's people's collective choices that are purely responsible for the massive gaps in wealth and representation. They don't want to accept that these inequalities are purely the result of injustice, so they look around the world and conclude that it must be the other way around, that race produces poverty. Allison and I talked together about statistical base rates— meaning the proportion of individuals within a population who have a specific trait—and she showed me that, no matter how you tried to slice a population, race itself never emerged as a clear, strong predictor of how people would behave, what choices they would make, or their intelligence, when other meaningful factors were also considered. We walked through these numbers, elaborating the ways that IQ tests themselves could be affected by education, family resources, cultural expectations, and physical health and well-being. In short, there was nothing solely attributable to "race" other than the way that society treated a person. What conditions anyone was likely to be born in could be tied to race, along with the legacy of how their previous generations had been treated and what they had passed on, because ensuring that subjugation had been the purpose of creating the legal and social category of race to begin with.

I didn't ever accept her arguments as soon as she gave them, but I always read the academic papers and talked about them with her. Weeks or sometimes months later we'd return to an argument, when she'd ask whether I still believed the argument for it. I'd usually admit that I'd accepted that a certain piece of evidence didn't work, and I had stopped using it. It felt like I had a toolbox of arguments, and realizing that one of my tools was faulty meant I needed to remove it from my ideological collection of arguments. No one piece of evidence, it felt to me, could demolish the underpinnings of a whole ideology, so I felt safe to engage in these debates and accept their consequences without the fear that my world was eroding beneath me. I felt more personally threatened when our conversations turned away from intellectual debates and toward my responsibility for the harm I was causing. Allison knew I justified my beliefs on the idea that they were true when it came to large numbers of people, so we started there.

Eventually I accepted what I'd heard my whole life from protestors, antagonistic journalists, and anonymous people in my inbox: that race was not a definable category of human beings in any way other than as a social category. It was instead a loose set of bone structures and skin colors, regional ancestries that overlapped between every population. Barring comparison to other racial groups in America, there's no commonality among White people or any other "race" that keeps them tied together. It's why Irish and Italian immigrants weren't "White" until they were—that is, until their inclusion served a more powerful political purpose than their exclusion.

There were small populations around the world with notable overlap that made them distinctive from people in other parts of the world, but most of those populations actually existed within Africa. One of the main points of evidence that human beings migrated from Africa is the unparalleled genetic diversity among the population there. To this day, an average person from Eastern Africa has much less in common genetically with an average person from West Africa than any supposed "White" person does with either of them. Yet the random collection of traits that went into creating the category of "race" during the colonial era, when skin colors and subtle differences of features were the easiest ways to distinguish people, would lump both people into the category of "Black."

In contrast, people descended from prehistoric humans who traveled across the world tend to share extremely close heritages, because there was a genetic bottleneck among the limited population that migrated to Eurasia. Consequently, the gene pool in Western Europe has been quite small and isolated over the last few thousand years. White nationalists sometimes latch on to this fact. What they don't follow is that any one of those genetically isolated Europeans has far more in common with anyone from Africa than most Africans do with each other. In other words, White supremacists latch on to the population isolation and relative inbreeding of Europeans to prove their uniqueness. They miss the point, however, that, just as all of Europe could fit geographically within Africa multiple times over, all the qualities they find so valuable exist along with so much more in people who never left Africa. If we valued the genetics of only one population, it wouldn't be the isolated ones of Europe.

AS THE SUMMER BREAK NEARED its end, and we prepared to return to Sarasota, another horrific banner of breaking news streamed across the cable networks blaring in my house. In early August, a Stormfront member had attacked a Sikh temple in Wisconsin on a Sunday morning. He murdered six people and wounded four more, families that were attending religious services in their own neighborhood. As always, journalists confronted my dad, me, and our movement with the culpability that we deserved. Once again, my dad abdicated responsibility for the reach of our ideology, and once again, I said nothing. He clarified, as he always did, that Stormfront moderators banned any illegal or violent discussion, so anyone who perpetrated violence was violating his rules. At the same time, he said the violence had been horrific, but he removed any doubt about the distance between our ideology and the murderer's when he said the tragedy could have been prevented, had the Sikh community not been living in Wisconsin. It was the same logic he had used in response to the Norwegian mass murderer only a year before. This argument always sat heavy in my gut as I followed his lead and tried to avoid my responsibility, and refused to discuss it.

Our ideology was clear about who was an enemy in our country. It was based fundamentally on the idea that it was clear who should be forced to leave if they hadn't been banned to begin with. Yet even my last refuge—the fact that my family, who clung to their surface support for nonviolence—melted away when the only thing grieving families could hear from us in defense was the same horror that motivated the killer.

That day, our frequent co-host, Roy, who I'd gotten to know years before when he started calling in to my online radio program, called me out for my silence. On air, he said he thought my liberal college friends had gotten in my head, and that I was leaving him and my dad to say the hard things they and the listeners knew needed to be said. He had assessed me right. I had always tried to avoid my responsibility for the people who increasingly cited the language of "White genocide" that I had put out into the world. I knew there was no line between their beliefs and mine other than the inhuman executions they'd brought to unsuspecting innocent people. My activism for the cause defined enemies and outsiders, and I stood at a central point to distribute and spread that message. I had done so since I was a kid. I had always justified my beliefs by arguing that they were true, believing I really wasn't responsible for anyone but myself because I condemned violence.

I had never had to make those arguments knowing that Allison was tuned in. As Roy called me out, it was clear that I had not ever been misunderstood. I was making a choice to side with my family and a movement that ruined the lives of so many people who could just as well have been my closest friends. I had nothing to say to either Roy, to my dad, or to Allison later on, when she confronted me about the shooting. As in the face of so many accusations on the Forum, I remained silent.

AS THE FINAL WEEKS OF the summer wore on, Allison and I continued to talk, but I knew she was conflicted about how close we had become so quickly. We had become companions who spent as much time talking as we could find, and the prospect of formally dating had crossed both our minds, although we didn't dare say it. One moment we could be talking about wildlife or grammar, fun facts about the world, comparing scores in online geography identification quizzes. The next we were debating just how harmful racism needed to be before I would admit it was not only wrong, but that the enormity of my responsibility required that I speak out. She believed I had done too much harm, been too loud a voice for me to just stop broadcasting those beliefs. But I refused to condemn my family, to say they were actively harmful. I refused to leave my community, to name White nationalism for what I should have been willing to call it: a movement motivated by hate and by misplaced fear.

Our debates about the flimsy arguments that underlay my beliefs continued, reinforcing just how little the way I had been taught to see the world actually corresponded to reality. I was beginning to face the fact that the imaginary so-called objective lines of race had long ago been disproven. The only thing that made demographics destiny was our society's unwillingness to move beyond it, to invest money and time into righting the inhumane decisions this society intentionally inflicted on people. I was coming to realize that the social lines people in my community thought were so real had never been anything more than ways to divide and dehumanize people, and I was in the middle of the side that would do anything to terrorize people back into believing in them.

Allison and I cared for each other, and we couldn't get enough of each other, but she also knew that she needed to keep some degree of distance from me for her own sanity and her own sense of morality. Once we both returned to Sarasota in fall 2012, planning future adventures together, I texted Allison after I'd left her dorm to ask if she would be willing to date. As frequently as we had talked that summer, I felt more known by Allison than I had by anyone else in my life, and I didn't know what to expect when we returned to campus. She'd previously told me via text that she didn't plan to go anywhere, but I was afraid of losing her like I'd lost so many other people before. By asking, I didn't even acknowledge the conflict I knew she felt by getting so close to me. I texted her, out of the blue, "Allison, would you like to go out with me (or is that something I shouldn't think about)?" She turned me down, explaining, "I think whatever undefined thing we have going on is nice. And I like it. And that's all I know." She followed up, "I don't mean to be ambiguous or difficult and am instead like always attempting to be as transparent as possible." I responded that I had wanted to be explicit and not keep the thought in my head and not name it.

I had a lot more difficulty with transparency than she did, and I didn't name any of the concerns I knew she had. I wasn't willing to even consider that my choices, the choices we'd talked about all summer, meant that a relationship with me, even if she wanted it, would mean making the same morally unacceptable calculus that I made every day. She told me how awful she found the impact I had on the world, and she somehow balanced that with my being considerate and understanding. Despite liking me personally, she knew that my loyalty to the White nationalist cause and to my family meant that the most ethical choice I would consider making at that point, when I admitted anything, was silence. And silence was a choice she couldn't live with.

Allison said she was hesitant about any relationship at that point, burned from a few recent negative experiences. She told me, "I know better than to put myself in a position that I'm not 100% sure I want to be in." Neither of us wanted to name the implicit statement there, that I was not someone she could align herself with. It was a familiar experience, but like with so many things with Allison, this time it felt different. She had come into my life fully knowing my reputation, and choosing to spend her time with me anyway. She also had made it more clear more thoroughly than anyone else I was close to that she was repulsed by my beliefs and my activism. She spoke the analytical language I asked for in refuting my points one by one. Trusting her and becoming so close while knowing she couldn't agree to become closer because she didn't want to be morally complicit in my choices was devastating.

In turn, I replied only by alluding to the amount I was beginning to rely on her. She reiterated that she had no more solid answers for me about her feelings or what she wanted. We agreed to move on, and we got ready for the semester ahead. I told her I wouldn't be too weird about it: "I will be focusing on work and appropriately relying on interactions with my friend circle (focused probably around you)." She told me what a big part of her life I'd become.

I was scared of the commitments and responsibilities that I saw wrapped up not just in romantic relationships, but also in my responsibilities to my family and my community. I told her I saw my relationships as "the most binding and obligating things possible." She, understandably, replied perplexed, wondering why, if I thought relationships were such a binding obligation, I'd risked starting one with her. "Why can't you be free," she asked, "but just free with another person? Don't ever settle; whatever it is you want, make sure you get it, because you can." Allison challenged me to see new options, different choices, previously invisible but often scary.

ALL NEW COLLEGE STUDENTS HAD to write and defend a lengthy academic thesis to graduate. All thesis defenses were publicly announced, and an audience of students usually showed up to support their friends as a panel of three professors grilled them. I enjoyed the distance my thesis had from the controversies of my life, which was the thing that had drawn me to premodern history to begin with. Mine looked at the introduction of the word and concept of "vampires" to the rest of Europe after the Austro-Hungarian Empire won Serbia from the Ottoman Empire. I may have also been very into vampires at the time.

The Austro-Hungarian imperial administrators sent back reports of villages where the locals believed they were plagued by walking corpses. The revenants, they said, returned to life at night and sucked people's blood while they were sleeping, and spread diseases. An Austrian official oversaw the exhumation of the supposed "vampire" by townspeople who chopped up the corpse, burned it, and dumped the ashes in the river. Afterward, the administrator said, people said the attacks ended. Readers throughout Europe were unsure whether the town really had a walking corpse problem. Serbs called them "vampires," which wasn't a known term outside of Balkan folklore until then.

Thus, the first writings about vampires weren't fiction, but a sophisticated international debate on whether such a thing was possible. Reading the arguments offered ways of thinking and of weighing evidence that were completely foreign. Arguments in favor of the possibility of walking corpses relied on whether physical life relied on a force in the body, whether that vigor could allow a dumb corpse to walk without a soul. It was a debate about whether souls were responsible for bodies walking around or simply higher-level thinking. Looking at a debate about what could or couldn't be true that took so many ideas for granted demonstrated that arguments on truth were cultural. They relied on prior understandings of the world, which in turn relied on the question of who we trust. This meant, at the most basic level, that we needed to be mindful of who and what authority we trusted. The arguments in the vampire debate felt detached from reality, but they were serious for the people making them, so I asked myself what grounded me in my sense of what was true and how what I decided affected everyone else.

THAT FALL, ALLISON AND I became closer, hanging out or studying together nearly every day. Matthew's dinners took on a new feeling of routine as I slowly became an unofficial roommate. Many late nights, after finishing work, Allison and I would watch TV or a movie. At first, I went home often, but increasingly she'd agree I could stay over. Usually one of us would suggest a movie, and, when it got late, she'd invite me to sleep in her bed rather than drive home to my place. Her bed was elevated with a pile of blankets and a yoga mat underneath like a permanent pillow fortress. On nights when we'd had an especially intense argument about my beliefs, one of us would often slip out of bed to move underneath, until we found each other again and talked it through more. As I became a part of her life, I started trying to integrate her into my own, which outside of New College still revolved primarily around my family.

I had withdrawn further from doing the radio show with my dad, calling in only infrequently, and I hadn't posted on Stormfront in over a year except to provide an update about my dad's health. However, taking what I had created the year before, my dad decided that there should be a second Stormfront conference in Tennessee, and he made it clear he expected me to be there. He'd concluded our get-together one year before with a closing speech praising what I'd created as the most meaningful and active gathering he'd seen in years, and promising they'd use the year to make it bigger and better next year. I, however, had not engaged in planning this second one. I'd been ambivalent at first, but over the following months I told him I didn't want a second seminar any more than I wanted to call in to the show every day. Looking back, the power I had had to convene a congress of White nationalists from around the world with only a few weeks' notice, largely because I felt lonely and asked them to come, chilled me even then. The weight of my birth and of my own activism wouldn't let me distance myself without being called out for dropping the torch. No one made that expectation clearer than my dad, who cherished all those years attending conferences together when I was growing up. He had concluded the first Stormfront seminar by telling the audience how proud he was to see what I'd gleaned from all those years, and how I'd put my insights into making something that inspired him and other White nationalists.

A year later, I was trying to distance myself from what I'd created. I didn't have the power to make them stop, no matter how little I now engaged. I didn't have control over anything, I realized, once I'd put it out into the world.

My discussions with Allison about White nationalism and my role in it only increased once we were back on campus that fall—from intellectual debates with academic papers to deeply emotional fights about the fact that I was hurting people I said I cared about. I'd agreed already that so much of the structure I'd built in my mind was factually flawed, but that still left me as a representative and a figurehead. I told her that I didn't accept that the movement, and especially my family, were as wholly broken as she said they were.

She felt like we had started going in circles, and to be fair, in those days I was still quite avoidant of conflict. She felt like I was slippery in my arguments, liberally wielding the power of omission, and she was worried I was keeping my full positions from her, that I was giving her a watered-down version of my beliefs. I told her I wasn't holding back, and in retrospect, I think I wasn't. The more we talked, the more I realized that every conversation I'd had about my beliefs had been either with journalists or other people in the movement, or they had been one-off conversations that were never revisited. Before Allison, I didn't know what it meant to argue these beliefs to someone I cared about but who was horrified by them. Even the few New College students who had asked me to explain myself had been an exercise in talking past each other. Neither of us really tried to understand the other, because the fact that we each believed we were right was so fundamental to our image of ourselves. We'd end exactly where we began, because it wasn't safe to consider any other option.

Allison knew she could listen to me and work to understand the world the way I saw it without giving in or surrendering her beliefs. Seeing her do that has stuck with me forever afterward. Few of us recognize the ways we shut down our ability to understand beliefs that make us recoil. Doing so can create such intense dissonance that it feels like it will undermine our sense of who we are. Instead, we argue with someone, or more likely avoid arguing with them, just to reinforce who we are and what we believe. Allison was showing me that she could learn my beliefs inside and out, so much so that she could argue them in my stead. I had believed my whole life that if White people took the time to understand the worldview I had been raised with, they would have no choice but to believe it themselves. That argument often appeared within the movement as the idea that once you understood the way the world "really was," you could never go back and unknow it. Seeing someone I trusted show that she could understand me fully and still be repulsed by what she understood shook my ideological foundations unlike anything I'd ever experienced, and I couldn't unsee or unfeel that.

As the patchwork of evidence I clung to fell apart, the real core that drove the elaborate arguments I used to justify my actions got increasingly exposed: there was no room for doubt in a community that demanded shared belief. Everything in the movement involved talk of enemies and comrades, true believers and sheep. I saw a community of people who had raised me—babysitters, teachers, parents of friends, and friends of my parents. In reverse they saw a bright kid who reflected their views back to them.

I sometimes told Allison I thought I had room and power to persuade them of new positions. There were no longer swastikas on

Stormfront because I'd lobbied my dad to remove them. She knew I condemned homophobia, and she asked me how I squared that with a community that hated gay people. I argued they could be persuaded otherwise, as long as I didn't tell them to break with their commitment to Whiteness. She showed me threads on Stormfront I hadn't seen that declared its official position was that being gay was a mental illness. I didn't have an answer for that.

It was my connection to this community, my obligation to show up for them that tied me to my identity as a White nationalist. To address her concerns that I was minimizing my own beliefs, that I was hiding arguments from her in the name of avoiding conflict—and to show her my community—I invited her to the upcoming seminar. I told her it would be an opportunity to see how I talked to people within the White nationalist movement, in private, away from antiracists, away from our community at New College. I told her how much I didn't want to go again this year, much less to participate, but that nevertheless I'd be giving the final talk with one of my radio co-hosts. I'd promised to join him in cheerleading our audience, telling them to keep their heads up when people called them racist. I was dreading it. Allison understood who I was, but I felt she needed to see the world that had driven all of my public actions over the years. I knew it was the people who kept me where I was, and I needed her to know them like I did.

She was understandably worried about joining me. Dealing with me—yes, a White nationalist, but also a fellow college student who had recently stomped around her dorm pretending to be a dinosaur—was one thing, but dealing with an entire population of White nationalists, including my family, was entirely alien and terrifying. Still, Allison was White, and she looked White. She wasn't Jewish, and she didn't have a name that seemed Jewish. I reassured her she could fly under the radar without having to do too much engaging, because I had seen plenty of people come into the movement over the years. For a group that was deeply suspicious and paranoid, they were always ready to accept recruits. I was also the guest of honor at the seminar, and my family was hosting it. I reassured her that I had no hesitation that she'd be safe.

That confidence was in reality founded on shaky evidence, more like wishful thinking. My family had moved the event from the conference center downtown where I'd hosted it the year prior into a resort in the mountains. They talked publicly about how much more security it offered, and implied that the reason they needed security was because of far-left Antifa. In reality, the previous year I had unintentionally snubbed representatives of a local White supremacist skinhead group who had asked to meet with me to offer their services as bodyguards. If Antifa actually showed up with the intention to create a physical altercation, the last thing I wanted was empowered skinheads to fight them. We'd just call the police, who would take our side over members of Antifa. We'd already faced bad publicity, and I had no intention of adding a riot to that. I didn't express this diplomatically enough, and the skinhead leaders felt snubbed. After the conference, they had announced my family were not welcomed in their territory, and they'd attack our event if we showed up again. Partly because of that threat, my family had moved the event somewhere more secure.

In retrospect, it was careless of me to reassure Allison that she'd be safe. I knew I had the trust and protection of the hosts, who would keep us secure from the endless threats that had become almost background noise, and back then my sense of when things were safe included a wide degree of constant threats. The skinheads weren't what I was worried about for her. It was antiracist infiltrators surreptitiously identifying her online that worried me, so we came up with a reasonable nickname and printed "Alice" on her badge. Even if I thought she'd be physically safe, I knew she wouldn't be comfortable in that environment, and I felt guilty that drawing her into my world meant taking her into such a volatile place.

She asked one of her closest friends and her mother for advice. Her friend told her that he trusted her instincts, and, if she thought it was important enough, then he would trust her too. Her mother was worried, and told her not to go, but ultimately to go with her gut. She told Matthew she was going to a family reunion; she knew he would never approve.

A family reunion was what my family had told the venue we were having, but it really did feel true to me. There would never be another place I could go where I'd feel more connected and beloved by the people I saw. Despite being the one place in the world where people would tell me I was exactly what they wanted and needed, that I didn't need to change, I still didn't want to go. I didn't want to face the responsibilities expected of me, which I had come to dread more and more as the months went on. I wouldn't name it, but I didn't want to be a hypocrite. I didn't want to expand the list of my crimes against so many people I cared about at New College. I wanted to withdraw from movement activism because I increasingly saw this racist movement for what it was: an insular world of people obsessed with an ideology that told them they were the best type of people.

In the days leading up to the Tennessee conference, an older man who wouldn't be able to make it sent me an email suggesting I share his idea that White nationalists always add the word "evil" to any antiracist group they were describing: "We need to imbed in our own psychology that our conviction is of the highest morality, and that those who oppose that effort are EVIL." I replied to him, "We should only be careful that we don't seem hysterical when we use the word evil." I saw these people who were my wider family, however, cutting themselves off from the world, justifying endless horrors. The people who loved me didn't care about the lives of the people I loved. Showing up to reassure them, to reinforce our connection, took away my ability to deny that I was embracing that horror.

I rented a car and packed a small bag for the weekend. I had long ago branded myself to be the best, most committed, most loyal in the community. I saw my life leading out from when I made that decision before I turned ten years old, and then when I'd reconfirmed it at nineteen, running for office and becoming a spokesperson for my own cause. I knew Allison wouldn't see a different version of me at the seminar, but it felt like a last-ditch effort to show her the people I couldn't turn my back on, and why I stayed silent.

A COUPLE DAYS BEFORE LEAVING town, I told my family I was bringing a friend from college, and Allison and I made the eleven-hour drive up to the mountains of East Tennessee. Everyone attending was staying in cabins around the central conference center, which had wide windows overlooking the beautiful mountain view as a backdrop for the podium. My parents greeted us as we arrived at their cabin. Their out-of-control but incredibly friendly German shepherd Freya jumped on both of us. The house was bustling with people doing planning and logistics for the conference the next day. My mother had name tags laid out on the dining room table for the next day. Large amounts of food were around the kitchen in delivery boxes and someone told us to grab a plate. My mom took me to the fridge to show me she'd specially stocked fresh grapes for me, because she knew they'd always been my favorite fruit. One by one, I introduced "Alice" to the bustle of the inner sanctum of far-right leaders who took a moment away from their phone calls and computer screens to say hi. Each one, although busy, said they were happy to meet her.

Most people assumed she was a supporter of the movement. I had never told my parents anything about her, and my dad, hanging back from most of the frenetic energy, was curious. He asked her what she thought of everything, and she replied that she was still getting used to it. He asked her directly if she believed in White nationalism, and she gave him the explanation she had decided to use ahead of time and repeated the next day at the seminar: she was "curious and still processing everything." To their credit, my family didn't ask me to clarify whether we were dating, which we weren't, but we'd also confirmed that we only needed the one room they'd planned for me.

All weekend, we sat in the audience listening to talks that made Allison feel sick; once, she fled to the bathroom to take deep breaths to avoid panicking. On my end, I was shocked to realize I was hearing the messages in a new light. The language I was familiar with, of "enemies," was constant. David Duke railed against Jews, describing the global conspiracy he'd staked his career to. Speakers described immigrants as hating White people, and as inherently violent. They were trying to organize the attendees against everyone they named as their enemies. I spoke last with my radio co-host, while Allison took notes in the audience. I told the audience what I did on the radio, that the most important thing was to remember they weren't bad people, to never back down no matter how many times someone called them a racist. It was the same message I'd given the previous year, but it felt hollow now.

On the drive back, Allison confirmed the crowd was as shocking as she'd expected. She asked me if I was aware I was the only one

who hadn't labeled someone else as an "enemy." She confirmed I said
the same things I always said to her, but she was more resolved than
ever that this wasn't a community in which I should feel comfortable.
They clearly loved, even adored me, she said, but it was still a group
of angry, bitter people who blamed the world's problems on everyone
they didn't see as part of their group. The hate and violence that came
out of the movement, she reminded me, was not a bug, not a glitch. It
was exactly what you would expect to be spawned from this ideology.

I BACKED AWAY FROM WHAT Allison was asking me to see, and she no
longer had patience for my doubt. How could I come to this precipice,
she asked, and say that I was too committed to my community to
distance myself? I told her I *was* distancing myself, that I was refusing
to engage on the radio, I was not posting on Stormfront, I was not
doing media interviews.

She said that didn't change anything for the people on our campus who were rightly afraid of me. I told her I hadn't said or done
anything on campus. I denied my responsibility for the movement,
and reminded her that she'd seen how I spoke at the conference. In
reaction, furious at how arrogantly I wanted to have it both ways, to
be seen as someone worth trusting while I gave nothing back to our
community, she threw my own words from Stormfront back at me.
"In case you think you have nothing to be sorry for (and I sometimes
think you think that's true)," she wrote me, "you've said things like
this: 'The Civil War was such a glaring act of oppression to White
America.'" She threw the antisemitic diatribes I'd repeated in discussions on Stormfront, which I had come to be ashamed of, back in my
face: "Jews are much different from other non-Whites," I had written.
"The fact that they worm their way into power over our society to tell
us how to think makes them different from everyone else. They are
responsible for the perversion of our information media." I'd viciously
argued to Stormfront members less than six years earlier, and Allison
now quoted back to me: "We have to drive on every day, all the time,
that Jews are NOT White and the facts of everything they've done
with their influence. This has to be the cutoff that Jews are expelled
and do not come back."

She found one that even I was shocked to see: "I'm ready for the return of political posters that will promise me White supremacy. Good honest pride is by nature intended to be power in any case."

NEW COLLEGE STUDENTS RETURNING FOR another year of my silence were just as hurt and traumatized by my indifference as ever, and they expressed that bitterness once again. Someone started a new Forum thread about me, which played out initially much like all the ones before it: "This hasn't happened in like a year so litmus test: derek Black, son of former kkk grandwizard don Black, goes to our school."

Again students engaged in yet another form of the same debate. At this point, defenses of me felt as hollow as attacks: "Is this supposed to get me to not talk to Derek? I hope not, because it's just making me not want to talk to you." Even if I wasn't prepared to abandon or condemn my family, or the entire community that had raised me and who I spoke out defending in all my public speech, I knew that there was no misunderstanding. The defenses of me weren't warranted, because I was hurting my fellow students. Anyone who didn't feel it was simply not the target of the movement I represented.

Allison urged me to finally reply. Seeing the discussion going nowhere, between students anguished by the daily fact of knowing I was on campus, publicly a racist, totally silent on the Forum, and apparently pleasant in person. She, frustrated, replied for the first time about me. She didn't say she was close to me or knew me personally, but said that I attended weekly Shabbat dinners, I was clearly friends with Jewish students and students of color, I had dated a Jewish student, and there was very little evidence of my engagement in the movement in the recent past (i.e., no Stormfront posts, rarely on the radio show). She told the forum to go engage in the kind of social justice change they wanted to see, but that "attacking him as a mass gang" was not the right move anymore.

She of course knew all this from her proximity to me, but she didn't claim that in her post. Each of her points were facts about myself that in many ways I was very proud of. My beliefs were dramatically changing as the pseudoscientific basis for them eroded, but the foundation for that erosion had been the hurt and pain I was causing the community and my care for Allison. What had begun as my question, "Where is the misunderstanding?" was landing squarely in my own lack of responsibility, demanding that I act.

Students responded to Allison with the inarguable missing piece: a message from me actually clarifying my intentions. "Derek isn't advocating his beliefs," one student wrote, "but he isn't publicly abandoning them either. If he does, I will gladly accept him as a friend and someone I can trust. Until then, I will eye him with the suspicion that he deserves."

Privately, Allison urged me to finally speak, to at least let the community know the extent that I wanted to change their fear of me, even if I wasn't ready or able to remove the source of their fear. We drafted a response together at a coffee shop and I posted to the Forum:

"I haven't defended myself on here or responded to anyone except when they've approached me personally because I've discovered it's a no-win, very hostile situation all around." I said what I'd privately been harboring for years, that I cared about the college community and didn't want to be the source of so much fear for them.

"I have done my best since arriving to New College to stay out of people's hair," I wrote. "Since returning after the big thread about me while I was abroad, I have tried hard to not do anything of note whatsoever." I told them about my experience of feeling constantly ostracized on campus, always weighing whether the discomfort of attending any public events would be too much to make it worth it. I told them about trying to escape: "During my first semester back I would go sailing to escape the occasional middle finger in the library, the murmurs when I'd get food in Ham, and the occasional threatening emails." Reading it now, the woundedness of it is a bit galling, but it was the first time I'd dared reach out to the community I felt so connected to, despite myself. I was doing my best to be honest.

I went on to detail a list of things that I wasn't, such as not being a Nazi or part of the KKK. I said that I didn't think a person's race or religion predetermined a person's life course, and I said that "I do not believe people of any race, religion, or otherwise should have to leave their homes or be segregated or lose any freedom or whatever other terrifying similar-vein ideas have been posted in threads about me.

(Whoa.)" I further clarified, "I do not support oppression of anyone because of his or her race, creed, religion, gender, socioeconomic status, or anything similar." I closed the message saying that if people wanted to message me directly, they were welcome to, but I wasn't going to debate publicly. I closed with: "Making these statements obviously does not instantly create comfort or security for everyone who's uncomfortable, but I hope it might help slightly."

I hit send, and Allison and I looked up as students stationed around the room started to look worriedly at their screens, nudging each other to show them what had appeared on the Forum.

CHAPTER 12

I AM PLANNING TO WRITE SOMETHING ABOUT YOU TODAY

I DIDN'T KNOW IT YET, or I wasn't able to acknowledge it, but my ability to be the heir and leader my family demanded I be had already been destroyed months before. When I couldn't find a way out without bringing on too much scrutiny, I still parroted the talking points I'd memorized years before. I was terrified at what this feeling meant for the future.

I'm ashamed of how much I pushed Allison to be my conscience as I fought each step away from White nationalism. People leaving the movement was nothing new. They did so for many reasons. Sometimes they were driven out of it by accusations of a lack of ideological or racial purity. Many more have left because of infighting. Many others left because they didn't see a future for it and didn't want to keep pouring their energy and sacrifice into a black hole. Others left after being outed publicly, running from the shame and consequences. Most of the time, people gave no reason at all for leaving and simply disappeared from gatherings. That option was less easily available to leaders, who were expected to show up, to be what the rest of the community needed from them. I had made myself a leader.

Several prominent leaders, unwilling to denounce the ideology but also unwilling to continue being its spokespeople, had decamped out of the country entirely. It was like the only future they could see for themselves after having tied their identities up so much with White power was starting again in a society that didn't have the same roles and identities for them to fall into. Most of the time, when I considered leaving my role as a White nationalist advocate, I couldn't imagine any exit other than accepting a mandate of silence and leaving the country like many before me had done. I could only imagine a life in hiding, trying to exist rather than live. I didn't see any kind of meaningful life ahead of me after this.

While my dad despised it when Stormfront users asked to have their records wiped from the site, he always complied. I think a part of him respected their need to leave a movement that seemed to do nothing but fail and hurt its own members. My dad had stuck around long enough to see most people come and go. Remembering the early days of Stormfront, he was annoyed to observe that nearly everyone who had logged on in that first year had moved on. He preferred those who left in silence, and he railed against "those with the loudest mouths" who subsequently denounced White nationalism.

Coming to accept that the supposed evidence for my beliefs was not only flimsy but irrefutably fraudulent hadn't actually led me to the obvious decision that I needed to denounce them. After nearly two years of seeing an entire school call me a bigot and an idiot and describe being afraid of me for my advocacy of a belief system I no longer believed in also did not leave me certain I had to denounce it. My message to the Forum, which I'd hemmed and hawed about, and dragged my feet writing, I'd written as carefully as possible so as not to cross a line that would mark me as a "loudmouth."

Allison had asked me to rank the positions I felt comfortable denouncing. Many were easy, such as denying I was a White suprem-acist. No one in my family believed they were racist or a supremacist. I confirmed that I didn't hate anyone, which everyone in my family would also say, but I meant it in a very different way now. I confirmed I didn't wish ill toward anyone, that I didn't support oppression or believe race predetermined people's lives. I could say I wasn't a member of the KKK, and I didn't agree with KKK ideology. She asked me if I felt comfortable denouncing neo-Nazis, and I pushed back, not because I identified as a neo-Nazi, but because I didn't want to offend the close inner circle of Stormfront moderators who would in fact have called themselves Nazis. Instead, I hedged that I didn't agree with the ideology of Nazism, so I could leave my diplomatic connections to modern Nazis unchanged. I parsed all these lines so carefully because I strongly suspected the message would leak, and I wanted my reputation within the movement to survive its publication, because I couldn't fathom losing the only home I'd ever known.

After posting my first response to the Forum, I felt relief for the first time at New College. I was overjoyed to see a string of private messages showing the relief of a community that just wanted this experience to end. In retrospect, these initial emails were the ones who forgave a bit too easily, who were looking past the fact that my email did not explicitly say I was no longer a White nationalist. "Derek," began a message that arrived within minutes, "I was glad to finally have you share your side of your story. I'm glad to have you as a friend." Other similarly relieved messages poured in. "I know it was hard for you to write this. I simply wanted to apologize for the crude hypocrisy you've been subjected to, and to simply thank you for your dignity and maturity."

Following expressions of relief came the harder, but fully well-deserved, wariness: "I'm very glad to hear that you hold egalitarian beliefs. Yet, I don't think that this e-mail answers all of the questions that individuals have about your worldview. Primarily, I think that some people might find it difficult to understand how someone who is against oppression could associate with your father's website." Another privately messaged me, "Maybe you *don't actually agree* with everything written on Stormfront, but your show is promoting a worldview in which these ideas have currency. And ultimately, I think that you are misleading us when you play down WN's White supremacist impli-cations." These were exactly the right questions, cutting through the questions of personal feelings and getting to the fact of my public role and responsibility. With only days left in the semester, I either begged off or suggested the students and I plan a time to return to the conversation when I got back the next semester. Zoë privately emailed me: "Hey Derek, I thought your forum post was good. It made me wonder what your beliefs actually are though? I guess I never completely understood them. Also, out of curiosity, has your time at NCF changed your beliefs at all?" I didn't respond at all, feeling guilty for spurning Zoë's olive branch, but even more so because I knew I had no answer I could authentically provide and feel proud about it. Everything I had said was true, but it was also so tenuous that I couldn't answer the most important questions.

I had essentially declared myself a non-racist White nationalist.
A growing number of private messages were basically asking me to
declare myself an antiracist. I couldn't do that, not because I was
actually ideologically opposed to any of the beliefs of antiracism, but
because I didn't want to lose my family.

IN THE LAST WEEKS OF the semester, I applied to the student funding
body that gave out money for ISPs and theses. I applied to study
French in Bordeaux. They funded a round-trip flight to Europe, and I
left almost as soon as I was home. I doubted the administration would
have been happy to know I made a stop first to visit David Duke, but
I wanted to leave before Christmas and avoid spending much time
at home. My flight landed in Venice, Italy, a little more than a week
before Christmas, and I quickly boarded a train north through the
mountainous countryside. I hadn't effectively communicated with
David about my precise arrival time, but I knew his address and had a
vague sense of the train schedules. I didn't have a cell signal in Europe
and, somewhat recklessly, I didn't have much of a plan to navigate the
small skiing town where he was living alone that Christmas. Along
the way, I'd learn after I arrived, he'd emailed my mom, who told him
which flight I was on, and he backtracked the schedule to guess what
train I'd arrive on. When my train came into his station, David was
waiting for me on the platform. I asked him how he'd known when I'd
arrive, and he said he hadn't. Not wanting to miss me "because your
mom would have been furious," he'd driven back and forth from his
apartment to the station for every train that came from Venice that
day. This was not the first time he'd watched a train disembark that
day; it was just the first time I'd gotten off it with my bags.

I was relieved to see David, but I had been worried and anxious
for the entire trip. When my flight landed and I connected to Wi-Fi,
I saw that Mark Potok, an anti-hate researcher from the SPLC, had
emailed me hours before. He was going to write about my letter to
the Forum. Now, as I had worried, I'd have to defend myself in front
of the world and each of my communities. My heart felt heavy.

Potok had written, "I'm writing because I heard about your post
to the students-only forum saying, among other things, that you're

not a White supremacist, a neo-Nazi, a Klansman or anything of that ilk. Someone sent me the entire post anonymously, but I've managed to confirm, from other students, that it did come from you. Several of them also said very nice things about you. I am planning to write something about you today."

I dashed off a quick reply asking for a few hours delay on the story so that I could collect my thoughts and because I genuinely would be out of Internet reach until then. I told David I needed to send an email as soon as possible from his apartment because the SPLC was writing a story about me, and I wanted to give them a comment. We drove the few minutes back to his apartment, and he agreed we could go grocery shopping after I was done instead of on the way home. While David recorded YouTube videos in his office, I wrote my reply to Potok from the couch, doing my best to straddle both worlds: "Everything I said is true, and I also believe in White nationalism. My post and my racial ideology are not mutually exclusive concepts, and people can believe both. White nationalism doesn't dictate specific creeds so much as my concern about White assimilation, which I still think is very much a problem." I still wasn't willing to admit the truth even to myself that there was little I actually believed in the movement beyond the fact that I didn't want to separate myself from my family. Potok replied, "Thanks for the replies, Derek. We are going to post it—I'm sorry, I'm not doing it to annoy or attack you, but because we're a kind of news organization and this is news for us."

I closed my laptop, and we went to shop for the ingredients to make Christmas dinner. David was living alone at that point, and his house was relatively dark. He told me not to come and go much, and not to talk to anyone. Each night I made my bed on the couch and then reassembled it in the morning, in case the landlord showed up, so it wouldn't look like he had a guest.

When the story came out the next day, they printed my attempt to "have it both ways," as Potok put it. I felt deeply depressed. I was worried about how David would respond, but he read the article and was entirely unbothered. To my surprise, he and my family were supportive when they read it, reassuring me that, like always, I was careful and clever and was a great spokesman for our cause. They all thought it was particularly politically savvy, offering a sophisticated and smart-sounding approach to White nationalism. I had carefully parsed the line of the fractious parts of White nationalism, and ultimately, I had come up on the hard edges. But I knew the New College community would be resoundingly less positive when someone inevitably found the article.

David and I spent six days together at his apartment, during which time he asked me if I would put my name down on a rental agreement so he could avoid having his own flagged. With European authorities trying to deport him, he needed a lease that would take them time to track down. When I refused, he seemed genuinely hurt. Living alone, with governments closing in around him, he was running out of options.

I was finalizing applications to graduate programs while I sat on his couch, and one day he suggested I swap my first and middle names much like he had done to exist in Europe all those years earlier, calling himself Ernest Duke. It had worked to distance him from his reputation until it hadn't, and he recognized in me the same feelings of exile and being hounded that he had known since he first spoke out publicly in college. I didn't take his recommendation then. I didn't want to hide. I thought, after everything I'd been through, that I could handle any ostracism I had coming.

When I left David's apartment two days after Christmas, taking a train to Slovenia and down to Serbia to celebrate New Year's on my own, he wrote saying, "Good luck and remember about creating that identity to get you through the next few years. Do it. If you don't, and something goes wrong, you will always regret not taking this step." That visit and those conversations were the most human and empathetic that I ever had with David, despite how frustrated I was at the time with his meticulous cleaning schedule, which I think he made us follow to keep himself busy, much like the YouTube videos he recorded incessantly while I was there. I had no way to know it yet, but it was to be the last time I saw him or spoke with him.

I FELT HOLLOW WAITING TO see the reaction of New College to the SPLC article. Once again, I was sitting alone in Europe, waiting for a new thread to pop up. I had told them the half truth, trying to reassure them, but I had only been able to go so far as saying that I didn't want to hurt them, not that I would do anything to stop doing it.

The commentary on my response was harsh, but it was hard to argue that it wasn't fair. "It looks like one of DB's homies took my suggestion for Derek to apologize to the SPLC if he really cared and forwarded the e-mail themselves," one wrote, "and I'm glad that person did so because 'I also believe in White Nationalism. My post and my racial ideology are not mutually exclusive concepts' is the truth we needed to hear from Derek."

I unloaded on Allison about how much more the Forum was now affecting me because I'd reached out to it. "What happened to me not caring what others think of me?" I asked her. "It was cowardly to send the second message."

Like a wounded child, I ranted to her about how I'd tried to distance myself from the thousands of posts on the Forum the previous two years: "I was OK with it because I felt like they were attacking an idea of me and not me." It's shameful to think back on my outburst, unable to see what hundreds of people had spent years communicating in every way they could imagine. "For a second I wanted it to be about me and other people and I feel almost betrayed. It's not my community."

Parsing my tantrum now, remembering that night—how they always seemed to come when I was alone—I can feel it like it's new. Nothing over those years had been anything but personal. My classmates who posted on the Forum had shared so much of themselves while I'd only watched like a voyeur to convince myself they couldn't possibly be speaking to me personally if I didn't speak back. That night I sat on the bottom bunk in a nearly empty hostel in Belgrade, Serbia. I had taken a bus into the Balkans to spend New Year's Eve closer to the towns where my thesis vampires had been recorded centuries before. Lying there, I wrote to Allison through my hyperbolic and injured feelings: "This situation makes me want to harden up and laugh in their faces in order to show they didn't affect me. It also makes me want to organize the biggest, hardest, wildest WN thing ever, just to show them how little I think of them." I never actually considered doing that, and the moment I wrote it I realized just how much this identity had long ago ceased being something I believed in and had just become a point of pride and of fear. I told her so a second later, "I'll work through it and be more sensible, but those are my emotions tonight. I need to get to thinking about ideas and their merit and not be personal about this."

All those years defending a dehumanizing ideology, trying to have it both ways, believing I could be friends to the same people who had everything to lose from it. I had justified that by retreating to "ideas and their merit," accusing the people who rightly called me a hypocrite of being "personal." That night I walked through the Belgrade Fortress, where couples came to sit on benches. I knew this situation was untenable, that I had to make a choice. I kept thinking about my email to Allison, where I'd acknowledged painfully that New College was "not my community." By that I meant that, even if they were the people spurring me to recognize that I needed to leave the people who had raised me, the people I wanted to protect there weren't offering me a new world. Taking another step publicly away from my White nationalist movement role would eventually break that community's confidence in me. I knew that when I fell, I would fall alone.

The next day, Salon.com ran a headline story announcing the radio show I'd started was going off the air. I sent the link to Allison, and she replied, "Huh. What's going on over there?" I didn't know, and I didn't really care to find out. I hadn't called in to the program in months, and I didn't want to be a part of it. My dad had kept going in every day, texting and calling me often, annoyed that I wasn't joining him. Despite reassuring me that my post on the SPLC was fine, he clearly understood privately that it represented my trying to distance myself from the movement, and from my role within it.

A MONTH LATER, WHEN ALLISON and I were back at New College for our spring semester, she took me aside one of our first nights home. She had asked if we could talk about something serious, and when we did, she was nervous and on the verge of tears. I'm not sure there was anything she could have told me that would have made me mad, seeing her so afraid to say it.

Weeks before, I had sent my response to Potok at the SPLC before Allison and I had a chance to connect. "I don't have many comments," I told him, "as I think of this issue primarily as a matter between me and my peers." I ended my response just with, "I feel that I considered my words and that my sentiments were reasonable and consistent." I had expected them to print exactly what I'd said on the Forum.

There was only a moment, however, where I imagined that future. A few minutes after I emailed him, Allison saw my email to her about it and replied. She gave me a lifeline, something to grab on to to try to preserve my relationship with my family a little longer. "I feel like coming from a blow-back perspective on your family's side/WN's side/ whatever," she wrote, "I feel like it's probably important to clarify that everything you said is true, *and you still believe in WN*." It was ironic that it was Allison who had given me the out in that moment to reaffirm my commitment to the White nationalist community I was still so afraid to lose. I emailed him back.

As we watched the fallout in the days following, Allison regretted her suggestion. "No, you shouldn't have sent the second email. You have no idea how sorry I am that I told you to. I incorrectly assumed that you cared more about saving face with SF/not causing your family trouble in WN communities than you did with NCF." It surprised me as much as her to realize after the fact that that hadn't been true. I had already made the choice to stand by what I'd said on the Forum, but I nevertheless jumped on the lifeline she threw me to backtrack, essentially to defend my family and prove that I wasn't distancing myself from them. Both of us regretted it.

When we returned to New College to begin the spring semester, Allison was terrified I was about to hate her. When I asked what she had to tell me, she revealed she had in fact been the one who anonymously forwarded my Forum post to the SPLC.

She'd created an email address under a fake name and sent it to Potok to try to convince him to take down my listing and biography from their directory of leaders of White nationalism, the one that the original Forum post about me had cited as evidence of my high profile. She argued to Potok that I was much younger, and had done much less, than anyone else listed, and that I was clearly trying to extricate myself from the movement, which would be more difficult if profiles like the SPLC's were kept up. She thought he would need her consent to use the post, and the worst thing that could happen was that he'd say no, but that wasn't the case. When he'd told her he would be publishing it, and appreciated her sending it to him, she begged him not to do it, but it was too late. He went through other students to confirm it was authentic and then emailed me.

I had never suspected that she was the one, but I genuinely wasn't mad—I would never have written the message without being ready for what could happen if it leaked. Like planting the *Details* magazine almost exactly two years before, I had an obnoxious tendency to sprinkle bread crumbs in places where journalists (or would-be student journalists) could pick them up, rather than taking the initiative to do and say what I knew I needed to.

If we were going to be as close as it seemed like we were headed, sooner or later she'd get burned by dealing with the press and, as painful as this one had been, there really hadn't been any harm done by being the vector for what I'd thought might happen regardless. We agreed not to keep things like this from each other.

MY FINAL SEMESTER AT NEW College proceeded relatively straight-forwardly, letting me experience college for the first time in an almost normal way. Allison's prediction while we'd been traveling turned out to be mostly true: "People are already going to believe what they're going to believe, people are already going to act how they're going to act. People are *sick* of hearing about it and talking about it." The radio show was finally off the air, and I had long ago withdrawn from reading or posting on Stormfront. It was a period when I was almost able to forget my role in the White nationalist movement, when I wanted to try to forget about it, but not to address it.

Allison and I felt like we had gotten through some of the worst of it. During the break, we'd kept up regular travelogues that went on for thousands of words. I saw later she'd said about me in an email to her mom, "I really really really really miss him. I also miss being picked up. (He's always picking me up, giving me piggyback rides, holding me cradling-style—this is actually how I get down from bed every morning. Going to say hi to Matthew is really fun like this)." At the same time, we agreed we had never started dating, even when Matthew and her other roommates questioned how it was we weren't dating if I slept every night at her dorm. Suspicious indeed.

Partway through the semester, Maynard stopped accepting my rent payments. He told me he'd keep the guest room open for me if things fell apart with Allison, but that he felt bad taking monthly payments for an empty room. When Allison asked me if there was anything she could do to make her dorm more comfortable, I told her, "I'm surprisingly comfortable with your room. This may be partly because I feel so comfortable with you."

Allison got back yet another amazing narrative evaluation from a faculty member for her time in Australia, "Allison, this was an outstanding, superb, WOW ISP! It is hard to believe how much you accomplished in only three weeks while you were there." Reading it reminded me of one of our earliest conversations, while we watched the stars late at night. I'd claimed that no one in college knew what they wanted to do afterward, and she'd been shocked to realize I didn't know what I wanted to do. She was going to be a clinical psychologist, she told me, and Matthew was going into finance. I told her when I imagined my future, the only thing I could come up with was fleeing the country and trying to find somewhere that no one would ever look me up on Google or care if they did. As a kid, I'd watched the movie *The Truman Show*, about a kid secretly raised on a TV set, who planned to escape by going to Fiji, where "you can't get any further away before you start coming back." When I joked with my dad that it often felt like I was Truman, he told me I might be onto something. How else could I explain the bizarre situation I was growing up in?

THAT SPRING BREAK, ALLISON'S SIXTEEN-YEAR-OLD sibling came to Sarasota from Ohio, and my fifteen-year-old niece came up from West Palm Beach for us to travel across Florida. I'd been admitted to a fully funded medieval studies graduate program in Kalamazoo, Michigan, and I knew I'd soon be leaving Florida. I didn't know when or if I would ever return to the place I'd spent almost all of my life. I'd driven across Florida numerous times with my dad as a kid, where the first fourteen hours of the trip were just trying to get out of the state. My family had lived in the state for generations, and it was a point of pride that I still held.

I wanted to show Allison, her sibling, and my niece the parts of Florida beyond just Disney World (which we did dutifully visit, along with Universal Studios). We crisscrossed the state in my car, which I'd done on weekends in the early days back at New College, when I had few social opportunities. We visited every region except the panhandle. We went to St. Augustine, the oldest colonial city in North America, and swam in the clear freshwater springs in the north, where my grandmother had grown up, and where my family visited every year growing up. It was an extension of the road trips my niece and I had taken over the years. Now that she was a teenager, it was nice to have a same-age gremlin with her in the backseat eating snacks, while Allison and I sat up front, and also to be on a trip where no one in the car wanted to argue for White power. We all went to a contra dance weekend in the hills where we stayed in cabins and caught up with some of the friends I'd introduced Allison to over the last year, who called themselves my "dance family."

The months went by quickly, while I wrote and then defended my thesis, and Allison and I spent our spare time planning various trips to places around the world—Thailand, Nicaragua, Peru, Argentina, French Polynesia—that we would actually end up taking over the course of the next decade. One weekend, we took a day trip to the Everglades that took us three hours each way. After I defended my thesis, we went to New Orleans for a few days, and drove all night back just in time for me to blearily present my thesis in the showcase.

THAT SUMMER, I WAS PREPARING to move away from Florida for the first time. I was twenty-four, and I had graduated from New College a couple of months earlier. My mother had asked me to attend the graduation ceremony because her mom wanted to see it. I was reluctant because I would still be the most infamous student walking the stage that afternoon. But, ultimately, she came into town with my grandmother, my sister, and my niece, and they stayed at a beachfront hotel, so I felt I had to go. They sat under the tent that was erected for the ceremony every year by the bay front.

I don't remember who first suggested that my dad not come. In the years since, my mom has guilted me that, in those last weeks before I denounced their ideology, I had insulted him by prioritizing the antiracists at the college. I remember being ambivalent and uncomfortable with his not being there. Even though my mother was the more ardent ideologue in our family, my father was the public spokesman for White nationalism.

Having suffered a stroke a half decade earlier, he still walked with a limp, and I worried students might corner him. I remember sharing this concern with both of them. I was still bitter toward the activist students who had made my life miserable on campus for years. I was still stubborn enough that I think I wanted him there to show that I wasn't intimidated. I remember hours before graduation, sitting inside College Hall, looking out the window at the water where the big white tent and stage for graduation were set up. A student I barely knew approached me and asked if my dad was there. I said no, and he walked off.

My mother reserved a room at an oceanfront hotel downtown, and we hung out by the pool. At the ceremony, when I walked across that stage to take my diploma as the sun set on the bay, someone yelled "Fascist!" Otherwise, things went smoothly enough.

I had become disaffected from our ideology, and everyone knew that, to some extent, because of how much I'd withdrawn. I had come to hear the tropes and arguments that I myself once honed and articulated as detached and brutal. The road leading to that moment was long. Thanksgiving the previous year had been awkward enough. I nodded and listened, but now I was repelled at hearing the same old things about supposedly violent Caribbean immigrants, Jews, and Black people. My parents perceived that I was trying to prolong my time away, and they frequently asked me when I intended to stop studying history and start making it.

AT THE END OF THE summer, I would be bound for Kalamazoo to start a graduate program in medieval history. I expected to lay low there. As it became clearer how catastrophic and yet necessary my break with White nationalism would be, the program seemed more like a retreat from the world. I would not only be studying monks, but trying to retreat into the scholarly cloister like the medieval authors I was researching. The program was funded, both tuition and a small living stipend, in exchange for teaching a college class and being a proofreader at the university's academic press.

For many people, I think, graduate school represents a kind of deviation from the regular course of life. It at least delays engagement with normal employment. For me, graduate school was a way to divert myself from a professional world that I was not at all sure would accept me. I still didn't have a plan for a life I'd always thought had been set in stone before I was born. My life in Michigan, instead, would be quiet, but it would also require energy and keep me from ruminating. I wanted to go somewhere as far away as possible. I wanted to stop reading the news, disappear into the library, and only speak about medieval history.

At the end of the semester, Allison left for a research internship at Virginia Tech in Blacksburg, Virginia, while I stayed in Sarasota to house-sit for two of my professors. The night before she left, we made dinner at their house, churned ice cream, and recorded videos of each other late at night talking about the future. We cried, because now we would be living across the country from each other, and the next morning I drove her to the airport. We never would return to whether we should formally "date," but we were each committed to each other going forward.

AS THE MONTHS WORE ON, it felt like a looming deadline was approaching. I felt shame at my past actions and fear that I couldn't imagine a future. I had initially thrown myself into medieval academics because I thought that was a space that was disconnected from modern politics. No one, I thought, could look at my medieval research and accuse me of working on something that would ever be considered dangerous or even relevant. Academia is a world where ideological strangeness is common, but I wasn't confident even in that context that a renounced White nationalist would be accepted.

Over the summer, to prepare for my future, I listened to dozens of hours of recorded lectures. One, by a professor from Tulane, was on the writings of Anna Comnena, the daughter of the Byzantine emperor and the main historical witness to the First Crusade in 1095. Comnena's record, while beautifully written, the professor argued, demonstrated the adage that those who could not wield power themselves wrote histories. She had attempted to seize power herself with the help of her mother at one point, but she had failed. Reading the history she wrote reminded me of the urgency my own mother used when warning me to make history, not to write it.

I found myself unexpectedly remembering one of the White nationalist conferences I'd attended as a teen activist, when I'd tried to retreat from the other young people there who represented the new generation of White power. We had finished giving interviews to a documentary crew attending the event, and to some local TV news reporters. Afterward, they invited me to hang out by the pool and talk, but I wasn't interested. I wanted to be alone, now that I'd done my duty. I went to the small hotel library and picked up one of the pretentiously placed books on their shelf, *Paradise Lost* by John Milton. I'd grabbed it to give myself an excuse not to hang out, although I realized when I said it that explaining I was busy reading a seventeenth-century epic poem retelling the biblical book of Genesis was much stranger than if I'd just said I was tired. I stuck to the bit, however, and I did finish the book that afternoon. At the end of a weekend congratulating ourselves on the progress we were making to reshape and overtake the society around us, it was Satan's verses that stood out. The fall of the world and the expulsion from the Garden of Eden didn't read to me like White nationalists were the protagonists. Satan rallied the forces of Hell, telling them, "Who can yet believe, though after loss, that all these puissant legions, whose exile hath emptied Heaven, shall fail to re-ascend, self-raised, and repossess their native seat?" Sitting on a couch that afternoon, I related to the pride of an angel who, "for the testimony of truth hast borne Universal reproach, far worse to bear than violence." Yet it was the passages by Satan that resembled the conversations we'd had all weekend. As the mouth of Hell opened and Satan's forces poured into the world, "To range in, and to dwell, and

over Man To rule, as over all he should have rul'd," I could only see
the future revolution we said we were preparing. After Satan succeeds
in tricking Adam and Eve, he relays the story back to his followers in
Hell, that his victory came at the cost that humanity would forever
"bruise my head," but, he tells his followers, "A World who would not
purchase with a bruise, or much more grievous pain?" As the other
activists came back into the hotel library asking if I was sure I wouldn't
join them, I remember thinking about Satan's lines and wondering what
the personal and social cost really would be to us and to everyone else.

Having grown up committed to leading the movement, realizing
now I had no option but to walk away left me feeling like I was in a
void. Losing the connections of my lifetime didn't feel like joining a
new world, but simply walking into nothing. I had tried all my life to
help lay the ground for all of our followers to fulfill a vision we had
of overthrowing the world. Now I didn't know what or where I could
go, what I could build.

I WANTED TO BE DONE with the harm both that I had caused and
that I had experienced. For me that meant accepting the identity of
"White nationalist" like a brand that I couldn't remove. I wanted to
back away quietly and never be heard from publicly again. I didn't
want to face the fear I'd held on some level my entire life: that my
parents' protection and care was dependent on sharing their beliefs. I
told Allison it felt arrogant to consider another interview or speech,
another campaign, another round of advocacy, even if this time it was
against my old positions. I wanted to show my disaffection slowly, with
silence. Allison's argument, in retrospect the most important moment
for the future of my life, was about responsibility.

I told her I wanted to write something that disavowed White
nationalism. Then, true to form, I promptly avoided the idea. But
since I had said I wanted to, Allison wouldn't let me turn away or drag
my feet anymore.

While I was lying in the sand on Lido Beach one afternoon, watching the sun set, an email from Allison popped up on my phone: "Are
you going to do this? If you're going to do it, get your stuff together
(I wrote 'shit together' first but I think that might be rude, but it's

really what I mean) and do it."

Different messages and points trickled in over the next few days: "I feel like you are a representative of a movement you barely buy into."

"You need to identify with more than 1/50th of a belief system to consider it your belief system. I can't be like 'oh the Holy Spirit sounds cool, but I'm not into Jesus' and call myself a Catholic."

"Your father certainly does not speak highly of his own career in White nationalism," she reminded me, "and he doesn't seem particularly happy with what he's done. So, get out of this, before it ruins some part of your future more than it already irreparably has."

And finally, "I will be here for you regardless of what you choose. But, love, if for whatever reason we stopped talking forever tomorrow, I would still with all my heart think that this is what would be best for you. For you, for your future career, for your future family. There's nothing good in WN. Aside for possibly a supportive community that shares a victim complex. But you can get that elsewhere."

Ideological identity, it finally occurred to me, was not actually about belief. It was based in who I was committed and connected to, who I cared for and felt responsible for. The pressure of belief was to signal loyalty, care, commitment.

I drove up to visit Allison halfway through the summer. One night, while Allison did laundry in her Virginia Tech dorm, I sat on a washing machine and started writing.

CHAPTER 13

YOU NEED TO MAKE NEW FRIENDS AND FAMILY

I'D NEEDED TO BE WITH Allison when I began the draft, and I was afraid to share it with anyone besides her, afraid it would leak early. But I needed someone to read it who wasn't so close. The next day, Allison asked her mom if she could proofread what I'd written. I hadn't met her yet, but she knew through Allison what was going on. Her mom agreed and gave helpful feedback. In contrast, I hadn't been able to get the nerve up to even suggest to my parents what I planned. I'd drafted both a description of the dehumanizing ideology that White nationalism was committed to and my detailed denunciation of it. I'd written about the reality I was finally able to admit: that I'd hesitated so long in taking the step of formally condemning something I'd much earlier ceased to believe in because I couldn't imagine losing my connection and relationships with my family. I wrote that I'd finally come to accept that the only moral decision consistent with my values was to speak out against the destructive movement I'd poured so much energy into helping build. Going silent, which felt like the safest course and the one that could preserve some semblance of my personal life, would leave me with only my advocacy for racism. Moving forward in any way required that I push back on what I'd participated in and which I now saw as so horrifying.

The weekend before I sent the letter, I visited home, hoping to tell them something, but I couldn't do it. I didn't know how to explain it, and I didn't think they would be able to understand. I'd helped my mom install more of the windows we'd been building for years. Late Saturday night, after eating dinner with both of them in front of the TV, watching cable news, I got in my car and drove around the town where I grew up. It was strange to see all the changes and new construction. I went to an outdoor bar that was still open for a few more hours, and sat at a hightop table and ordered a beer. On my laptop, I added a few final details to the letter.

The next day, I worked with my mom, who had taken off work while I was able to be around. She asked me to stay in town that week, helping her before I left for grad school, and it was momentarily tempting to tell myself I could wait another week to send this thing, to be able to talk with her before I did it. Feeling my resolve ebb, I told her I needed to go, that I had a lot to prepare before I would be ready to leave the state. I was avoiding the news, but it was hard to miss the verdict the night before finding the killer of Trayvon Martin not guilty of murder. Relying on Florida's "stand your ground" law that had passed only a few years before and which didn't require people to try to flee before using lethal force in a fight, the jury had said George Zimmerman was not responsible for following the Black teen, accusing him of shoplifting, fighting him, and shooting him in the street. I knew what my dad would say on the radio the next day, if we still had a radio show.

So I sent the letter to Mark Potok from the house I'd grown up in, with my family all around, not suspecting what I was doing. I couldn't talk to my parents about what I was going to do, and I knew I didn't want to be there when the letter went up, which from that moment could be any time.

IN THE MORNING A COUPLE days later, the article went online on the SPLC website: "Activist Son of Key Racist Leader Renounces White Nationalism." At the top of the page, they ran a close-up of the picture of me when I was nine years old with the governor of Mississippi, a few months after I'd done my first interview on *The Jenny Jones Show*. "Derek Black," the headline ran, "son of the former Alabama Klan leader who now runs the largest racist Web forum in the world, has renounced White nationalism, saying that he has been through 'a gradual awakening process' and apologizing for his past activism." The article was fair. I'd written directly to Mark Potok, the same person who had written the article about my message to the Forum eight months earlier. He'd started his career as a journalist, and had joined the SPLC as an investigator in 1997, just when I was an eight-year-old about to start my own activism. My family despised the SPLC, and I had passionately shared that feeling. Even being prepared to condemn everything I'd ever said, I was still bitter from years of guarding my privacy desperately from them.

While my dad was in the hospital following his stroke five years earlier, the same blog had published a series of articles calling for my mom to be fired from her job. They focused on the fact that she had been listed as the main contact for her boss's charity school in the Everglades that served almost entirely Black and Latino kids. Commenting on the news stories that they picked up on their blog, the SPLC commented, "Chloe Black is married to one of the most active white supremacists. We do not understand why she has not been fired."

Going back and forth from the hospital to where she worked every day, she was the only source of income for the family. Her office told her they wanted to support her, but she needed to distance herself from my dad. She wrote a short email that, like my first Forum post, hadn't been untrue as far as she saw it: "I am not involved with the Web site and do not agree with extremist or racially prejudiced views." People on the anti-Stormfront White nationalist part of the Internet attacked my parents for the sleight of hand, but neither of them took it especially seriously. She kept her job.

I'd thought Potok was the most straightforward writer at the SPLC. He seemed to follow journalistic standards I was used to with newspapers and TV, where some ground rules made things at least somewhat predictable. Journalists usually uphold basic rules. I could ask that I'd tell them something only if it was "off the record." If they agreed, then they wouldn't report or even repeat what I then said. I was fastidious about the terms of those interactions. Among White nationalists and antiracist groups, on the other hand, there were no rules, other than to keep things to yourself if you don't want them used against you.

I wanted to make my announcement to the SPLC, because no publication was more widely read by both antiracists and White nationalists than their "Hatewatch" blog. There was nowhere more appropriate to make my statement. The fact that the venue would offend my parents so much was devastating, but that was exactly why it was the right place.

Potok printed my letter in full at the end of his article, as I'd requested. That morning in July, his write-up started: "Black, 24, wrote that he had come to see the arguments of White nationalism as 'principally flawed,' adding that he had realized that American society is marked by an 'overwhelming disparity between White power and that of everyone else' and that White nationalism was really about 'an entrenched desire to preserve White power at the expense of others.'" The article went on, quoting the letter I'd finished and sent only a couple days before: "'Advocating for White nationalism means that we are opposed to minority attempts to elevate themselves to a position equal to our own,' wrote Black, who recently finished his third year at the elite New College of Florida."

"Black was explicitly apologetic," Mark Potok wrote, quoting the recognition of my faults that I'd avoided for so long: "I acknowledge that things I have said as well as my actions have been harmful to people of color, people of Jewish descent, activists striving for opportunity and fairness for all, and others affected." I'd tried finally to be explicit and take responsibility for what I'd said and done: "It is an advocacy that I cannot support, having grown past my bubble, talked to the people I affected, read more widely, and realized the necessary impact my actions had on people I never wanted to harm." Potok commented, "It was a remarkable statement for Black."

Reading it now, I can't help but cringe at how stilted and precisely I wrote it, but I remember the sense I felt in that moment, like I was jumping off a cliff into the abyss. I didn't know how to do it, didn't know where I'd land. I didn't know if anyone at all would be with me after I made it through. I described what I was doing and feeling as clearly as I could.

ON THE WEDNESDAY MORNING IN July that my letter went up, I woke up to countless emails and texts. A message from the New College communications department, who I'd never heard from before, with word that journalists were trying to get in contact with me, warning me of what I already knew: "Expect them to reach you directly, regardless of our protection of your information." I had already heard from various journalists that my name was blowing up in discussions across both White power and antiracist spaces. They wanted comments that I wasn't interested in offering. My dad's moderators seemed to be removing threats from Stormfront as soon as they saw them, but the wider White power Web wasn't as sparing. I didn't look up any responses from White nationalist pages.

I'd woken up late in a dark bedroom, blinds shut, blocking out the world. I saw a text from my dad: "I think you've been hacked. Call me back." I dialed him, and he asked if I'd seen the SPLC article, that someone from New College was playing a prank on me. I told him it was real. His familiar jokey tone ended. He said he needed to go, and hung up.

Allison had spent the previous weeks grounding me in the seriousness of what I had done by advocating for this scourge of an ideology. "It does very, very, very much bother me when you act like you've done nothing wrong or hurt no one throughout your WN career," she wrote me, "that your actions haven't had impact or that you haven't perpetuated racism." Watching the sun set on the beach one afternoon, I'd messaged with her, arguing this movement was populated by old people who were fading away, that Obama was president, and the future of the country might be fine, that the movement had only ever been a few hundred or a few thousand people. I admitted the horrors done in the name of this movement, but I told her I didn't see what I could do to stop it now. She argued back, "*It was wrong*, and WN hurts people and perpetuates stereotypes and harm and hatred. You contributed to that—unequivocally—and I don't necessarily see you ever acknowledging that." It was the push that I needed to make the choice I increasingly knew was right.

I knew how to apologize in aggregate for the harm I'd caused, how to speak to the media and apologize to a group, but I still couldn't do it personally. I couldn't tell my family I regretted and despised what they'd taught me, and what they still dedicated their futures to. I couldn't face myself, someone who'd told everyone my whole life that I wanted to believe things because they were right, not because they were convenient or felt right. I couldn't face the individuals I'd hurt and tell them I was sorry.

I could justify myself and explain that I'd grown up surrounded by the movement, that I'd made my choices knowing White nationalism was my parents' passion for decades before I was born. I had seen from my earliest memories that understanding their ideology, embracing it, and developing it was the main way I knew for them to be truly proud of me. I knew before anything else that the world despised everything they stood for, and that they found safety only among other White nationalists. They had been called stupid, ignorant, hateful, and backward since they were teenagers, and they had found a bitter community running from that same characterization. Embracing and sharing their worldview was the only reason they respected anyone, so I should have been able to forgive myself for directing all my abilities toward understanding it as well as they did, trying to make it my own. "I do not think this part will be easy," Allison had written me, back when I was still hesitating to write the letter. "In fact, I think that it will be by far the hardest part."

In my letter, I explained why it had taken me so long to get there, that I'd been unwilling to drive a wedge between myself and my family, even after I'd come to no longer believe in their ideology. I wrote that it was accepting the harm I had caused that had finally driven me to be honest about my slow disaffiliation from White nationalism. Over my life, I had believed that my beliefs were independent of my loyalty to my family and community. I hadn't thought I was trying to make them proud by parroting their beliefs. I'd argued with the critics of White nationalism as strongly as my family ever had. Finally coming to the place where I knew it was my family that I had to condemn meant accepting that I had done all of it out of love and fear, that loyalty had driven me to craft arguments for things I now saw were abhorrent. It meant realizing that I had pieced together an elaborate intellectual argument to support something that was so obviously wrong because I had been a child afraid of what it meant if it *were* wrong. Making this statement against my family meant accepting how much less power rationality, argument, belief, or fact actually held when identity and safety were at stake. I should have been able to feel that my justifications for my arguments had risen from my fear of losing the people

I cared for, even if that fear was so deep, I kept telling myself. The fact that I hadn't felt it unmoored me. I expected not to wake up as me that morning, and yet I was still me, only without a purpose or a foundation or a community.

Even as I had pushed back on Allison, I knew she was right. I had known it for a long time, but I'd forced her to be the one to say what I needed to do. The gap between what I knew was the right thing to do and the consequences of actually doing it had been unimaginable, but now I only regretted how long I'd dragged my feet. Accepting the movement was wrong, that I needed to get away from it, and that I had hurt people and could never take that back filled me with shame. Once I had taken the leap and made my peace with condemning this movement, however, I realized that changing my ideas had never been that hard, not really.

Over the days after my statement went online, I came to know what it meant to lose nearly every connection I'd ever known. The fact that I knew there were still people arguing online about this ideology felt hollow. Arguing about facts felt like a game in the face of so much loss of connection, family, and friends. It was like seeing that the world was a hologram and continuing to go to work. Allison reminded me that I still needed to make the arguments against White nationalism. I argued against the antisemitic conspiracy theories, against the faulty statistics and biology, against the ignorant views denying the role of wealth and policy in ruining people's lives.

I'd wanted White nationalism to be wrong for much longer than I'd actually had the arguments to dismiss it. In many ways, that situation had begun the moment I started to care for a community that told me over and over again how much hurt I caused them. If race was a social fiction, then the gap in experiences people had in this world based on the randomness of their birth was a crime. Getting the advantage of being born defined as White and then using that definition to make things worse for everyone else was beyond a wasted life. It was a repulsive, bitter, narrow, and stupid way to live. I didn't want to admit my own fault, but once I did, I realized it was the first step to moving beyond that shame. The thing that I couldn't solve, because I couldn't

take them with me, was the need to condemn the choices my family
continued to make.

I'VE BEEN HIT MANY TIMES with a sense of desperation when I've
relived moments from that morning. Allison told me students were
talking about the letter on Facebook, but she'd only been able to check
it occasionally between internship work. On the Forum, yet another
thread appeared: "Before any of you fucks take credit for 'changing'
Derek Black, stop stroking your egos. Just because he's renounced his
White supremacy doesn't mean all you asshats get to take credit for it."
The irony of seeing that opening post—promising yet another round
of meticulous dissection of my character and morality, and speculation
about my motivations—was how much I desperately wanted to believe
that I didn't owe my transformation to so many people who'd made
me feel like shit for years.

The Forum poster chastised the community, "All of you 'social
justice activists' are just glorified bullies who love that they have the
power to shit on others," she posted while I privately felt validated.
"People can change themselves, and I don't think the NCF community
deserves any credit." It had been half a year since I'd gnashed my teeth
and declared they weren't my community, that I thought they weren't
treating me as a human, when they had all the right in the world to be
wounded and angry. I didn't imagine this school ever welcoming me,
offering the sorts of connection and deep history I'd known before,
even as I desperately, secretly wished they would. I'd written a letter
condemning my family without being able to answer what, if anything,
could ever replace it. Meanwhile, my dad and David had taken to the
radio for a special emergency episode, so that David could pontificate
on his theory that I was suffering from Stockholm syndrome. Having
spent years with my "liberal captors," David argued, I must have come
to sympathize with them.

One of my friends from first year, who I'd commuted with to Habitat for Humanity when I got back, agreed with the opening message
that the condemnation hadn't done any good: "Students were even
attacking admissions for letting him slip by, and it's possible that if
admissions had not let him slip by and he had never attended New

College this process would have taken longer or ended differently." He continued, "I have a feeling some of the more mature and supportive people at NCF might have had a role in the process," and the first poster concurred: "Some of the more mature and supportive people probably did. Those are individuals, not the larger community."

At that moment, staring at the loss of my family, who bitterly, and of course correctly, blamed my desertion on the influence of the New College community, it was absolutely galling to admit the central and important role that the constant condemnation and ostracism had actually played. It had not been "persuasive" in the typical sense, of course, because I'd been repelled and sometimes afraid of many of those students. The strong, consistent, and informed condemnation had hurt. But I knew even then that it had been their reaction—and the arguments they made for *years* that it didn't matter if I was interpersonally kind if I advanced a cause that attacked the very people I purported to be friends with—that had driven me to reassess my choices.

LATER THAT AFTERNOON THE SPLC collated and then published the reactions of White nationalists, which I was trying not to read myself. "Derek was here all weekend, helping us build and replace old windows," my dad had written on Stormfront. "He's made it annoyingly obvious over the past few months he was no longer interested in WN activism, but he always said he was still WN. But he didn't give us a clue as to what he planned today." They went on to quote the suggestions of violence and murder directed toward me across the rest of the White power Web, describing it viscerally. Others debated my language, my arguments against the movement, and worked furiously to either denounce me or explain how I'd lost my mind. The SPLC article helpfully summarized what was apparently happening out there: "Numerous posters on racist websites theorized that Derek Black had taken up with a Jewish, liberal or non-White girlfriend; that he was secretly gay; that he was acting out of anger at his father; that he was being blackmailed by the SPLC with an unspecified secret; or that he was still a believer, but wanted a normal life." Any of these explanations sounded fine to me, and I wished they'd just decide on one and go with it.

I had wanted to avoid doing any more interviews that week, but I had also expected my dad to do the same. Yet, when my decade of White nationalist advocacy ended, my dad and I were once again offering interviews to the press, only now from opposite sides of the ideological spectrum. The *Daily Beast* published an article about my public and unexpected denunciation of White nationalism. My dad told the reporter, "I'm baffled. I'm disappointed in many ways. . . . I regret that I've lost a comrade in arms . . . It's gut-wrenching for me because Derek and I have traveled around the country since he was nine years old. But he's still my son and I love him." Nevertheless, typical of our relationship, my dad took the opportunity lash out at how I'd said it. "He's a good writer," my dad told them, "and if he were to come up with his own conclusions about this, he would have written something more original, not just regurgitated the same anti-White, multicultural standard bullshit that's taught in colleges everywhere."

Assuming my family would also avoid the press during such a personal moment, I was genuinely surprised to see their hand-wringing. Even my sister, Erika, who hadn't spoken in any article about our family to that point, "sounded equally mournful, telling the *Daily Beast*, 'This is a really sad time for us.'"

Initially, I followed the advice that the communications officer at New College offered: "You can tell anyone who reaches you that the letter speaks for itself." Galled by my family's display of mourning, however, I reached out with an addendum that the reporter added to the already-published piece. It was the last time I spoke out to any press for years afterward.

In that final statement, I dashed off a more bitter denunciation of all the students who had ostracized me. Sparked by my dad's and David's condescending speculation that I might have Stockholm syndrome, I clarified that "in the process of rethinking my ideas on White nationalism, people who disagreed with me were critical. But it's important to point out that the so-called activists who never spoke to me personally but chose to denounce me publicly, intimidate my friends, or otherwise try to peer pressure me did not have a positive impact." I felt like I couldn't let my dad and the crowds of middle fingers at my college unite. It would take me years to recognize that what was most painful and caused me to claim that "these expressions did not act as catalysts or contribute to my changing mindset," was simply not true.

I had spent my life thinking I could point to my White nationalist advocacy as proof that I knew how to stay strong in my convictions, never giving in to my desire to be kind and humane. The long process of accepting that my values would not let me choose to stay with my family, which I so strongly still wanted to do, was the first time, I was realizing, that I had actually done what I'd preached all those years. Whereas before I rose toward the praise from my community, now I had fractured that community, and I didn't see myself as joining any other. The closest thing I read to a welcome that day was from one of the students who had surrounded me at the party that first night back: "Now that DB is no longer a White supremacist, he can go on to be a low-key racist (much like many folks in the NCF community)."

AS MUCH AS I HAD considered what I needed to say publicly, it was the break from my family that I thought about the most that week, rather than anything I could do to fix what I'd done wrong. Overcome by feelings of shame, I retreated from everyone who reached out, and I imagined a future only of trying not to hurt anything, like walking clumsily through a store filled with fragile objects in every direction.

Zoë wrote me, replying to a thread we'd dropped months before: "Congratulations on graduating, I hope that next year goes well for you! It would have been good to mend some ties, but maybe we can someday in the future. I would like that. I heard about your letter, and I'm happy (/proud?) for you. I know that can't have been easy. I hope you're doing well."

I replied, "The letter aftermath has been sort of rough, but I feel like it's in-character to surprise people with stuff I publicly think/say. I kind of hope I become a little less notorious or at least more consistent with myself." Still, after all that time, I wasn't yet able to apologize, or speak like a human.

Zoë responded reassuringly, "To my mind, forming your own (kind of idiosyncratic) opinions is very in character for you. I'm really sorry to hear that about your family. Maybe with time they will come around." I didn't reply right away, because after spending so long figuring out what to say, I was still at a loss. I was trying only to move on to the next day, the next thing, to go for a drive, or bury myself in work.

The things I remember most clearly from that time aren't reading the article or Allison's responses. They're not seeing the Forum thread pop up, the endless texts and emails from press, friends, or enemies, not my sister's seemingly enraged calls, telling me she was coming to pick up my niece early, who I'd asked to come visit me that week. She was coming to take her away, I remember her saying, because now, of all times, she thought I was suddenly a bad influence.

Instead, what I remember most clearly is the curiosity I felt while writing a letter to my medieval history professor right after I'd read the SPLC article. I attached a picture I'd taken the day before at the Ringling Museum of a page from a medieval manuscript I was writing about as part of my summer internship. I asked him for help transcribing and dating it: "Could you take a look at an example of its script and give me your thoughts? I'd also be interested in what you think its purpose was. It's clearly a small book for carrying around, only about four inches high and three or so across." He replied a couple hours later with a kind note and some helpful feedback.

Distracting myself from what I was feeling with work was typical, and I was glad to have things to think about. The rest of me was contemplating what a future completely devoid of one's past could feel like. I had written Allison a few days earlier, "From like the age of nine, I consistently wanted to be a person who knew and could speak and read Latin. If I specialize this way, I'll become the person my childhood-self always wanted me to be."

IN THOSE FIRST COUPLE DAYS, I got a lot of nice messages from some of the people I'd been close to in my earliest days at New College, my closest friends asked how I was doing, or asked about my safety or plans. With few exceptions, I didn't reply. I relied for support almost fully on Allison, who was 800 miles away and in the middle of a summer research position.

Until I wrote my letter abdicating White nationalism, my mother ended every phone call with "I love you." That week, she emailed me, "You need to make new friends and family." She had always been my most ardent fan, and also the person who had pushed me to be ambitious and had encouraged me at every step. I knew her love wasn't dependent on sharing her ideology, but I realized that day that her respect, her sympathy, her encouragement, and her confidence in me were over. I had relied on my mother's care my entire life, and I knew in that moment I had lost the trust of the person I'd always counted on during any challenge. My mom's rejection felt like the most final confirmation that I could never again go back or feel the protection she'd always given me.

Although my dad didn't tell me he loved me until years later, during another especially scary medical event, I never doubted how much he cared about me. The only thing he cherished as much as me was the White nationalist community and movement he had built. In the days after he learned I'd condemned his identity, he had called, saying he'd thought it through, and had decided it would have been better had I not been born than put him through this pain. Although he called back a few minutes later to say he was sorry, that moment has never really left me, because it did feel like one era of my life had come to an end that night.

I MET WITH MY OLDER sister in a dark parking lot on the Gulf Coast of Florida on a Friday evening, the night after my letter condemning our White nationalist community was published and my family had spent the day processing it. My sister and I had planned for my niece to stay with me during my last couple weeks of the summer before I moved. When the end of July came, I would be heading out to Michigan, finding somewhere to live, and beginning work on a master's degree. Instead, my sister texted me saying she wanted to make the three-and-a-half-hour drive from the Atlantic side of the state to pick up her fifteen-year-old daughter and bring her back home. When I had told my niece what I had done, she'd called me stupid and said, "Our family will never forgive you." I took her out to lunch and we had crab soup by the beach, then went thrift shopping. The hours waiting on my sister to arrive felt like a clock ticking down to the end of my family.

My sister's sudden apparent lack of trust was galling. My niece was like a younger sister to me. I changed her diapers, walked around the yard with her to calm her down for naps, gave her bottles when her mom was at work. I had picked her up from school every day for years when I was a teen, babysitting her while she did homework, or unhelpfully trying to convince her to play hooky and go see a movie or walk with me to the playground. My sister had trusted me enough to let her daughter join me on a two-week road trip across the country when I was twenty-one. Three years later, a few weeks after graduating, and a day after publicly condemning the White nationalist movement that she and I had each grown up at the center of, she was driving across the state because she seemingly no longer trusted me. I had said I would bring my niece back in a week like we had planned, but she told me she couldn't in good conscience leave her daughter with me after how I'd betrayed our family. We met in a parking lot because I no longer trusted her to come to the house where I was staying.

For my parents, my denunciation of their beliefs was a blow to the passion of their lives by the child they had expected to embody it into the future. They and I had spent the previous day and a half in constant tearful phone calls, with them vacillating between saying their goodbyes, and then calling back to pick up where we'd left off. My sister, on the other hand, hadn't contacted me since the letter had gone public until she declared her daughter had to come home. The night before it had appeared, she'd called me when I'd taken my niece to the dollar theater, and I'd stepped out of the movie to answer. I'd normally have let it go to voicemail, but I suspected that was the last time she'd greet me warmly. Hearing her curtly announcing her plans to come get my niece seemed to confirm that.

My sister's embrace of our parents' cause inspired me when I was a child. We often talked on the porch late into the night about the worldview we had inherited, about how we could and should shape it into the future. We talked about why we thought it was righteous, and how we felt like we were standing on the turning point of history. I learned about gender politics for the first time from her, when she complained that the movement didn't value contributions from women like my mother, whose contributions were as essential but invisible. Without her, we agreed, neither David nor my father would have been able to build the organizations or conduct the national messaging campaigns she facilitated behind the scenes.

I always told Kristine she should run for office. As the daughter of David Duke, she'd have instant name recognition, and the media narrative about us being born to run wrote itself. I confirmed the power of her name recognition in 2000, when, with her permission, I sold her Palm Beach County sample butterfly ballot on eBay. The buyer asked for me to confirm that, in fact, David Duke's daughter's name was printed and visible on the label. He wanted it for a private museum he was curating on Southern American history. She always demurred from public positions, and instead completed college, cared for her daughter, and started working. When I ran for local office, she supported me because, she told me, I was important to the future of our family's movement.

When Kristine arrived in that parking lot years later to pick up her daughter, she asked to hug me and made a prediction that she's upheld ever since: that it would be the last time we ever hugged. She then told me it would likely be the last time we ever spoke, and that promise has also held true, including no response to my Christmas and birthday gifts or messages. She told me she had a few last things to say. She told me she wanted me to know that I was treading on our family's name and accomplishments, that I hadn't ever achieved any-thing worth the notoriety I received, and, if I had any self-respect, I would go away quietly to try to make something of my own and leave their legacy alone. At the time, I partly believed her, and going away silently was the only thing I wanted.

WHEN I PUBLICLY CONDEMNED WHITE nationalism, the days that followed were a slow-moving breach that felt like it was widening into an unbridgeable chasm. Over those days, though, it did become clear that my dad wanted to maintain our relationship in some form, and we made plans that I would come to visit him for his birthday the following week, before I left for Michigan.

When I arrived, though, the rest of the family refused to let me inside either my own house or my grandparents' house, where my dad's sixtieth birthday party was happening. With me sitting in the driveway, they sent my cousin's husband to carry the message that I wasn't welcome.

Instead, my dad left his own birthday party to get in my car, and he and I went to the bar and grill we'd been to a hundred times before, where I'd hosted all my earliest press conferences, just as he'd showed me. We then went to the spot by the ocean where he'd taken me to see the first sunrise of the New Year throughout my childhood. Over burgers and on a bench by the sea, we talked about what led me to condemn our movement. Despite living in his shadow, trying to make him proud of me my whole life, I had always known he respected my thoughts and opinions. It sometimes felt like he cared about what I thought too much, because the pressure to make the right calls as an adolescent could be overwhelming. Now, that same curiosity was in his eyes, and I tried to explain how race was an idea that had developed historically, that crime couldn't actually be tied to it, that IQ couldn't really be tied to it. I told him that the fact that White people had so much more wealth couldn't be explained or justified, couldn't be rationalized. It was only a crime, a violation from history we needed to change.

He thought my arguments were bizarre and tired. He said he'd heard this all before, although I didn't believe him. He admitted that the way I made them had the same style and spark he knew so well. He said it felt strange to see me, that he had expected me to seem different. Instead, I was the same person, and so was he. We loved each other, but we only knew how to express that love through our ideas and our identities as activists.

Eventually I needed to get back on the road to drive the twelve hours north to meet Allison in Virginia. We drove through the night, covering the final six hours north to her family's house in Ohio, where I met her mother and saw for the first time where she'd grown up. I asked if she waited at the front door for someone to come, and she just led me around the side to go in directly. The house was warm, and her mom greeted me after years of hearing about each other. It felt like being transplanted into a new kitchen table, in a new part of the country, a new place to call home.

CHAPTER 14

TRYING TO BECOME BETTER

JOURNALISTS' INQUIRIES DIDN'T STOP AFTER the flurry of news that followed my public renunciation, but they did significantly slow down as I tried to settle into my new life. I either ignored or rejected them. It felt like I lived almost in hiding, spending my days in the Western Michigan University library stacks in Kalamazoo, reading medieval texts, taking Latin classes, worried that journalists or angry White nationalists might show up at my house one day. Just before class, I'd flown back to Florida for one night to make my court date to confirm my legal name change. I swapped my middle and first names, as David had originally suggested, although for different reasons than he'd intended.

Any possibility of having to acknowledge my previous life felt like an intrusion and a threat to the privacy that I'd just started believing could last. I introduced myself as Roland to new acquaintances, my given middle name, and, like always, I didn't disclose my background to the other students in my medieval master's cohort. But here, the equivalent of being outed on the Forum happened without my knowing it. My reliance on anonymity ruptured soon after I arrived to the program, and people chose their sides a year before I knew they were even discussing my past. Not everyone in my program, I learned long after, believed I'd truly renounced my life in White nationalism, or that what I'd done was enough to warrant their acceptance. For the time being, however, I tried to live my life as if I would never have to answer more questions or revisit my legacy. On my own, halfway across the country, I focused on my academic work, and centered my social hangouts mostly on group bike rides on Michigan nature trails, hikes in the dunes and hills, and reading Latin with a friend every Sunday. I wanted my students and new friends to know the version of me I was learning how to be. I took that desire to an unhealthy degree sometimes, once answering "no" to a clerk at CVS who asked me at

2 a.m., while I was buying some junk food, if the phone number I'd entered in the rewards account of "Derek," was mine.

I'D PERHAPS ABSORBED THE WRONG lesson from finding my Sarasota landlord Maynard so easily when I showed up in Sarasota without a home. I arrived in Kalamazoo with a couch I could stay on for a few days while I looked for apartments. I'd found it through Couchsurfing, a website that connected hosts and travelers across the world and didn't allow payments. Allison and I'd used it several times over the previous year on trips, and the intimate community feeling it fostered reminded me of earlier road trips where I'd slept on the couches or in the spare rooms of White nationalists around the world. My host in Kalamazoo was an immigration attorney, fighting for undocumented workers largely from Central and South America. Just over a month from publishing my letter renouncing White nationalism, it felt nice to recognize that I was on the same side as him, although he didn't know who I was. Years later, he told me he probably wouldn't have invited me into his house if he had. I couldn't blame him for the reasonable call I hadn't given him the choice to make, but he said he didn't have any regrets, and in retrospect he was glad he hadn't known.

As the days went by, I messaged with Allison, who was moving back into the dorms at New College for her final year, and I found a room in a house to rent. We were beginning a long-distance relationship that would last for years. We were committed to that future, but it was deeply uncertain.

I didn't know how to just exist. I leaned on anonymity, because I couldn't imagine how to have the conversations necessary to explain my history. I spent hours in the library stacks, presented at academic conferences, volunteered for committees, participated in student organizations. Allison and I talked every night and messaged throughout the day. We shared interesting articles, still discussed racism and sexism and transphobia, but now without the antagonism.

I knew intellectually what I believed, but I didn't know how to embody it. Some of the memes I sent Allison that year are conspicuous in retrospect. One showed a Great White Shark with the caption, "Did you know? The ocean gets its saltiness from the tears of misunderstood sharks who just want to cuddle." We sent each other love notes and edited each other's schoolwork. She came to Kalamazoo that October for the first time during New College's fall break. Sitting across from my desk at the academic publisher where I worked part-time, studying to take the GRE exam she needed for her PhD program applications, she wrote, "This week with you has been amazing. It makes me very very happy to be around you and cuddling with you and loving you and seeing you and it's just been mega great and I can't wait for Dec/January." At winter break, she came back, and I took her across the Midwest for her grad school interviews. In one of her required diversity statements in those applications, which I helped edit, she'd written—among her other experiences and advocacy—that she had worked passionately "to educate and inform others about those whose voices may be harder to hear." It felt like a callout.

Her family took me in, inviting me to my first northern Christmas in their home that December, and caring for me when I had my wisdom teeth taken out while I was there. Allison and I went on road trips across Michigan, and I'd gotten gifts for my family members that holiday, but none of them replied or told me they'd received them. I heard later that my dad had eaten the chocolate I sent.

I visited New College during my spring break, which didn't align with theirs. Back on campus, things felt oddly familiar. Matthew and Allison and their roommates were in a new and better dorm. He still hosted Shabbat each Friday, and I saw mostly familiar faces on campus. Nevertheless, I stuck close to the dorm and to them, worried about how I'd be received on campus, even coming on a year after my public condemnation. I met with professors, and we finally took pictures of us all at one of Matthew's weekly gatherings. I still couldn't find the nerve to bring up my appreciation that he'd welcomed me to those dinners week after week. I wasn't proud of my past or even of leaving it, and I wasn't ready to acknowledge my shame. Allison likewise didn't want to talk about our experiences, which felt like something we had barely gotten past. When Blair, the student who'd intervened my first week back on campus years earlier, when I'd been surrounded at the party, came up to me to tell me how impressed he was at the courage I'd shown, I could barely acknowledge it. I dismissed him, said thank you with an eye roll. He replied that, no, he really meant it, and was so impressed. I said thanks again, and we separated.

Allison and I sat together on her bed as she accepted an offer to start a PhD in clinical psychology at Michigan State University. That meant she'd be less than an hour-and-a-half drive from me starting in the fall, but we had sworn to each other we wouldn't sacrifice professional decisions for each other, and when I graduated my master's program I'd be moving on to a PhD program at another university that could be anywhere. She sent me her thesis acknowledgments section to edit, and I only replied, "Like." For a section that thanked her family and Matthew, it hurt that she couldn't reference me. We didn't share photos of each other on social media or tag each other, and though we privately sent love notes back and forth constantly, she couldn't risk publicly naming me.

I returned to Michigan, and Allison followed soon after, and we toured apartments she might move into in the fall. At the end of my first year in Kalamazoo, I came back to New College to attend Allison's thesis defense almost a year to the day of mine, and to see the cohort I'd joined the school with graduate that spring. Everyone I'd gotten to know at orientation, and that one peaceful semester, would walk the stage that day. Because I had been a transfer student, Juan and Moshe had been two of the only students graduating with me a year earlier than the rest. I watched Allison's thesis defense and absentmindedly stole one of the glass snack dishes that the student-run cafe had brought when she asked them to cater it. That small plate still decorates our apartment, holding loose change, keys, and shells.

I HAD DROPPED THE MESSAGING thread with Zoë after my public letter, uncertain, ashamed, and unable to figure out what to say. I hadn't picked it up again when I was back a few weeks earlier. With graduation looming, I knew it might be my last chance. I wrote them, apologizing for not replying to their message, and promising, "I'm trying to become better at dealing with uncomfortable things." It still felt overwhelming to finally name what I'd avoided saying for so long, but I finally apologized, and it felt like letting a breath out that I'd been holding for years.

For a week, they didn't respond, but, a couple of days before their thesis, Zoë replied, "I think it would be nice to talk while you're here. I have trouble talking about things over email." That night we met at the bar just off campus. I apologized again and we talked about how those times had felt. When trivia started and the bar got loud, we decided to leave. We drove to a late-night diner. I remember them asking on the way if there were things I missed from my days as the White nationalist heir apparent, and I said I missed when people cared what I thought, the feeling of influence and power to be able to announce an idea or an event and see it happen shortly after. Zoë said it was scary that I'd ever had that power, and asked me if I was finding meaning in my life these days. I said I liked research, but I didn't know how to move on, and I felt like I was living in hiding. We stayed out late eating midnight breakfast. When we split up, back on campus, I wished them luck on the end of the semester, and they said it was nice to finally mend some of what we'd left so frayed.

TIME SEEMED TO ME TO move faster after we had all graduated, scattered across the world to jobs, grad school, the Peace Corps, and dozens of other eclectic landing spots. We communicated that summer through a shared email travelogue Allison organized between us former Shabbat attendees. That summer, I was in an intensive summer Latin course at the University of Toronto, which occupied me all day, every day. It was a busy summer, and focusing on work so intensely, in retrospect, was a sign of just how seriously I was avoiding the fact that I couldn't see a place for myself in the world.

Allison was working at an intense summer camp with social justice values, never off the clock, lacking cell or Internet reception, and navigating complicated social dynamics and occasional serious injuries. Matthew wrote that he was starting a job in finance in Atlanta.

IT BECAME CLEAR TO BOTH Allison and me that I wasn't handling well the new role I found myself in. I buried myself in academia to the exclusion of everything else, worried about even reading newspapers. At the end of the summer of 2014, Allison messaged me, "Everyone NCF on my newsfeed is posting stuff about #Ferguson." I told her

I didn't know what she meant. She replied, incredulous, "What?????
Literally all the past 2 days it's all there's been, even my phone has
been giving me NYTimes alerts about it. The police of Ferguson,
Missouri are occupying the town b/c protests and demonstrations." A
day later, at the closing dinner of the Latin course, one of the students
pointedly told me about police brutality against Black Americans.
I hadn't thought it was a targeted comment until he named David
Duke as someone who must love to see the terror White supremacy
perpetrated on the world.

I didn't know what I could do, what I could say. Despite continued
journalists' inquiries, angry midnight messages every now and then
from my family, and the occasional random call from some right-wing
figure who still had my number but hadn't heard that I'd condemned
their ideology, I refused to engage.

In the summer of 2015, I was once more burying myself in intensive
Latin study, but this time even more wholeheartedly. I had made a
pilgrimage to Milwaukee to spend the summer with about twenty others from a wide array of backgrounds to study under Father Reginald
Foster. He was a legend among Latinists, the irreverent former secre-
tary of Latin letters at the Vatican—meaning the personal scribe and
translator for the pope—for forty years. He had retired and returned
to Milwaukee several years earlier, after he got into trouble for telling
Bill Maher in the documentary *Religulous* that he thought the opulence
of the Vatican didn't accord with the message of Jesus: "If I were the
boss I wouldn't be living there. I mean, Jesus would probably be living
in some barracks out in the suburbs of Rome."

Back in his hometown, Father Foster brought a renegade version
of his unique summer Latin course that he'd taught every year at the
Pontifical Gregorian University in Rome. He taught us without any
payment every day but Sunday for six hours. We sat in a semicircle in
the basement of the church of the Order of the Discalced Carmelites
that he belonged to. I'd arrived in Milwaukee without knowing how
to find him, but I knew he planned to host summer school, so I rented
a room and stood outside the Carmelite church a few hours early,
assuming they'd know something. Right on time, a medical transport

van pulled up and he descended in a wheelchair, his legs wrapped in gauze. He yelled, "Are you a Latin student?" I said yes, and he asked me to get his bags and bring them in.

For the rest of the summer, the eclectic group, including a high school teacher, a graduate student, a novitiate priest, a monk, several extreme traditionalist Catholic priests, and several students in their twenties who had traveled from around the world showed up and spent the day translating Latin passages as he brashly critiqued us. After class, he'd hold speaking circles for us to practice spoken Latin while sitting on the curb. His spoken lessons had become a small pedagogical revolution in the field since he'd started them decades earlier.

OVER THE PREVIOUS YEAR, I'D begun to send articles to Allison for us to talk about issues of racism, sexism, transphobia, and classism as often, if not more so, than she initiated those discussions with me. Despite engaging privately, I was still terrified of being drawn into public discourse, because I could see no outcome other than being shamed for the horrible things I'd once said and done. Apologies to individuals felt hard enough, but at least through private engagement I could ask them to tell me their experience and learn what could constitute repair. A public apology for crimes against society, against the world, would be so broad and yet so vague that I did not see any way forward other than to keep hiding, hoping no one would ask me to face something I had no answer for.

One Friday afternoon, during our half-hour Latin class break, I checked my phone and my stomach dropped. With the subject line "Washington Post story request" the email was from a *Post* journalist named Eli Saslow. He began the email, not even perfunctorily clarifying whether he had the right person, "Dear Roland, I'm guessing you're away from school for the summer, but I wanted to update you before I move too far ahead with this story for the *Washington Post*."

Eli had learned about my story when he went on Stormfront following the path of a young White supremacist mass murderer, who earlier that month had attacked the Emanuel African Methodist Episcopal Church in Charleston, South Carolina, and killed nine Black worshippers on the same day that Donald Trump had announced his candidacy for the presidency. Both those news stories had already been weighing on me, and the idea of someone writing a story about me in connection to them was horrifying.

"I want to write about this," he continued, "because I think you have thought through—and lived—some of these issues in ways that are complicated, smart, hopeful and nuanced, which is an important thing." He assured me in the email that he wanted to write the story "in a way that makes you feel comfortable and that gives you some measure of control over what I include about your life now." Having spent a lifetime responding to journalists and now fleeing them like I was being hunted, that offer still felt unusual for the level of care he seemed to be implying, but I was mostly in damage control mode. He concluded the email, "I'd probably want to come out and spend some time with you, and take my time to get this right."

I wrote to Allison, forwarding his message, telling her I was alarmed he'd identified me so confidently. I had expected being listed under a different name to be more of a deterrent to being found than it ever actually was. It had delayed the inevitable, and it had allowed me to teach without my reputation getting in the way. The search results for "Roland" led my students to my teaching profile, rather than to my legacy of White supremacy and hate. Journalists like Eli looking for me had access to the court records of my name change, people-searches that brought up my lease in Kalamazoo, and simple online searches could turn up my New College alma mater at Western Michigan University. When I ignored him, he then followed up in a way that worried me he was threatening to proceed without me. "I'd love to talk and gauge how you're feeling before I start moving forward with phone calls to friends, family, etc., so if you are getting these emails will you please let me know?"

Over the weekend Allison and I talked about it, about how he seemed genuinely unique in his style, care, and the length of his articles. He tended to give many thousands of words to his subjects, and he had previously won a Pulitzer Prize. I was deeply uncomfortable in the way I was living, and a journalist willing to take the time to hear me out about what had happened at New College could at least help me share the experiences I had never explained to anyone but Allison.

I was already unnerved to receive Eli's emails at all. When I didn't respond, however, he affirmed all my worst stereotypes of journalists being invasive and aggressive by reaching out to my landlord (though, to his credit, Eli didn't explain anything about my background). I replied to Eli and shut down any hope I'd cooperate for the story. "No," I wrote, "I'm not interested in this and I consider your messages and calls to people I know an invasion of my privacy." He didn't acknowledge what had pushed me away so forcefully, but his response was professional, and I hoped that would be the end of it.

OVER THE NEXT YEAR, THE idea of speaking out felt just as disconcerting, but it also began to feel necessary. My family and their movement kept appearing in the press, and the social interconnections, ideological foundation, and political talking points they had spent their lives producing were glaring at me as I kept trying to avoid the movement altogether. Staying silent was beginning to feel like a choice I could no longer ethically make.

In August 2016, Hillary Clinton gave a speech in which she accused Donald Trump of "taking hate groups mainstream and helping a radical fringe take over the Republican Party." She named White nationalism and called it the "paranoid fringe in our politics" that now "had the nominee of a major party stoking it, encouraging it, and giving it a national megaphone." She condemned Trump for retweeting "White supremacists online, like the user who goes by the name 'White-genocide-TM.' Trump took this fringe bigot with a few dozen followers and spread his message to 11 million people." She went on to condemn David Duke outright, quoting from the radio show I'd originally convinced him to start. "On David Duke's radio show the other day," Clinton reported, "the mood was jubilant." She described a line of David's I was familiar with because it was the message I had been raised under and had tried to enact in the world myself. White nationalist messages had not taken over the Republican Party, but they were coming closer than ever. Clinton called out the messaging my family and I had helped foster, saying: "Racists now call themselves 'racialists.' White supremacists now call themselves 'White nationalists.'"

Clinton concluded that speech with an event from her own family's political history. Recalling his 1996 acceptance speech for the Republican presidential nomination, she described how Senator Bob Dole declared, "If there is anyone who has mistakenly attached themselves to our party in the belief that we're not open to citizens of every race and religion, then let me remind you, tonight this hall belongs to the party of Lincoln and the exits, which are clearly marked, are for you to walk out of as I stand this ground without compromise."

Listening to Clinton's speech made me realize that we had both learned different lessons from the past decades of American political history and from that election in particular. Where she saw progress, I had grown up among adults who saw reactionary hostility to racial diversity as the most powerful subset in conservative politics. Dole may have won that primary, and Clinton's husband may have been reelected to the presidency, but the lesson should not have been that racism was defeated.

Bob Dole's speech appeared to Hillary Clinton like a victory of moderation over radicalism and racial hate. It looked to the followers of Buchanan, and to the supporters of David Duke, on whom he had built his base of support, as a temporary defeat in a much longer revanchist strategy that had begun decades earlier and would continue into the next century. The story of racist progress in America over the last few generations is full of moments like these. Few of them amounted to definitive victories of racism or of antiracism. Yet it seemed like the mainstream press preferred a sanitized vision of American progress that denied how thoroughly conservative politics relied on White power positions and messaging.

From the time I was a kid, begging my dad to take me along with him as he visited old comrades and attended conventions, I'd seen what drew people to White nationalism. Most people I met came from relatively privileged backgrounds: private schools, suburban homes, reasonably well-paying careers, or owning their own businesses. They were mostly men. They were motived by the overarching desire to reject feelings of shame. They identified Whiteness as their own greatest source of pride, and it was only friends within the movement who validated that pride. I remember once speaking to a musician who had recently come to the movement. He had been alarmed to discover, as he put it, "that this is all there is." I responded by telling him something like, "This is enough."

IT FELT LIKE I SPENT the rest of the spring and summer of 2016 sitting in Michigan and Chicago breweries while TV chyrons scrolled through Donald Trump's various outrages. I had watched his declaration to run for president while he called Mexicans rapists the year before. I had seen that he had secured the Republican nomination in the same way. When one of my grad school friends commented that they hadn't thought the victories would come so quickly, I said that didn't seem odd, but I hoped a defeat in the general election would prevent the GOP from risking so much on campaigns touting White racial aggression in the future.

As the months leading up to election day approached, it had become obvious I needed to do more to counter the messaging of this movement. Clinton was making speeches about how "White nationalist" messages were dominating the Republican's campaign. I had lived in the shadow of Donald Trump's Mar-a-Lago home my entire childhood, and he was now threatening to bring the movement I had hoped to lead closer to power than it had ever come. I got back in touch with Eli, whose aggressive messages had put me off, but whose long, narrative style was the only format I could imagine using to talk about my experience. I didn't think my story could make any sense without all its nuances.

I wrote him apologizing for being rude the previous year and asked to talk off the record about what kind of story he'd want to write. "Yeah, I imagine I have something to say about it, maybe something worth saying, but there's lots of ways to do that wrong, so I'm extremely cautious. I also have selfish motives, not wanting to get in the middle of any of this." In the weeks leading up to meeting with Eli in August of 2016, I sent Allison my commentary on the national news. "He might muck everything up," I wrote her once about Trump's campaign for president, "but it feels like it gives him too much credit to think he could navigate actually becoming a dictator. He's literally just a guy who doesn't read much and doesn't know much. I mean, I guess being ignorant doesn't mean he wouldn't know how to consolidate power." For the first time since my days as an outspoken White nationalist strategist, I was trying to employ those same instincts, but now against the movement I'd helped foster.

Watching the election campaign, I told Allison that I was starting to feel implicated as I heard talking points from the movement appear in the news and from candidates. As jarring as the first interaction had been, we agreed that Eli was the best writer to share what had happened to us at New College. Neither of us had ever talked about it with other people after my letter to the SPLC. I'd explained my beliefs, but I'd never told anyone how they'd changed.

I DIDN'T INITIALLY TELL ELI anything about my life. I had moved on to start a PhD at the University of Chicago, and I'd asked that my department not list my name on the website along with all the other students. Allison was still living in East Lansing, where her PhD program in clinical psychology at Michigan State University was progressing. If the interview didn't go well, I wanted to limit the amount of information I gave him in case he decided to proceed with the story without my consent.

So I agreed to an interview, but I asked to meet in Ann Arbor, home of the University of Michigan, forty miles from Allison's apartment. I was hoping that a neutral location unconnected either to Allison or me would make things more difficult for Eli to track me down if I bailed. We met at a diner, and after breakfast we walked around the city, and I realized quickly I was feeling comfortable and growing in my confidence that I could trust him. For the first time, I described what I had experienced at college a few years before. I still didn't want him to know many details before I was sure this was the right way to go, so I refused to tell him anyone's names. To keep things straight, that afternoon we created a code system: Matthew was "Shabbat Friend" and Allison was "Sailing Friend." I held all day that Sailing Friend was obviously not also my partner, though by the end of the day he ventured to guess that they were one and the same.

When I got back to Allison's apartment in East Lansing at the end of the day, I told her I liked him, and that I thought I wanted to go forward with the story. The problem was that I clearly couldn't tell the story on my own. My perspective was only one side of what had happened at New College. Hers was another, and many other people at school had each experienced their own slice of the dramatic and traumatic years we spent together.

Over two full days, Eli and I walked around Ann Arbor and then Dearborn, which I suggested at the last minute because I'd been wanting to visit several Arab restaurants and museums. The hours flew by: stopping for breakfast at a Yemeni bakery, lunch at a famous Lebanese restaurant, coffee in the afternoon, and long walks through parks and museum exhibits I didn't have time to actually study. Eli kept notes and would regularly ask me to clarify something I'd described or where on the timeline things fell.

For the first time I was telling the story of the years that led to my breaking with my family and everything I'd known until then. When I got home the second night, I told Allison how surreal it had felt that I'd never told anyone, and Allison and I had never needed to tell it as a story. As she and I discussed it that night, an email from Eli popped up asking for source material, including Forum posts, conference itineraries, and campaign documents. It was clear that the subject of our bizarre and difficult time at college was about to grow beyond us. He ended his email asking if I could forward him "emails from Sailing Friend sharing articles about the concept of race and its invalidity and structural inequality."

The next day, Eli talked to my dad, who told him he thought I was choosing to speak out again because I "missed the attention and havoc." I wrote Eli explaining how much my dad was misunderstanding me, that what made this all worth it for me was sharing my perception of the imminent threat of White power in our politics, which was something I was "willing to give up some privacy and tranquility to spread." It boiled down to the fact that "the problem is not some wicked feeling in the hearts of a few people, which is what everyone seems to mean when they say 'racism.'" Looking back, I can see pretty clearly how much I wanted to turn the conversation away from me, away from more attention that had made me self-conscious and ashamed. Instead, I wrote, "It's the fact that our ancestors established a global system where people of European descent dominated the power, wealth, land, etc. and identified people who look like us as the in-group." Since condemning my family and stepping away from the movement, I had expected never to speak publicly again. Yet, over those years I couldn't help thinking about what I *would* say if I were to return to public advocacy. It felt inane, but one of the main things my family and other White nationalists had criticized me for was the tone and phrasing of my letter. I wanted to figure out how to express the realities I'd come to understand in ways that White nationalists would be able to hear. "The result is 'White privilege,'" I told Eli, "and that doesn't mean every White person is rich, it means that we all live in a society made for us and the negative consequences of that are huge for everyone else."

"Since dropping out," I told him, "I've had to watch as White race politics continue to loom large, but now I have watched the same things that I once thought could propel the WN agenda play a huge role in this country and the world." Eli agreed that these issues were a big part of the story, but also that the story couldn't be foremost about arguing these issues that had been so hard-fought for me. It was also a story about me, about how it was possible for people to change their minds. To write it, he needed to focus on my conversations with people, my relationships, my sense of community, who had ostracized me and who had reached out. He needed to understand where I came from. It was also becoming clear that the story was incomplete without Allison's perspective. She trusted my judgment of journalists and of his character, but she didn't know Eli herself. She composed an anonymous email for me to send him, inviting him to come to her apartment.

She told him she was conflicted with "a compulsion to be open and honest and to see Derek's story told accurately, but I am nervous about the tricky balance of being open and honest while also considering the implications of whatever stories I tell." To keep her from being publicly connected to me, we still didn't post pictures together often, even on our private social media. When we went to a romantic cabin on the shores of Lake Huron in northern Michigan, her Facebook post about it described the isolation and nature, but didn't mention that anyone had joined her. It was the practical thing to do, but it hurt that we kept our names disconnected outside of the most private spaces. We loved each other and were building our lives together, but we also could not imagine a future where the shadow of my unresolved past didn't loom behind us, waiting to jump out again.

For so long, we had hoped that the hard days were behind us. It felt like we had come through it and could now live our lives. Talking about those days publicly would end a period that had felt like peace, if in retrospect it looked like hiding. The presidential campaign of 2016 was revealing new forms of cruelty in the political mainstream, and I increasingly felt implicated. I had already put Allison in a terrible position by always making her the one who had to name what I needed to do next. Now I still needed her to speak. What had been important and powerful was our privacy and trust, which we now needed to figure out how to share with the world. I hated feeling like I was sucking her into my vortex more than I ever had before.

WHEN ELI'S STORY CAME OUT on the front page of the *Washington Post* in October 2016, Allison was staying with me at my apartment in Chicago. We woke up and pulled out our computers to read it online in the Sunday morning light that surrounded my bed. We read the cover with a slight cringe: "The White Flight of Derek Black." It felt strange, disorienting, and unnerving to see my face on the cover of the newspaper and my name in the headline. Interacting with journalists had once been familiar territory, but that had come from years of advocacy and media training by my family. That morning, I didn't think I had a cause to advocate for, or a community to stand with.

Although I'd urged Matthew to withhold his name from the story, he asked me why he shouldn't want to accept that recognition, unless I was asking him to stay anonymous. I told him I would never ask him not to do it if he wanted to, and I appreciated him being willing to be publicly named. I expected my story to draw another round of condemnation, but this time it would be national. The Trump campaign for the presidency was in its final weeks, and most commentators expected him to lose. I thought my story would land like it had on the Forum, as a disconcerting story of "one fucking guy" who had spent a lifetime saying the most vile things and didn't deserve much credit for stopping.

I hadn't thought much about the immediate future other than trying to anticipate the potential backlash I might face from friends who I hadn't told, or people from the university that had admitted me without knowing my background. At first, I wondered whether the discrepancy between the Roland they knew and the Derek who appeared in the story might mean that no one in my life made the connection. Over the coming days I was disabused of that hope.

The next morning, I received an email from a faculty member that started, "I'm quite sure I've never seen one of our PhD students in medieval history appear on the front page of the *Washington Post* before." After I sent the article to another advisor, he responded, "I do not believe in much else, but I believe that people can learn, though as a society we do little to show we believe that."

When I responded with my thanks and shared that I was receiving offers from literary agents and book publishers, I got back some of the most helpful advice I ever heard: "If you have means enough to live, use that freedom to learn what you want to be and can be. You will have in due course occasion to digest and recount what you have to tell, and by waiting you will have perspective." Seven years later, I'm not sure I'm any wiser, but I know more and have done more than I could have imagined then, and I finally feel less afraid.

I WATCHED OVER THE NEXT couple of weeks as celebrities and global politicians reshared the article across social media with affirming statements, and I once again experienced that sense of distance between who I felt I was and who people wanted or needed me to be. I was drawn again to the sense of purpose that advocacy can bring, but I dreaded the self-consciousness and the perceived need to assume a role that people expected me to take on.

The days after the story came out felt like a waking dream. I imagined being recognized while I walked around Hyde Park. No one did, but they did start emailing me after they'd seen me in a workshop or recognized me from a class. This became relatively common and made me extremely self-conscious in every new room I entered. What was completely different from any other time I'd spoken publicly were the waves of positive letters and invitations to work in antiracist causes and in opposition to antisemitism.

While quotes from Allison featured in the story as things said by anonymous "friends" and she had been actively in conversation with Eli to flesh out the story, she had decided to withhold her name to protect her privacy; thus, Matthew and I became the only two named figures in a story that was spreading on social media and leading to dozens of invitations to speak, travel, and accept humanitarian awards from social justice organizations. We started to say yes, and Allison traveled with us often as my partner, but it was only when the organizers cared enough get to know us all personally that they realized how essential both of them were to the complete story.

DONALD TRUMP WON THE PRESIDENCY a little over two weeks after Eli's story came out. What had initially seemed to land as an optimistic story of change for an audience that expected Trump to lose became instead a warning about the power of the movement. The night before the election, the *New York Times* predicted Trump had a 15 percent chance to win, and op-eds appeared arguing it wouldn't be enough for him simply to lose, but that it was important that he lose by such a margin that no one would try such a hateful campaign again.

After Trump's upset victory, the messages I received were more frantic, focused on attempts to understand the structure and history of the White nationalist movement, how they thought, and what they wanted. The morning after Trump's electoral victory, I went to a cafe and wrote an op-ed for the *New York Times* with what I wanted to say publicly for the first time. I expressed the despair I felt at realizing so many of the expectations I had held about the future of our country and that I had condemned only seemed to be confirmed.

It felt bizarre to think of the alternate timeline I could have been experiencing. It was a world where I would have been with my family and White nationalist leaders I knew, gathered somewhere together as shocked as the rest of the country. I knew they'd be planning rallies, dealing with a deluge of calls and emails from alarmed journalists, as well as a flood of new recruits and people interested in their movement. I would have been one of the most prominent faces of the movement that night, being asked to speak on behalf of it, and asked by the community what I thought we should do next.

In the op-ed, I described my background, my experience of leaving it, and how I was ashamed to admit I had ever deluded myself into thinking that it was ethical to ignore the core beliefs of this movement, and the broader implications of how deeply racist ideas ran in our society, because our society was racially unequal and unjust. So long as that was true, White people would continue to buy into fears of losing their position. That motivated members of the movement decades ago, and it was continuing to drive it now.

I knew my story was being received as one that proved that civil conversations and debate could change even the most hardened racists, so I thought the most important thing I could contribute was to clarify what I finally had space to admit. It had been those private and welcoming conversations that had made an impact on me, certainly, but I never would have been motivated to answer for myself had I not faced severe backlash and condemnation from my community first. That backlash was, in fact, critical. I made a summons to readers that I was really making to myself, reminding myself that I couldn't justify continuing to turn away.

IN THE WEEKS AFTER THE 2016 presidential election, the *New York Times* ran an article entitled "White Nationalism: Explained" that was as surreal to me as anything I had seen over the previous months, because they were treating the White nationalist movement as a serious intellectual threat. As millions of people reeled in shock at Trump's electoral victory, the *Times* drew a distinction between "White supremacists" and "White nationalists." It reassured readers that "for many White people, of course, the growing diversity is something to celebrate. But for others it is a source of stress. The White nationalist movement has drawn support from that latter group."

At the end of November, Richard Spencer's National Policy Institute meeting had gathered in downtown DC and brought together all the old faces I knew from the conferences I'd attended in the DC area growing up. I could predict the speeches before I even saw videos, including the one that spread virally of Spencer at the lectern later in the evening Hitler-saluting and screaming "Hail Trump, hail victory" while the audience chanted it back. I could immediately imagine the chagrin and rolled eyes of some of the professors and uptight White nationalist gentry who had spoken earlier in the day. The moment encapsulated just how little in the movement had changed, despite the grandiose articles about an alt-right umbrella that represented a new coalition. White nationalists were the same people. They had the same beliefs, and they acted the same. Only now they had direct lines into the White House.

AROUND THAT SAME TIME, ELI proposed expanding his original story into a book. That meant going back to speak with more people, and it meant revisiting whether Allison still wanted to remain anonymous. She talked with me, with her friends, and with her academic advisors. The advice she got back was that it was better to live a whole life, not to divide herself into categories and try to keep them separate. Publishers and agents urged me to tell Eli not to write a book about my time at New College, because it would preempt anything I had to say myself, and he told me he would do whatever I decided. I told him to do it, because he could reach out and capture the personal stories of so many New College students I still didn't have the nerve to email after all these years, afraid to barge back into the lives of the people I had cared for and hurt. Their stories weren't mine to tell.

I always contacted them first, letting them know I trusted Eli, but that it was up to them whether they wanted to participate. He was able to talk to my friends, Forum posters, organizers of the teach-in, faculty members, administrators, staff, and members of the community. The number of interviews he conducted with my former classmates and faculty expanded eventually to over a hundred people. Speaking through a mediator had long ago become the main way I knew how to face the parts of myself and my past that I had been afraid to reckon with. Slowly, however, I was coming to recognize that I needed to learn to speak directly.

THE FIRST PUBLIC EVENT I spoke at was at Georgetown University, a couple of days after Trump's inauguration, and three and a half years after I had condemned White nationalism. On my trip in, live coverage of the recent Women's March played on the airport TVs. Blair, my friend from college who had pulled me out of that first party, now worked in DC and we met for dinner in Dupont Circle, and afterward we walked through the monuments along the Tidal Basin. The white marble was brightly lit, and the cold early January air meant we had the walk mostly to ourselves.

The next day, I went to Georgetown to speak in front of an audience that still seemed shaken. In the moments before we went on, I met the student organizers of the event and the professor of history and African American studies, Dr. Marcia Chatelain, who they'd selected to moderate the conversation. She said she thought there was a lot of trepidation over what would come next. I asked whether she thought they'd hold their fears against me and whatever role I had played in fanning those fires. She was surprised by the question and said she didn't think that was anyone's reaction. It was my first time speaking to an audience about White nationalism—my first time advocating *against* it in front of people—and describing the goals and structure of White nationalism as a social movement.

How to do that was perplexing. I had spent a lifetime absorbing the lessons and history of White nationalism, and then contributing to it myself, but my experiences talking about it in the years since had been limited. I was conflicted about whether spending time talking about White nationalism could even help push back against a social wave that was simultaneously so much bigger than my experiences and yet deeply personal. I found myself talking about what it felt like to live within the movement, the ways that community reaffirmed belief, what they thought they believed, and what had happened to break me out of it. I argued that day against the idea that civil discourse alone could combat racism. I argued that White nationalists were using the media in ways I had done myself years before, and that it was unacceptable for journalists to play into these strategies. Careless coverage would actually build this movement they were only now beginning to pay attention to. I warned them that the sensationalist coverage of my former movement was often just a distraction at a time when we needed to engage in critical thinking to chart a way forward.

The next day, as I landed back in Chicago, I was thrilled to read my message reflected back at me in the Georgetown student newspaper. These were opinions I'd privately harbored for years since condemning the movement, but leading such a private life had meant I never expected to see them broadly considered in print. It felt like the first step to not just shouting stop, like I had when I wrote my public letter, but to actually pushing back using the perspective I'd gained since then.

I didn't know if I was being an activist, an advocate, or a witness. For most of my life, I had acted strategically for my cause. Now, for the first time in my life, I didn't know what I wanted to accomplish.

AS THE MONTHS HAD GONE on, Matthew, Allison, and I each tried to navigate a world that seemed to ask us for reassurance, but needed what we said to be neat and simple. We felt like our experiences were messy, frequently unpleasant, and we were never sure whether there were broad takeaways that anyone should be drawing from us. We decided that, so long as people were using us as examples, we had an obligation to provide some more context.

Matthew messaged us that he'd received an invitation for him and me to travel to New York for an event that would honor both of us with an award in the name of Elie Wiesel, author of *Night*, one of the foremost advocates for memorialization of the Holocaust. Wiesel had passed away several months before, and his only son, Elisha, didn't understand at first why I was reluctant to accept an award. The more we spoke, the more I understood the unexpected sense of commonality I shared with him. The gulf between our experiences was vast, but I was surprised to recognize a shared burden under the shadows of expectant and proud fathers. I love my father and have deep empathy with his experience, but I am ashamed of choices he made. I was trying to be more like him by carrying out the values I held, but his choices left me feeling hurt and used. Elisha had grown up likewise being told about the greatness of his father, but, he remembered, "When I was young, I'd think 'Oh God, here comes another guy telling me how great my father was.' Now, I'm trying to be more like my father was."

When Matthew, Allison, and I met Elisha, we talked late into the night, telling him the full story of Allison's role, and why she had chosen not to appear in the story. Elisha asked if the three of us would consider speaking publicly together with him as the moderator, and we accepted. It would become the first of many public talks that Allison and I gave together, in which she could finally express her ambivalence at the role she'd played at New College.

I remember her advice back then, to someone who had asked how to be better at persuading other people: "I believe the way to impact a specific person is to *be* a specific person in their world." For her, how-ever, that choice had a weight to it. She had chosen to become *a specific person* in my life, which had placed the priority on me, rather than her becoming more involved in social activism, or simply standing as an ally against what I once stood for. Although our personal relationship grew and expanded over the years in ways neither of us could have ever expected, we still looked back on our origins with uncertainty. "As someone who thinks it's important to be an ally to people of color and use whatever power I have as a White person to act against racist agendas," Allison remembered once, she didn't believe she should have prioritized me. As I've written this book, a comment she made then has stuck with me throughout all the scenes: "Everyone argues with people in college. It regularly strikes me as crazy that arguments I had with a specific person in college are now receiving attention."

FOR MYSELF, I WAS LEFT with the question of my own role going forward. Invitations kept coming in, but it wasn't uncertainty about whether I could tell the full story, but rather my uncertainty about whether I really belonged anywhere I was being asked to go, that gave me pause. A part of me enjoyed once again being able to participate in activism, to write speeches, and plan out messages. It felt meaningful in a way that purely academic work never had. I was still scarred by the realization that the last time I'd engaged in those feelings, I had deceived myself so much. The words I had put out into the world had hurt people, and I could never be sure the extent of the damage I was personally responsible for.

In the fall of 2017, after the horrific Unite the Right march on Charlottesville, Virginia, during which an antiracist protestor was murdered, organizers for the Obama Foundation invited me to present on radicalization and White nationalist organizing at their inaugural summit. They were bringing five hundred civic leaders together in Chicago during the first year of the Trump administration and had heard me speaking to the press.

It felt presumptuous and ridiculous for me to speak to this audience of activists from all over the world. I had won my first and only election in 2008 partly by fearmongering against Barack Obama's first presidential campaign. I asked if I could just be there rather than speak. I attended quietly, and I met several people who are close friends to this day. I had many awkward conversations with people in the hallways, explaining what had brought me there. I sat next to Obama himself at a session on how to prevent hate and radicalization online. We shook hands at the end of the summit. He said he was glad I'd come, but I don't think he knew who he was talking to right at that moment.

I'd been in correspondence with the United States Holocaust Memorial Museum in Washington, DC, about doing an event with Matthew about my experiences. I was intrigued but also deeply unsettled about the idea. In accepting Elisha's award, I remembered the organizers giving me a standard offer to invite people to the event who I knew might like to support the group, but most of the network of benefactors I'd left behind would have accused me of supporting a global conspiracy to bring down Western society. Yet I felt welcomed in that remarkable space, and I had done all I could in advance to make sure there wasn't some misunderstanding. I still wasn't sure if I should be anywhere important, be given any platform to speak, and second-guessed anyone who invited me to do anything as having maybe not thought it through well enough.

After the Charlottesville march, I was worried my story would be used by people to argue that civil discourse—at the expense of civil disobedience and resistance—was the most effective or only way to combat Nazism, White nationalism, or White supremacy. I certainly know the power for radical change that can come from love and friendship, but it's a nightmare to me to become a figurehead for a message that lets people off the hook from going to protests, making public statements denouncing racism, condemning it loudly, and other uncomfortable actions.

Watching the violence in Charlottesville, led by people I knew, with antiracist friends in the crowd opposing them, I felt horrified and implicated. Suggesting that the best course of action is to let White nationalists speak their views more widely so that we can debate them is extremely counterproductive. Antiracism has the moral high ground that I once tried vainly to claim for my family's movement. It is a movement whose most basic principle is that there's no theoretical bounds to the sphere of people the movement cares for and seeks to protect. Elisha wrote me at that time, asking if I was working on writing something publicly to contextualize that terrible outburst of White-power violence that David Duke had been central to. I responded that I'd been working on a response all summer, long before the riot had happened, because I knew something like it was coming. When the time actually came, I realized I couldn't contextualize the moment as being any less horrifying than it seemed. It was genuinely a moment when a broader cross section of the White power movement than had ever seen before had come together. I made the mistake of looking at David's online statements to quote him, and I was disturbed at how callously he dismissed the violence. Writing for the *New York Times* again less than a year after Trump's election, I realized the most important thing was reminding everyone constantly that this is only a fringe movement if our institutions expel its ideology. White nationalist ideas aren't alien to our culture, as some people tried to claim in the aftermath of that moment. If they were, the rally would never have happened, and the president would never have defended it. White racism is baked into the fabric of our lives, and the most radical forms of it only remain marginal when we work constantly against it.

The tensions surrounding my work in these spaces and my own history have often hit me unexpectedly. The next summer, I worked for months at Facebook as part of a team of researchers and product designers hoping to "increase empathy, understanding, and humanization of the 'other side.'" We often had to navigate our own experiences of alienation and double standards, even (and maybe especially) within a project meant to find ways to facilitate that experience for others. Near the end of the project, many of us went into town to see the new Spike Lee movie, *BlacKkKlansman*, based on the experience of a Black police officer, Ron Stallworth, who went undercover in the 1970s and struck up a relationship on the phone with David Duke. Stallworth remembered: "Sometimes my conversations with David Duke were light, personal discussions about his wife, Chloe, and their children. How they were doing and what was going on in their lives."

The portrayal of David as a young man was eerily familiar, down to his vocal inflection and quirky turns of phrase. It was surprisingly endearing and nostalgic for me to sit in the theater, seeing this depiction of David as a man who, "when you took away the topic of white supremacy and K.K.K. nonsense . . . was a very pleasant conversationalist." All the humor and any attempt to take the sting out of the White nationalist movement took a hard turn at the conclusion, which jumped to present day, showing the hate and violence of Charlottesville, David pumping up the rally there, telling the crowd "this is a first step toward taking America back," hours before one of the White power marchers drove a car into a crowd of antiracist counterprotestors, killing Heather Heyer. Many of us came out of the theater shaken, tears forming, without words. I left my temporary role there at the end of the summer, and less than a month later Facebook reorganized staff internally, telling employees to shift priorities "away from societal good to individual value." The team I had worked with soon disbanded, and several of them left the company.

MY DAD CALLED ME IN early 2019 to let me know my grandmother had passed away, that her funeral would take place soon in Athens, Alabama, and that he'd like me to come. I wanted Allison to join me. At that time, my family still occasionally sent random bouts of antagonism toward both me and Allison. My parents told me they would commit to not saying a word about anything related to race. I believe they gave it their best effort, but racist comments that I knew they thought were so universal as to be innocuous still snuck through. At the memorial, I met cousins I'd never heard of, and I learned it was because their families had distanced them from mine because of our politics. My dad and I both intended to say a few words about what his mother meant to us, so we spent the morning quietly preparing short speeches in our heads. Yet, when we expected the pastor to invite people up, he never did. The proceedings instead were formulaic, reading off the bare facts of her life. At the last moments of the generation that raised him, he and I were both silent.

ALLISON AND I HAD ALREADY discussed wanting to marry as the new year dawned in 2020. We had qualms about what marriage symbolized. It had been nearly nine years since we had met and started to spend all the time together that we could find. We didn't have a first date, because we had so ambiguously transitioned from acquaintances to friends who could talk for hours to friends who stayed over nearly every night in the same bed. We had navigated six years of long-distance communication and come back together to share an address for the first time in 2019 in Washington, DC. Allison was completing the last year of her PhD program, and working at the children's hospital, and I was working on my dissertation. We attended couples counseling to work through some of the more tumultuous parts of our relationship history, and we emerged on the other side more excited about commitment and the future with each other than ever before. We had an upcoming appointment scheduled for the afternoon of March 17, 2020, at an ethical jeweler, where we planned to look at rings. Throughout the early months of the year, our biggest concern had been how to keep a wedding small and relatively private without offending our families. My number of relatives was small, however, compared to the (to me) innumerable uncles and aunts and cousins in Allison's wide family.

Then the first local lockdown order was declared the day before our jeweler appointment. In the face of a global pandemic, an in-person ring appointment was easy to let go of, and we started to count the days of being trapped at home. As the days turned to weeks, and the initial declarations of two-week orders were extended indefinitely, we realized there wouldn't be any near end. By the end of April, while everything around us remained still, we knew we wouldn't be able to invite relatives or friends for an in-person wedding anytime soon.

So we found a large cabin in the Blue Ridge mountains in Virginia, suddenly vacant during what was normally prime spring vacation season, and fashioned several days of our own private marriage ceremonies, laying on couches and chairs writing letters to each other, writing our own vows, and cataloging the ways we meant so much to each other. We brought ingredients to make all our favorite meals. We recorded ourselves and our meals and formal preparations using a tripod and a drone and sent out an announcement video to our friends and family. Showing how little we understood about the pandemic even at that point, we concluded the video with the promise of a "small one-year anniversary TBD." I wouldn't have changed our marriage ceremony even if I could have.

Allison entered my life at a moment that I felt least like someone worthy of being trusted or loved. I had known even then that my loyalty to the community that raised me had led me to betray all the people who'd chosen to be close to me. She showed me new ways to exist, and we created even more together as we grew up after college. We had influenced each other in so many ways over those years. It's impossible now to distinguish the ways we've influenced each other versus the things we discovered together that now feel most fundamental to who we are. It's impossible for me to imagine my own life story without her intervention. She showed me that I could love other people fully and unafraid, and I showed her how wide the world is and that we could experience all of it together.

THE POLITICAL SCIENTIST COREY ROBIN described my situation in a way that I still ponder sometimes: "Black has changed sides, but he hasn't changed the sides." What then is left? I don't want to live with ghosts. I want to live with my family. I even want the community that raised me to change and grow with me. I am afraid that we will lose everything because we're too afraid to change, to admit that the enemy we imagined out in the distance was never real and no one was guilty but ourselves for continuing to make the same choices despite having a way out.

As a part of the movements for antiracism and against antisemitism, yet someone with a very different experience than most people I work with, the most painful experience has been learning just how often the unity White nationalists imagine about the other side is nonexistent. Once in Berlin, I found myself seated at a long table in a private discussion as part of an American delegation of activists, scholars, and community leaders who confront the history that has allowed prejudice to grow. I almost broke down as the group facilitators tried to address a heated conflict between Black antiracist activists and activists focusing on antisemitism. Instead of unity, it felt more like antagonism. I was deeply affected by it, because I personally identify with both causes, and the near universal overlap in these fights sometimes seems obvious only to me in these settings.

I still don't have answers to fix things, and I accept that there really never is one obvious solution. New College, the place I finally had the time and the commitment of a community to take a breath and assess who I wanted to be, left me with several general lessons. There is almost never one correct answer to any problem. Instead, there are more and less rigorous ways to answer a question. The most important of them is not any academic analysis, but the question of who your decision affects, and who you care about. Answering the question of who I consider a part of my community, and constantly trying to expand the boundaries of that answer, is the only way I have found to decide what is right. My experience at college wasn't one that gave me many explicit answers. Instead it planted me in a small physical area with hundreds of other people trying to answer the same questions.

THE WHITE NATIONALIST MOVEMENT IS a shallow ideology rooted in fear of change. It has a legacy of horrible atrocities, willful ignorance, and people clinging to the banalities of familiar things even as they watch their house rot away around them. This community is depressing and twisted, but its malevolence should be familiar. The fight between visions of antiracism or White nationalism has played out unnoticed by most people. It is the history of our society played out in microcosm. The stakes of that story are continuing in front of all of us, growing in intensity until no one can ignore them. The outcome of this fight will be the foundation of our future.

Ibram X. Kendi, the prominent antiracist author (who I've had the privilege of working with several times over these last few years), describes the view of American history that argues that progress toward racial justice is inevitable "does not explain why the mass incarceration of Black and brown bodies followed the racial justice movements in the 1960s. It does not explain how Jim Crow could emerge out of the ashes of slavery, and why slavery expanded out West after Congress voted to outlaw the importing of slaves in 1807." Under these broad changes were activist movements—either antiracist or White supremacist—that drove the culture forward. Those movements were filled with people who dreamed of things bigger than themselves, but their visions were so powerful that they often made the rest of us forget that they were individuals like any of us. My story is small, just like theirs were. We all make our decisions starting from the questions of who we care for, who we love. Everything flows from there.

When it comes specifically to the White supremacy that suffuses our society, there are a lot of incentives and reasons for everyone to condemn racism and create a different world. Antiracism is genuinely a more freeing, honest, humane, and intellectual framework for life than White supremacy. The former asks people to expand the limits of what they believe is possible and who they believe they can care for or be cared for by. The latter demands that its adherents keep other people away, guarding against categories of bodies that can't ever be defined. It tells them to be afraid and jealous of other people, to isolate themselves. Countering White nationalism means transforming our entire society into an antiracist one.

Antiracism has the stronger factual support for its foundational argument that racial groupings can't be defined in any consistent way beyond legal and social categories. White nationalists believe race predicts behavior, intelligence, culture, morality or any other of a long list of things they value and attribute to being recognized in society as White. Yet if evidence and arguments were the main factors that caused people to reconsider and abandon strongly held issues of their identity, a racist society never could have taken hold in the first place. Simply talking to people, or even just interacting with others in your daily life, would be enough to "prove" over time that things as subjective, random, and contextual as all the personal qualities like creativity, intelligence, risk-taking, criminality, or altruism that White nationalists attribute to "race" have more overlap between races than distinctions.

Yet people rarely make the most important decisions about their faith, ideology, or community because they shopped around and accepted the most rigorously verifiable belief system. We instead make those choices about identity and loyalty—I made and continue to make them—based primarily on the question of who we care about. Usually without consciously perceiving it, our hunt for evidence often works the other way. We try hard to justify and defend what we believe with objective facts, because discovering we no longer believe it may mean the end of many of the most important trusting relationships in our lives, or force us to make changes that we're not quite ready to make.

After having spent too many years listening to certain evolutionary psychologists describe how they thought "races" evolved different behaviors, only to realize the enormity of their willful ignorance of the evidence that there aren't behavioral differences attributable exclusively to race to begin with, I'm aware of how easily a smart person can convince themselves of almost anything. Whether it's a social or professional interest, the problem with treating our funda- mental beliefs and ideologies as something reasoned and considered, something subject to debate, is that the stakes of being wrong aren't just being embarrassed but losing your community and possibly your own identity. The fact that so many people continue to tolerate White supremacy even passively shows the power of identity and the desire to belong and support the status quo, no matter how destructive it is. Every day that racial hierarchy continues to be a fact of our society drags down the total GDP of our society, creates political and social instability that threatens to undermine the government, alienates generations and regions from one another, and burdens society with maintaining the largest incarcerated population in the world.

The foundational beliefs of White nationalists—that racial groups are more than a social category and Jews around the world are conspiring to destroy "White" people—are a particularly good example of something that, if it isn't patently ridiculous, has a century of rigorous proofs demonstrating that it's false.

This belief system only makes any sense if you're trying to justify what many average White people want to be true: that the relatively greater social status granted to them just from being born "White" is not the result of an elaborate social crime. White racism needs to be true for their relative wealth, access to better jobs and networks, having generally less trouble at upward social mobility, and generally more humane experiences dealing with police and the carceral system than non-White people to be anything more than the fruit of injustice. White nationalism tells anyone who would rather look away from this reality that nothing needs to change, and no moral outrage is required. Antiracism is the more difficult sell because it asks that we change, and change is uncertain.

IN HIS ACCOUNT OF INTERNMENT and torture in the Nazi death camps, Jean Améry wrote about his experience of homesickness after the war. "Anyone who is familiar with exile," he wrote, "has gained many an insight into life but has discovered that it holds even more questions." His answer, "first and tentative," to the question of how much home a person needs was: "all the more, the less of it he can carry with him." Home is a place, but it is also an idea, and it is possible to lose both of them in exile, only to find a new home again. Some people who find themselves in exile, Améry wrote, are able to find "transportable home, or at least an ersatz for home." Religion, money, fame, and esteem can all stand in for home. At times all of them have tempted me.

Améry observed that the non-Jewish German writers he saw in "self-exile . . . exclusively because of their ideology" could "live in the illusion that they were the voice of the 'true Germany,' a voice that could be loudly raised abroad for the Fatherland enchained by National Socialism." I have long since realized I cannot redeem my family any more than I can redeem any of the big questions of my nation or our world. Amanda Gorman, the poet who recited her work at the 2021 presidential inauguration, in another poem described the blend of horror and intimacy I've felt at watching the people I am a part of ruin themselves. "What can we call a country," she asked, "that destroys itself just because it can?" Her answer is the only one I have ever been able to offer to something so enormous and devastating: "Our only word for this is *Home*." Having asked myself these questions about what it means to go home when that is impossible has prompted for me what Améry called "the realization, which at first seems trivial, that there is no return, because the re-entrance into a place is never also a recovery of the lost time." There is only a search for something new, which we've never known before, and we need to be willing to purchase that world whatever the cost.

EPILOGUE

ON JANUARY 6, 2023, TWO years to the day after the far-right attack on the Capitol in DC, Blair, my friend from New College who had pulled me out of the party where I'd been surrounded and who I'd walked through the monuments in DC with before my first public talk at Georgetown, texted me in the middle of the afternoon. It was a link to the announcement that Governor Ron DeSantis had appointed a new slate of far-right trustees to New College's board, effectively stripping control of the school from its current administration. He only captioned the link "Pretty scary." I replied, "I only understand that appointment in a world where the right in Florida now sees NCF as some kind of leftist training ground at taxpayer expense."

Over the next two weeks, I dropped all my work to field interviews as the world suddenly tried to learn about New College of Florida. Even people who had heard my story didn't immediately connect me to this announcement. I've been criticized by New College alumni for years for sometimes not directly naming our alma mater, but instead referring to our college as "a small public liberal arts college in Florida." I often left out the name of the school because, before early 2023, it was incredibly rare that I'd receive any hint of recognition when I did name it.

Two years earlier, I had given a talk at New College with Allison and another alum from our time there, James Birmingham, who had been a major Forum presence against me. After years of me speaking at other colleges, it was stressful to appear back home.

For many years after my story became public, the New College administration didn't acknowledge any of the press or my public statements. Before the talk, the outgoing president requested we speak. I had warned him I didn't have only positive things to say about New College. He was open to hearing the critiques, which mainly came down to the fact that New College should have done more.

Universities often like to brag about their commitments to free speech, but in my case, they seemed to freeze more than make a choice.

Looking back, instead I can't believe they never even sent an email out acknowledging the uncertainty and fear that had accompanied my being there, never offered support or even condemned White supremacy in a statement. The moderator of the event I had spoken at, New College's first diversity officer who was hired in 2019, summarized our talk: "It was a humbling revelation, learning that it wasn't just Derek's presence but the absence of an institutional response—a failure to affirm institutional support for community members who believed White nationalist ideologies to be an existential threat—that left the community feeling unmoored."

Within a month of the appointment of these new trustees in 2023, however, that officer was out of the school. The DeSantis administration announced that they had appointed the right-wing activist Christopher Rufo, who popularized using "critical race theory" as a catch-all talking point that has been marshalled to ban schools from teaching the history of racism. This erasure of history serves their political ends, because it removes context and takes away the tools to understand the scars and grooves carved into the world around us. Announcing the new trustees, representatives of the DeSantis administration said they hoped to transform New College into "the Hillsdale of the South." That private, conservative Christian college in Michigan has been central to the conservative movement's overhaul of antiracist and social justice curriculums in private and voucher high schools across the country. Since its foundation, New College has seemed to attract ambitious and visionary monikers. In 1961, *Time* magazine described it as the "Ivy League among the Spanish moss" when its academic program was still being designed and its campus being constructed before it opened in 1964. Dreaming of making it into a mimic of Hillsdale, a school whose "1776 Curriculum" is designed so "students acquire a mature love for America" and teaches that the civil rights movement created "programs that ran counter to the lofty ideals of the Founders" is a step down.

Coming shortly after his being reelected, DeSantis's assault on New College fit within his larger attempts to censor education in the lower grades, notably banning discussion of queer identity in schools. A week later, DeSantis came to Sarasota to announce that his administration would ban diversity, equity, and inclusion (DEI) programs in colleges across the state and the teaching of critical race theory, and give trustees the power to fire faculty. At the first meeting of the new trustees, they fired the school's president. They bought out her contract and put in as interim president the former Republican speaker of the Florida state house and DeSantis's first commissioner of education (and gave him a salary twice what the previous president had made, nearly equal to what the president of Florida State University was paid, which had a student body of 45,000 students, compared to fewer than 800 at New College).

Soon after taking the position, the new president announced a slate of millions of dollars in new funding being allocated by the Republican-controlled Florida legislature, which they had denied the school for decades. Offering $10,000 in scholarships exclusively for new students to the school, he promised that New College would become a place where students could "explore their intellectual curiosity, pursue their passions, and gain a better understanding of the world without having to abandon who they are and what they believe." It was hard not to feel singled out by that specific language. He later publicly announced that he was on a "mission to eliminate indoctrination and re-focus higher education on its classical mission."

In those first few months, the trustees denied tenure to five professors who had been approved before the arrival of the new trustees, fired the librarian, and created a sprawling athletics program where none had existed before and on a campus without facilities for such a program. One morning during finals week while I was on a video call with organizers opposing the attacks on the school, DeSantis unexpectedly showed up at a New College administration building to sign new legislation that banned teaching, in general education courses, "theories that systemic racism, sexism, oppression, and privilege are inherent in the institutions of the United States and were created to maintain social, political and economic inequities." The legislation also allowed university presidents to hire and fire faculty, banned spending on DEI programs, and limited tenure protection. During the live broadcast, the chants of New College students outside protesting the event distracted from the ceremony.

Afterward, the American Association of University Professors made a statement that the legislation "cements the decline of Florida's higher education system by enshrining into law culture-war-inspired censorship." A student protesting that day told the press, "It's not some kind of, 'Oh Florida is a little kooky.' This is fucking fascism. . . . Everything here he is doing is completely strategic." It made me proud to see the continued activism of New College students, their refusal to defer to authority or to formality. The diagnosis was correct, but it took a student standing near the bay during finals week to say it.

I WAS INVITED TO COME down to campus at the end of the spring 2023 semester for the graduation ceremony by fellow alum X González, one of the founders of March For Our Lives following the 2018 attack on their high school in Parkland. X had graduated from New College the year before and they invited me to help advocate against the DeSantis takeover.

The day before I went to Sarasota, Allison, Matthew, and I drove from our homes in Baltimore down to the National Zoo in DC. Allison and I had moved to Baltimore for her postdoctoral fellowship in the summer of 2020, and she had accepted a position to stay on as faculty, so for the first time we felt like we were able to start putting down roots; Matthew had moved to Baltimore a few years before us after finishing an MBA at Columbia University. We talked about what was happening at New College and in Florida more broadly. We also talked about our lives, our work, and the uncertainties we were feeling about having edged into our thirties. This era of our lives was bringing with it greater stability—none of us felt quite so self-conscious as we had during our twenties—but also a sense that, for everything we'd accomplished, it was never quite certain whether we were doing what we felt we should be doing.

On the way out of town, I realized a big part of my anxiety about going back to campus was fear. For all that I had processed my experiences there independently and in therapy, my time at New College had been one of the most traumatic experiences of my life. Things that I downplayed in retrospect—like the night I was surrounded at the wall or the endless moments I faced middle fingers or feared that White nationalists might come to campus and incite violence to "protect" me—lurched back into my mind. I knew logically that New College had saved me, but I still associated it with shame and fear. Landing at the Sarasota airport, however, filled me immediately with a feeling of home that I haven't often experienced. Other alums who Allison and I had gotten to know in the Baltimore area had also come down for "the last normal graduation," as people had started to call it.

For all my outspokenness over the years, and how tied to New College my own story became, it wasn't until it was threatened and the alumni community came out in support of it that I felt like a part of its community. I could immediately employ my media connections and public speaking experience, just as other alums engaged their own points of connection and influence. I was no longer an outside entity, a symbol of hate that the community needed to wrestle with. For the first time, my background felt only relevant to the extent I could use it to draw attention to the plight of our alma mater. After so many years of insecurity, it was a bittersweet relief to recognize that, in the moment that our community was at risk, I was simply another person seeing my world being overtaken.

I HAVE VISITED MY PARENTS in Florida a few times since condemning their beliefs, with regular calls on birthdays and holidays. Each time I visited felt like it had been a long time since those nights in 2013, after I released my public letter condemning White nationalism without warning them, when they struggled to understand how our family could go forward without a shared ideology. Each visit felt like a long time since I had tried to assert that "family ties are separate from politics," and my dad had responded that that "obviously wasn't true with a family centered around political activism" and my mother told me I needed to "make new friends and family." Visiting Florida was a reminder of the past I wanted more than anything to leave behind.

When I returned to West Palm Beach for the first time in the spring of 2017, I was surprised both by how much and how little seemed to have changed. The trees I had planted in the yard when I was small were taller and some were bearing fruit. I was allowed to come into the house, and my bed, that my mom and I had built, was still standing. My things were still in my room like I'd left them, dusty and disorganized.

After the pandemic started, I didn't visit my parents for several years. They were both entering their seventies with medical issues and were caring for my nonagenarian grandmother. None of them were willing to receive the Covid vaccine. When my dad asked me to visit, and I tried to make it contingent on him getting vaccinated first, he told me that if he ever adopted one of my liberal opinions, the first one he chose would not be to follow Dr. Fauci. Eventually, I accepted that I couldn't make my family's choices for them.

AS I LANDED IN SARASOTA in mid-May 2023, I messaged Allison, trying to reassure her, because she was sad that she wasn't able to come down herself. I didn't think it would be a weekend that we'd look back on sentimentally. "The reason I'm going," I emphasized, "is to try to put myself out there as a weapon or shield to try to fight them." It was disturbing to believe the school could be destroyed. I had come down to do the kind of activism I'd done before I got to New College, but which I learned a new purpose for while I was there. It has felt good to try to help the school that helped me—not just open the door to combating White nationalism, but also plant the seeds and experiences for later on in my life, in the emerging understanding of my gender identity in my early thirties. Its culture and the people I met there helped me accept that I fit under the trans umbrella, a group whose rights are now under vicious, loud attack in Florida. I can't imagine how horrible it would have been to grow up in the current political environment as a child who, until puberty, was quite happy about being often perceived as a girl, and who then hid that part of myself. It felt so strange how tied my life always was to Florida politics, how they seemed to come for me in personal ways beyond my control or expectation. It seemed sometimes like my life could be explained as a product of Florida as much as any other aspect of my family.

THE NEW COLLEGE 2023 GRADUATING class put together their own alternative ceremony off campus, because the official event had invited a Trump health appointee to rant against Covid vaccines.

When we arrived at the alt-graduation, it was beautiful to see the community so vastly unchanged, even if I didn't know the students personally. Many of the faculty members came up to talk, and I realized I now had institutional memory more similar to theirs than to the students'. When I'd graduated, I hadn't even thought about the wide alumni community out in the world. I had only been concerned about the students sitting out in front of me, and I wished the same were true for this class too. I tried not to be invasive or to draw attention to myself beyond the few scheduled interviews we planned. This class needed to navigate activism, media interviews, and online harassment in ways that I'd been afraid my presence on campus a decade earlier would have brought. We'd avoided that attention then, but this tiny school that had shaped my education and career, that had introduced me to the most long and meaningful relationships of my life, and had forced me to confront my own hypocrisy and stand up for my values now became a boogeyman for right-wing trolls across the world. Students spoke casually about having their accounts attacked and hacked, of doxxing attempts, and threats to the school from around the world.

The chosen graduation speaker at alt graduation, Maya Wiley, was a prominent civil rights lawyer. Like any typical graduation speaker, she talked about the students and praised their accomplishments. She also named both X and me, sitting in the back row. I felt like an interloper and hoped people didn't turn to look at me.

The next day, X and I gave an interview together during which we shared pained grimaces as the host read each of our stock introductions. Afterward, I mentioned how funny and reassuring it was to be with someone who had as little worry about agreeing to a last-minute interview as I did. We each knew we would hit our marks; we'd turn our pain and feelings into talking points that could help serve our cause, help our friends do the organizing and activism they needed to do. Listening to us doing it, being able to pass the responsibility back and forth when it got too emotional, or when one of us simply ran out of steam, felt like being at home. And it occurred to me only in that moment how awful it really was to have developed that skill so young. Any teenager who is good at interviews and speeches has learned too well how to keep themselves bottled up. We had learned too well and too early, I thought, how to try to be what people needed from us.

That night, I talked with Allison, telling her about graduation, sharing what being back on campus and seeing how much continuity there was around me felt like. Even without knowing a single student, I felt a sense of kinship. No matter what happens on campus, they couldn't take our home away from us who have already come and gone. The campus was a nest that taught us how to be a family together. But none of us ever expected or wanted to stay there forever. If they burn it down, we'll deal with the loss and know what we carry inside. They're too late to take anything from us. What they want is to take away our future siblings and to make sure they never learn what they lost. That's what we're trying to save.

But New College is a microcosm, the wildest and most predictive I've ever seen, and its struggles and reckonings seem to operate on a five-year timeline ahead of the rest of the country. While I fight to save New College, I also know that means I need to be simultaneously gearing up for the ever-increasing role that White identity politics and White grievance play—explicitly and implicitly—in the Republican Party.

It's not like there weren't explicit White nationalists at New College when I was there. None were public like me, but they made themselves known to me. It's not like there wasn't entrenched White supremacy and racism at New College, just as there was everywhere. The activism and community building I saw at New College was that of a community that wanted to become a place that did not accept bigotry. Even as it fell short over and over, every generation always brought us one step closer by trying. After failing repeatedly, the community was a hyper-local space where we cared about each other, because everyone, just by being there, was in some way a part of us. While New College is a combination of all the unique institutions built within it, its transformative power comes from the simple fact that its members continued to live together. This small community that knows us at our best and our worst, that caused us to be accountable to what it means to be a human being, is a harder thing to lose than the people attacking it believe.

Even as I left Sarasota in May seeing such rapid change taking place, I knew many of the most severe policies had not yet gone into effect. In the fall, across Florida teachers began a school year with new rules that had taken effect over the summer, declaring chosen pronouns illegal for both teachers and students, imposing bathroom mandates that allowed for criminal prosecution of anyone found using a bathroom that didn't correspond to their reproductive function. The law defines women as the sex with the "reproductive role of producing eggs" and men as the sex with the "reproductive role of producing sperm." The creepiness of identifying every person to a breeding role seemed lost on the legislature. The penalty for a violation was up to a year in prison.

During his first run for governor in 2018, DeSantis actually claimed to reject anti-transgender legislation. "Getting into bathroom wars," he said, "I don't think that's a good use of our time." Yet, several years into his administration, going from banning discussion of slavery to criminalizing gender presentations followed Rufo's observation that "the reservoir of sentiment on the sexuality issue is deeper and more explosive than the sentiment on the race issues." On one hand, DeSantis and his department of education teach students about the "personal benefit" of slavery to enslaved people, and on the other they attack and try to criminalize queer people out of society. This constellation of bigotries is not new.

In Berlin today, in the center of the city along the river, there is a memorial to the first gay liberation movement and the first center for transgender medicine. Founded in 1919 by Magnus Hirschfeld, the Institute of Sexual Research stood there until 1933. Hirschfeld and the institute provided sex education, contraception, and conducted research on gender and sexuality, in addition to lobbying for the repeal of Paragraph 175, the law criminalizing homosexuality. It issued identification cards to transgender people in an effort to prevent them from being arrested. They provided the world's first gender-affirming medicine, including conducting gender-affirmation surgeries, and prescribing hormones for medical gender transition.

Many people today have seen the horrific images of the book burnings conducted in Berlin at the outset of the Nazi regime by the

German Student Union, a group of far-right college students. Less often are they aware that these images of one of the first and largest of those book burnings were taken in front of the Institute for Sexual Research, and show its massive library of over 20,000 books being destroyed. Three months after Adolph Hitler was named chancellor, the Nazis marched to the institute, broke in, and dragged the contents of its library outside to be burned. Nazi newsreels projected the image around the world with a voiceover declaring they were consigning "the intellectual garbage of the past" to the fire.

Yet in Florida, and in dozens of other states, gay, lesbian, transgender, and gender-diverse kids and adults are being persecuted by a government that increasingly sounds a familiar note.

It is clear where this path leads, because it is not one unfamiliar either to Americans or Europeans. It is a path that does not distinguish between racism and transphobia, that targets immigrants, and anyone who is not seen as White. The story of my life ran through New College and it freed me. Yet the story of our country also seems to be running through New College. What the outcome will be can't be known, because it depends on the choices of all of us.

ACKNOWLEDGMENTS

OVER THE YEARS, ALLISON AND I have incorporated some of the more outlandish, disconcerting, or patronizing things people have written about her into our in-jokes. An author once referred to her relationship with me at New College as "some combination of girlfriend, therapist, amanuensis, prosecutor, and priest." Once we looked up the meaning of "amanuensis" (a "literary or artistic assistant"), we started using it every time one of us edited the other's papers during grad school. Her feedback on the early drafts of this book, however, truly earned that title. I am forever conscious of having placed the burden of my own choices and their consequences on Allison, as I've leaned on her strength and conviction. This book could not exist without her, nor could the adventures and love that are still yet to come.

Thanks to Marc Skvirsky, whose friendship, honesty, and boundless curiosity and personability introduced me to so many incredible friends and guided me, not only with his feedback on this book, but as I have navigated my life.

When I first met Eli Saslow in Ann Arbor, Michigan, in the fall of 2016, I told him that I'd reverse the tables one day and write a profile on him. I still plan to. His work to understand the nuance of my experience changed how I see myself. We met at a moment when I couldn't imagine speaking again about the things that caused me endless shame. Eli, more than any other individual, is responsible for showing me that it was possible to draw something meaningful from an experience that I wanted only to leave behind. I hope he enjoys my own twist on the genre of Derek Black stories that he pioneered.

Emma kept me grounded and sane, and jumped on the phone to talk me down whenever I was convinced that my editor hated me and everything I'd written. She pumped me up after too many late nights writing and encouraged me to carry on. Without her enduring friendship, kindness, and patience, nothing about this process would have felt so meaningful.

I hope my parents can appreciate the history I wrote while living through it happening all around me.

Larry Weissman and Sascha Alper believed in me and this book for over half a decade, despite my decisions that prolonged the process by many years. Their reliability when so many people come and go still leaves me awed.

Zoë showed me that a long and complicated friendship can be exactly the right ground to grow ourselves anew. They encouraged me to find and embrace queer community. We've thankfully learned how to communicate beyond cryptic song lyrics, but the music they shared while I wrote is infused throughout this book.

Many people have come into my life since everything changed for me, and I can't name them all, but: Elisha and Lynn Wiesel invited me into their lives and community; Ibram X. Kendi gave me a seat at the table; Khalil Gibran Muhammad sat beside me in those heartbreaking days after Charlottesville; Aimee Segal brought me into the work of memory, and showed me what it means to stand behind the vow "never again"; Jonathan Lyon and Matthew Kruer, my long-suffering doctoral advisors, showed me patience and care despite my many peradventures, while Michael I. Allen improved my Latin dedication and gave me some of the most important advice I've ever received at just the right moment; Willemien Otten helped me connect my life experiences to my academic research; Kathleen Belew recognized me in an audience, and we bridged the gap between the past and present; Dr. K met me at age nineteen, told me I still had time, and asked me if I'd heard of New College; once I was there, Carrie Beneš and Thomas McCarthy began my career studying medieval history, while Susan Marks taught me how to engage human problems through religious scholarship; Catherine Turner brought me into community; Blair Sapp repeatedly showed me the narrow path between community, loyalty, and your own values; Matthew Stevenson offered me an invitation that changed everything, and remains my favorite dinner guest; I hope Juan recognizes himself in this book, a fellow transfer student; X González and Leo Muñoz also knew how alone it could feel to be a teen activist in front of a crowd, and a New College education taught us how to take control of who we were outside its walls.

Lee Bailey, for choosing me back as a sibling; Julie Gornik, for trusting me before she knew me, and for taking me in when I had nowhere I called home; Baltimore City, despite its very real problems, for giving me a home; my Baltimore book club, who will kindly refrain from nominating this book for us to read; all my Chicago grad school compatriots, who met me on the other side; Diane Tachmindji, for the friendship I never anticipated, but am so glad to have; Lisa Conn, who offered to share an unexpected candid photo of the two of us flanking President Obama, for her enduring curiosity and empathy ever since; the crew I got to know through Facing History and Ourselves, for showing me how to engage the past in education, particularly Maureen Loughnane, Daniel Braunfeld, Leora Schaefer, Pam Haas, Liz Vogel, and Judy Wise; my individual and marriage therapists, past and present; Jamison Stoltz, who taught me to lay the foundation boards of this book before I worried about the fine details; and all the rest of the staff of Abrams Press, who saw my vision from the start.

NOTES

Chapter 1: A Personal History of White Nationalism

1 **The episode they invited:** Markus E, "Jenny Jones - Hateful Web Sites on The Internet," YouTube, March 4, 2017, www.youtube.com/watch?v=egvhRytVNPA.

5 **In an interview nearly:** "Don Black, Birmingham, AL, 1985-03-24," Evelyn Rich papers, 1954–1993, David M. Rubenstein Rare Book & Manuscript Library, Duke University, Box 1, Folder 6, p. 17.

10 **The bombing killed:** "16th Street Baptist Church Bombing (1963)," National Park Service, September 19, 2022.

10 **doctoral dissertation:** "Don Black, Birmingham, AL, 1985-03-24," Evelyn Rich papers, 1954–1993, David M. Rubenstein Rare Book & Manuscript Library, Duke University, Box 1, Folder 6, p. 1.

12 **"used the N-word":** Don Terry, "Hatewatch Exclusive: Racist Serial Killer, Facing Death, Recants," Southern Poverty Law Center, October 17, 2013.

12 **Franklin's grandparents:** Mel Ayton, *Dark Soul of the South: The Life and Crimes of Racist Killer Joseph Paul Franklin* (Washington, DC: Potomac Books, 2011), 17.

13 **"just started hanging out":** Joe Eszterhas, *American Rhapsody* (New York: Alfred A. Knopf, 2000), 324, cited in Ayton, *Dark Soul*, 27.

13 **legally changed his name:** Ayton, *Dark Soul*, 3.

13 **"We weren't friends":** Rachel Monroe, "How Does a White Supremacist See America Today?," *New York* magazine, October 12, 2015.

13 **"traditionally conservative":** David Duke, *My Awakening* (1998), chapter 4.

15 **"become a soapbox":** Kathy McAdams, "Free Speech Alley System Is Criticized," *Daily Reveille*, 1969.

15 **"Chloe began to cry":** David Duke, *My Awakening*, chapter 27.

16 **free-speech lawsuit:** Brian Fairbanks, *Wizards: David Duke, America's Wildest Election, and the Rise of the Far Right* (Nashville, TN: Vanderbilt University Press, 2022), 53.

16 **compensate David and the Klan:** Ibid., 55.

20 **"every right-thinking White person":** "White Citizens' Councils (WCC)," The Martin Luther King, Jr. Research and Education Institute, Stanford University, kinginstitute.stanford.edu/encyclopedia/White-citizens-councils-wcc; citing, Joe Azbell, "Council Official Says Negro 'Bloc' No Longer Threat in Elections Here," *Montgomery Advertiser*, January 26, 1956.

20 **power of their economic control:** Ibid.

20 **King demanded:** Martin Luther King, Jr., "Desegregation and the Future," Address delivered at the annual luncheon of the National Committee for Rural Schools, December 15, 1956.

20 **"19th Century standards":** King, "Statement on petition by the John Birch Society and the White Citizens' Council," May 26, 1966.

21 **headline about that election:** "Black Wins B'Ham Race," *Tuscaloosa News*, October 29, 1979.

23 **Buchanan sounded:** Patrick J. Buchanan, "Address to the Republican National Convention," August 17, 1992, Houston, Texas.

23 **Donald Trump told** *Meet the Press*: "Donald Trump Discusses His Bid for the Reform Party Presidential Nomination," *Meet the Press*, NBC News transcript, October 24, 1999.

23 **"woke ideology"**: "Are G.O.P. Voters Tiring of the War on 'Wokeness'?" *New York Times*, August 6, 2023.

23 **"immigration invasion"**: "Texas's use of 'invasion' clause against immigrants is racist and dangerous, rights groups say," *Guardian*, May 29, 2023.

23 **"crime in our inner cities"**: "Trump claims 5K murders in Chicago during Obama presidency – that's incorrect," *NBC News 7 Chicago*, July 13, 2016.

25 **the *New York Times* ran a story**: Richard Fausset, "A Voice of Hate in America's Heartland," *New York Times*, November 25, 2017.

25 **drew harsh criticism and backlash**: "About That Nazi Next Door," WNYC, November 26, 2017, www.wnycstudios.org/podcasts/otm/episodes/about-nazi-next-door.

27 **six times the wealth**: Derenoncourt, et al., "The racial wealth gap, 1860–2020," *Manuscript, Princeton University and University of Bonn* (2021).

27 **Black people are imprisoned**: Ashley Nellis, "The Color of Justice: Racial and Ethnic Disparity in State Prisons," The Sentencing Project, October 13, 2021, www.sentencingproject.org/reports/the-color-of-justice-racial-and-ethnic-disparity-in-state-prisons-the-sentencing-project/.

28 **American academia**: Khalil Gibran Muhammad, *The Condemnation of Blackness: Race, Crime, and the Making of Modern Urban America* (Cambridge, MA: 2019, revised edition; originally published 2010), 20.

Chapter 2: Operation Red Dog

29 **"broad-based social movement"**: Kathleen Belew, "There Are No Lone Wolves: The White Power Movement at War," 278–288 in *A Field Guide to White Supremacy*, eds. Kathleen Belew and Ramón A. Gutiérrez (Oakland, CA: University of California Press, 2021), 280.

30 **Dr. Belew's other classification**: Ibid.

33 **He was caught**: "Jerry Ray Acquitted," *Times-News*, November 25, 1970.

34 **designed in Huntsville**: John Noble Wilford, "Wernher von Braun, Rocket Pioneer, Dies," *New York Times*, June 18, 1977.

34 **"The rockets worked perfectly"**: Ibid.

34 **von Braun had joined the Nazi Party**: "Wernher von Braun and the Nazi Rocket Program: An interview with Michael Neufeld, PhD, of the National Air and Space Museum," National World War II Museum: New Orleans, September 10, 2019, www.nationalww2museum.org/war/articles/wernher-von-braun-and-nazi-rocket-program-interview-michael-neufeld-phd-national-air.

34 **In exchange for bringing weapons**: "Two Guilty in New Orleans for Plot on Dominica Invasion," *New York Times*, June 21, 1981.

34 **"Nazi and Confederate flags"**: Ibid.

35 **"Bayou of Pigs"**: Stewart Bell, *Bayou of Pigs: The True Story of An Audacious Plot To Turn A Tropical Island Into A Criminal Paradise* (Missassauga, Ontario: Wiley, 2008).

35 **implicate mainstream officials**: "Judge denies Connally subpoena in trial of 3 alleged mercenaries," UPI, June 14, 1981.

35 **The law was famously used**: R. Kent Newmyer, "Burr versus Jefferson versus Marshall," *Humanities* 34:3 (May/June 2013), www.neh.gov/humanities/2013/mayjune/feature/burr-versus-jefferson-versus-marshall.

35 **covert wars:** Jules Lobel, "Rise and Decline of the Neutrality Act: Sovereignty and Congressional War Powers in United States Foreign Policy," *Harvard International Law Journal* 24 (1983): 1–72.

36 **"not designed for":** Robert F. Kennedy, "Statement to the Press," April 20, 1961, reprinted in M. Whiteman, *Digest of International Law* 231 (1968), 11, cited in footnote 16 of Jules Lobel, "Rise and Decline of the Neutrality Act: Sovereignty and Congressional War Powers in United States Foreign Policy," *Harvard International Law Journal* 24 (1983): 1–72.

36 **CIA actions:** Lobel, "Rise and Decline of the Neutrality Act," 71, "Finally, recent experience with respect to Nicaragua strongly suggests that a piecemeal approach to paramilitary action abroad contains serious flaws. Congress should prohibit all aid and assistance for paramilitary operations abroad irrespective of whether they violate the Neutrality Act, or, at least, provide that such operations cannot be undertaken without prior congressional approval by means of a joint resolution."

36 **train Nicaraguan exiles:** Patrick E. Tyler and Bob Woodward, "U.S. Approves Covert Plan in Nicaragua," *Washington Post*, March 10, 1982.

36 **"war on drugs":** Ashley Nellis, "Still Life: America's Increasing Use of Life and Long-Term Sentences," The Sentencing Project, May 3, 2017, www.sentencingproject.org/reports/still-life-americaos-increasing-use-of-life-and-long-term-sentences/.

39 **"reluctant to join the Klan":** "Don Black with Dr. Buford B. Sanders, Homewood, AL, 1985-03-12," Evelyn Rich papers, 1954–1993, David M. Rubenstein Rare Book & Manuscript Library, Duke University, Box 1, Folder 6, p. 2.

Chapter 3: Stormfront

43 **"electronic tools":** Keith Schneider, "Hate Groups Use Tools of the Electronic Trade," *New York Times*, March 13, 1995.

43 **"a new model":** Ibid.

43 **"newfangled Internet":** Don Black, History of Stormfront, October 21, 2011, web.archive.org/web/20111226124913/http://www.stormfront.org/forum/t832625-42/

44 **"I spent all night":** Ibid.

45 **saw a declaration:** Stormfront website, web.archive.org/web/19970302003250/http://www.stormfront.org/.

46 *Nightline* **in 1998:** "Hate Web Sites and the Issue of Free Speech," *ABC News Nightline*, January 13, 1998.

48 **an honest computer consultant:** Quoted in David Schwab Abel, "The Racist Next Door," Broward-Palm Beach New Times, February 19, 1998.

50 **"small and plain home":** "Should the Internet be Regulated," *Morning Edition*, April 12, 1995.

50 **"Hearings on the proposal":** Ibid.

50 **"election-year chatter":** Timothy Noah, "Cyberpundits Shake Up Political Commentary," *Wall Street Journal*, October 14, 1996.

52 **"a limited fringe":** Michel Marriott, "Rising Tide: Sites Born of Hate: Racist pages are growing in number," *New York Times*, March 18, 1999.

52 **"restore White majority rule":** Thomas B. Edsall, "Buchanan's Bid Transforms the Reform Party: Candidate's stands draw extreme right support," *Washington Post*, July 23, 2000.

52 **"a means of planting seeds":** David Schwab Abel, "The Racist Next Door," Broward-Palm Beach New Times, February 19, 1998.

Chapter 4: The Heir Apparent

55 **"Twelve-year-old Derek":** Tara McKelvey, "Father and son target kids in a confederacy of hate," *USA Today*, July 16, 2001.

58 **"going to the circus":** "Stormfront Press Coverage," Stormfront, https://web.archive.org/web/20000301184318/https://www.stormfront.org/dBlack/press.htm

59 **"I've come expecting":** Susan Eastman, "Ordinary White Folks," *Weekly Planet*, December 9, 1999.

61 **"That's the advantage":** "Don Black with Dr. Buford B. Sanders, Homewood, AL, 1985-03-12," Evelyn Rich papers, 1954–1993, David M. Rubenstein Rare Book & Manuscript Library, Duke University, Box 1, Folder 6, p. 17.

68 **oval mass of granite:** Lorraine Boissoneault, "What Will Happen to Stone Mountain, America's Largest Confederate Memorial?", *Smithsonian Magazine*, August 22, 2017.

69 **"The new secret organization":** "Klan Is Established with Impressiveness," *Atlanta Journal Constitution*, November 28, 1915.

70 **"reunion of Klan groups":** Evelyn Rich, "Interview with Edward R. Fields, Vice-Chairman of The National States Rights Party and founder of The New Order of Knights of the Ku Klux Klan," Atlanta, GA, March 5, 1985, Evelyn Rich Papers, David M. Rubenstein Rare Book & Manuscript Library, Duke University, p. 2.

74 **videos of that day:** terranaut, "2000 election fiasco and recount in west palm beach courthouse, from first to final day." YouTube, September 24, 2019, www.youtube.com/watch?v=h37v5WToyWc.

74 **Tucker Carlson said on:** *Washington Journal News Review*, Michael Kingsley and Tucker Carlson, C-SPAN, November 13, 2000.

75 **"not the focus":** Ibid.

75 **"anarchists' write-up":** "Anarchists Blitzkrieg Nazi Picnic in St. Louis," quoted in "St. Louis, 2006: White Supremacist Picnic Disrupted," *Trebitch Times*, April 13, 2015, trebitchtimes.noblogs.org/post/2015/04/13/st-louis-2006-white-supremacist-picnic-disrupted/.

76 **first day of classes:** E. Culpepper Clark, *The Schoolhouse Door: Segregation's Last Stand at the University of Alabama* (Oxford: Oxford University Press, 1995), 63.

76 **voted unanimously:** Ibid., 107.

77 **master's degree:** "An Indomitable Spirit: Autherine Lucy," National Museum of African American History and Culture, October 11, 2017, nmaahc.si.edu/explore/stories/indomitable-spirit-autherine-lucy.

77 **lie in state:** Andrew Glass, "Rosa Parks Mourned at Capitol, Oct. 30, 2005," *Politico*, October 30, 2017.

Chapter 5: Palm Beach County Republican Executive Committee Member

85 **local paper quickly expanded:** "A Local Election's Results Raise Major Questions on Race," *New York Times*, December 11, 2008.

86 **racist rants:** Brian Todd, "Ron Paul '90s newsletters rant against Blacks, gays," CNN, January 10, 2008.

86 **campaign refused:** "Paul keeps donation from White supremacist," Associated Press, December 19, 2007.

87 **"family meeting":** "Duke's Conference Goes On in Memphis," Action News 5, November 8, 2008, www.actionnews5.com/story/9316842/dukes-conference-goes-on-in-memphis/.

88 **"Great White Hope":** Nate Penn, "Derek Black: The Great White Hope," *Details*, May 2009.

90 **headline photo:** "A Local Election's Results Raise Major Questions on Race," *New York Times*, December 11, 2008.

91 **Italian newspaper:** Mario Calabresi, "Fermeremo Barack Obama siamo il nuovo Ku Klux Klan," *La Repubblica*, October 29, 2008.

Chapter 6: New College

102 **consistent rankings:** Mark Schreiner, "Florida Colleges Make Princeton Review Rankings," WUSF Public Media, August 5, 2014, wusfnews.wusf.usf.edu/university-beat/2014-08-05/florida-colleges-make-princeton-review-rankings.

103 **whiter than other public schools:** NCF Racial/Ethnic Diversity, www.collegefactual.com/colleges/new-college-of-florida/student-life/diversity/#ethnic_diversity; UF Enrollment & Demographics, ir.aa.ufl.edu/facts/enrollment/.

106 **densest Jewish population:** "Palm Beach County: More Jewish than New York," *Palm Beach Post*, October 23, 2005.

111 **'interesting group of people':** "A profile of the first-year class: the class of 2010," *Catalyst*, September 11, 2010, ncfcatalyst.com/a-profile-of-the-first-year-class-the-class-of-2010/.

111 **drug and party culture:** Ibid.

122 **into the headline:** Nate Penn, "Derek Black: The Great White Hope," *Details*, May 2009.

Chapter 7: Dude You're Famous on the Forum Now

127 **129-square-foot rooms:** München Wiki, "Studentenstadt Freimann," last modified May 16, 2023, www.muenchenwiki.de/wiki/Studentenstadt_Freimann.

142 **weekend before mine:** Arthur Goldwag, "The National Policy Institute Conference: Immigrants Ruining America," Southern Poverty Law Center, September 12, 2011.

Chapter 8: Middle Fingers, Murmurs, and Threatening Emails

144 **"plagued by crime":** Todd Ruger, "Newly released records suggest the two British tourists killed in Newtown in April staggered into harm's way while drunk," *Sarasota Herald-Tribune*, July 27, 2011.

145 **Hiss, a philanthropist:** Robert Plunket, "Brilliant, Imperious and Public-Spirited, Philip Hiss Helped Establish Sarasota's Claims to Fame," *Sarasota Magazine*, December 14, 2021.

145 **very high academic standing:** Philip Hiss, "Sarasota's Broken Promise," *Architectural Forum*, June 1967, p. 71, https://usmodernist.org/AF/AF-1967-06.pdf.

145 **a close community:** Ibid.

145 **"wild-eyed socialist":** Pat Haire, "Daydream Believer: Once Dismissed as a Wild-Eyed Hippie, Maynard Hiss Did Much to Shape Today's Sarasota," *Sarasota Magazine*, June 1, 2004.

158 **Highlander hosted:** Joyce Denise Duncan, "Historical Study of the Highlander Method: Honing Leadership for Social Justice," dissertation, East Tennessee State University (2005), 33.

Chapter 9: We Want Him to Come Back

168 **"These forums have"**: Rheana Murray, "Former KKK Leader Says Jewish Center Shooting Suspect Went 'Insane,'" ABC News, April 15, 2014, abcnews.go.com /US/kkk-leader-jewish-center-shooting-suspect-insane/story?id=23336358.

169 **"the kind of people"**: Alyssa Newcomb, "Stormfront Website Posters Have Murdered Almost 100 People, Watchdog Group Says," ABC News, April 17, 2014, abcnews .go.com/US/stormfront-website-posters-murdered-100-people-watchdog-group /story?id=23365815.

169 **White nationalist terrorist**: Tore Bjørgo and Andres Ravik Jupskås, "The Long-Term Impacts of Attacks: The Case of the July 22, 2011 Attacks in Norway," *Perspectives on Terrorism* 15 (2021): 5, citing something called "*Klassekampen*, 19 August 2011."

170 **"I was never kicked out"**: Heidi Beirich, "White Homicide, Worldwide," *SPLC Intelligence Report* (Summer 2014).

171 **"What about Zionism"**: David Schwab Abel, "The Racist Next Door," *New Times*, February 19, 1998.

171 **"too many sociopaths"**: Heidi Beirich, "White Homicide, Worldwide," *SPLC Intelligence Report* (Summer 2014), p. 3

Chapter 10: That's Your Poison

187 **Virginia Assembly passed a law:** "Slave Law in Colonial Virginia: A Timeline," www.shsu.edu/~jll004/vabeachcourse_spring09/bacons_rebellion/slavelawincolonial virginiatimeline.pdf.

187 **argued the axiom**: Edmund Morgan, *American Slavery, American Freedom* (New York: W. W. Norton, 1975), 330.

Chapter 11: A Commitment to Them, and Them to You

197 **an average person from Eastern:** Ning Yu, et al., "Larger Genetic Differences within Africans than between Africans and Eurasians," *Genetics* 161 (2002): 269–74.

198 **gene pool:** Ewen Callaway, "Most Europeans Share Recent Ancestors," *Nature*, May 7, 2013, citing Ralph, P. and Coop, G., *PLOS Biology* 11 (2013).

Chapter 12: I Am Planning to Write Something About You Today

229 **Satan rallied the forces:** John Milton, *Paradise Lost*, book 1, lines 631–634.

229 **the pride of the angels**: Ibid., book 6, lines 31–34.

229 **Satan's forces poured into the world:** Ibid., book 10, lines 492–493.

230 **victory came at the cost:** Ibid., lines 501–502.

Chapter 13: You Need to Make New Friends and Family

234 **"Activist son":** Mark Potok, "Activist Son of Key Racist Leader Renounces White Nationalism," Southern Poverty Law Center, July 17, 2013.

234 **He'd started his career:** "Mark Potok," Southern Poverty Law Center, www .splcenter.org/about/staff/mark-potok.

235 **for my mom to be fired:** Heidi Beirich, "Stormfront Founder's Wife Fronts for Minority School," *Intelligence Report*, August 29, 2008, www.splcenter.org/fighting-hate /intelligence-report/2008/stormfront-founders-wife-fronts-minority-school.

235 **her boss's charity school** John Lantigua, "Local organizer, other supremacists say Obama's run boosts their cause," *Palm Beach Post*, July 26, 2008, web.archive. org/web/20080807002909/http://www.palmbeachpost.com/localnews/content /local_news/epaper/2008/07/26/m1a_White_supremacist_0727.html.

235 **the SPLC commented:** "Billionaire won't fire assistant for KKK link," *Page Six*, October 9, 2010, https://pagesix.com/2010/10/09/billionaire-wont -fire-assisant-for-kkk-link/.

236 **his write-up:** Mark Potok, "Activist Son of Key Racist Leader Renounces White Nationalism," Southern Poverty Law Center, July 17, 2013.

241 **reactions of White nationalists:** Mark Potok, "Racists React with Shock, Anger to Fellow Activist's Renunciation," SPLC, July 18, 2013, https://www.splcenter.org /hatewatch/2013/07/18/racists-react-shock-anger-fellow-activist's-renunciation.

242 **unexpected denunciation:** Caitlin Dickson, "Derek Black, the Reluctant Racist, and His Exit from White Nationalism," *Daily Beast*, July 29, 2013.

Chapter 14: Trying to Become Better

254 **"If I were the boss":** Eugen Ghencioiu, "Senior Vatican Priest - Father Reginald Foster - interviewed by Bill Maher," YouTube, September 14, 2011, www.youtube .com/watch?v=iTV-VgrbnZU.

257 **Hillary Clinton gave a speech:** "Hillary Clinton's Alt-right Speech, Explained," *Washington Post*, August 25, 2016.

258 **Bob Dole declared:** "GOP Leaders Have Talked About Racism and Their Party in the Past," *US News and World Report*, August 14, 2017.

263 **When Eli's story came out:** Eli Saslow, "The White Flight of Derek Black," *Washington Post*, October 15, 2016.

265 **op-ed for the *New York Times*:** R. Derek Black, "Why I Left White Nationalism," *New York Times*, November 26, 2016, www.nytimes.com/2016/11/26/opinion /sunday/why-i-left-White-nationalism.html.

266 **ran an article entitled:** "White Nationalism Explained," *New York Times*, November 21, 2016.

269 **Georgetown student newspaper:** Jesus Rodriquez and Tara Subramaniam, "In First Event After Defection, Former White Nationalist Derek Black Reflects on Racial Climate," *Hoya*, January 27, 2017.

270 **"When I was young":** Rick Lyman, "Elie Wiesel's Only Son Steps Up to His Father's Legacy," *New York Times*, May 12, 2017.

272 **Writing for the *New York Times* again:** R. Derek Black, "What White Nationalism Gets Right About American History," *New York Times*, August 19, 2017.

272 **part of a team of researchers:** Jeff Horwitz and Deepa Seetharaman, "Facebook Executives Shut Down Efforts to Make the Site Less Divisive," *Wall Street Journal*, May 26, 2020.

273 **Stallworth remembered:** Julie Miller, "*BlacKkKlansman*: The True Story of How Ron Stallworth Infiltrated the K.K.K.," *Vanity Fair*, August 10, 2018.

273 **The portrayal of David:** Ibid.

273 **telling employees to shift priorities:** Horwitz and Seetharaman, "Facebook Executives."

275 **"Black has changed sides":** Corey Robin, "The Plight of the Political Convert," *New Yorker*, January 23, 2019, www.newyorker.com/books/under-review /the-plight-of-the-political-convert.

277 **prominent antiracist author:** Ibram X. Kendi, "Racial Progress Is Real. But So Is Racist Progress," *New York Times* Opinion, January 21, 2017.

278 **largest incarcerated population:** "Crime Is Down, Yet U.S. Incarceration Rates Are Still Among the Highest in the World," *New York Times*, April 25, 2019.

279 **In his account of internment:** Jean Améry, *At the Mind's Limits: Contemplations by a Survivor on Auschwitz and Its Realities*, trans. Sidney Rosenfeld and Stella P. Rosenfeld (Bloomington: Indiana University Press, 1980), 42. Originally published as *Jenseits von Schuld und Sühne* (literally *Beyond Guilt and Atonement*).

279 **"all the more":** Ibid., 44.

279 **"self-exile":** Ibid., 45.

279 **described the blend of horror:** Amanda Gorman, *Call Us What We Carry* (New York: Viking Press, 2021), 166.

Epilogue

282 **"It was a humbling revelation":** Bill Woodson, "We didn't get it then, but we get it now," New College of Florida, February 1, 2021.

282 **right-wing activist Christopher Rufo:** Trip Gabriel, "He Fuels the Right's Cultural Fires (and Spreads Them to Florida)," *New York Times*, April 24, 2022.

282 **central to the conservative movement's:** Valerie Strauss, "New Breed of Charter School Pushes Limits on Separation of Church, State," *Washington Post*, June 8, 2023, www.washingtonpost.com/education/2023/06/08/new-breed-charter-schools-/.

282 *Time* **magazine described it:** "I. M. Pei Architecture at New College," New College of Florida, www.ncf.edu/alumni/foundation/pei-for-the-future/pei-architecture/.

282 **"1776 Curriculum":** Tyler Kingcade, "Conservatives are changing K-12 education, and one Christian college is at the center," NBC News, July 20, 2023.

282 **DeSantis came to Sarasota to announce:** Benjamin Wallace-Wells, "What Is Ron DeSantis Doing to Florida's Public Liberal-Arts College?," *New Yorker*, February 22, 2023.

283 **Offering $10,000:** "New College Offers $10,000 Scholarships to Draw Students," *Tampa Bay Times*, April 4, 2023.

283 **"mission to eliminate":** Divya Kumar, "At New College Orientation, Students Express Hope and Hesitation," *Tampa Bay Times*, August 20, 2023.

283 **first few months:** Andrew Atterbury, "New College scores millions in Florida's budget amid DeSantis revamp," *Politico*, May 4, 2023.

283 **sign new legislation:** Divya Kumar, "DeSantis Signs 3 Bills Bringing Major Change to Florida Universities," *Tampa Bay Times*, May 15, 2023.

284 **made a statement:** Ibid.

289 **rules that had taken:** Mark Joseph Stern, "Ron DeSantis' Attempt to Erase Trans People From Florida Schools Is Now Underway," *Slate*, August 8, 2023, slate.com/news-and-politics/2023/08/florida-ron-desantis-attacks-trans-students-teachers.html.

289 **law defines women:** Steve Contorno, "DeSantis signs into law restrictions on trans Floridians' access to treatments and bathrooms," CNN, May 17, 2023, www.cnn.com/2023/05/17/politics/desantis-signs-anti-trans-bill/index.html.

289 **The penalty for a violation:** Chris Geidner, "Ron DeSantis Just Took Two Big Steps to Make Trans Lives Illegal," *Rolling Stone*, May 17, 2023, https://www.rollingstone.com/politics/political-commentary/ron-desantis-trans-lives-illegal-1234736648/.

289 **DeSantis actually claimed to reject:** Ibid.

289 **Rufo's observation:** Trip Gabriel, "He Fuels the Right's Cultural Fires (and Spreads Them to Florida)," *New York Times*, April 24, 2022.

289 **"personal benefit" of slavery:** Kevin Sullivan and Lori Rozsa, "DeSantis Doubles Down on Claim That Some Blacks Benefited from Slavery," *Washington Post*, July 22, 2023, www.washingtonpost.com/politics/2023/07/22/desantis-slavery-curriculum/.

289 **Hirschfeld and the institute:** Brandy Schillace, "The Forgotten History of the World's First Trans Clinic," *Scientific American*, May 10, 2021, www.scientificamerican .com/article/the-forgotten-history-of-the-worlds-first-trans-clinic/.

289 **identification cards to transgender people:** Ibid.

289 **world's first gender-affirming medicine:** Ibid.

290 **Nazi newsreels projected:** Ibid.

Acknowledgments

291 **"some combination of girlfriend":** Corey Robin, "The Plight of the Political Convert," *New Yorker*, January 23, 2019.

INDEX